Opera in the Jazz Age

Opera in the Jazz Age

Cultural Politics in 1920s Britain

Alexandra Wilson

OXFORD

UNIVERSITY PRESS

OXFORD
UNIVERSITY PRESS

Oxford University Press is a department of the University of Oxford. It furthers
the University's objective of excellence in research, scholarship, and education
by publishing worldwide. Oxford is a registered trade mark of Oxford University
Press in the UK and certain other countries.

Published in the United States of America by Oxford University Press
198 Madison Avenue, New York, NY 10016, United States of America.

Library of Congress Cataloging-in-Publication Data
Names: Wilson, Alexandra, 1973– author.
Title: Opera in the jazz age : cultural politics in 1920s Britain /
Alexandra Wilson.
Description: New York, NY : Oxford University Press, [2019] |
Includes bibliographical references and index.
Identifiers: LCCN 2018018677 | ISBN 9780190912666 (hardcover : alk. paper) |
ISBN 9780190912680 (epub)
Subjects: LCSH: Opera—Great Britain—20th century. | Music—Social
aspects—Great Britain—History—20th century.
Classification: LCC ML1731.5.W52 2018 | DDC 782.10941/09042—dc23
LC record available at https://lccn.loc.gov/2018018677

1 3 5 7 9 8 6 4 2

Printed by Sheridan Books, Inc., United States of America

For Sebastian

CONTENTS

FIGURES

ACKNOWLEDGEMENTS

Any large-scale book project takes a period of many years to 'brew', and I first started thinking tentatively about the subject of opera in 1920s Britain around a decade ago. Most of the research proper, however, was carried out during the academic year 2014–2015, when I was lucky enough to be the recipient of a British Academy Mid-Career Fellowship. This funding scheme is highly competitive and I am extremely grateful to the BA for awarding me the Fellowship, as well as to Helen Greenwald for refereeing my application in what must have been effusive terms. I must also thank the staff in the research office at Oxford Brookes University for their assistance in managing the award and Paul Whitty, School of Arts Research Lead, for championing my work, offering guidance, and helping me to access institutional research funds to support this project. Joanne Cormac provided able teaching and administrative cover during my period of leave.

Suzanne Ryan, Editor in Chief, Humanities at Oxford University Press, New York, was enthusiastic about this project from the outset, and offered valuable guidance at the proposal stage and thereafter. Victoria Kouznetsov, Editorial Assistant, Music Books, worked with me tirelessly and with great patience in preparing the manuscript for submission. I am extremely grateful to them both, as well as to Tim Rutherford-Johnson, copy editor, and all the staff at OUP who worked on the book during the production process.

I was pleased to be invited to present my research-in-progress to colleagues and students at the University of Bristol, the Institute of Musical Research, and at Royal Holloway, University of London. I also presented conference papers on this subject at the 77th Annual Meeting of the American Musicological Society (San Francisco), the Royal Musical Association Annual Conference (University of Birmingham), the First Transnational Opera Studies Conference (Bologna), the Music and the Middlebrow Conference (University of Notre Dame, London Global Gateway), and several conferences at Oxford Brookes University under the auspices of the OBERTO opera research unit. All of the feedback I received from audience members at these events helped to shape the book.

In terms of wider public engagement, I was delighted to be commissioned to write articles on my 1920s interests for *History Today* and *Classical Music Magazine*. Soprano Samantha Hay and pianist Luke Green kindly helped me to recreate a 1920s celebrity concert at Oxford Brookes in 2015. I am extremely grateful to BBC Radio 3 for giving me the opportunity to make a radio documentary about operatic culture in 1920s London ('A Flapper's Guide to the Opera', broadcast October 2017). Ellie Mant skilfully produced a wonderful programme, and contributors Oliver Double, Paul Rodmell, Catherine Tackley, Elin Manahan Thomas, and Michael Volpe helped to bring the subject matter to life.

Most of the research for this book was conducted at the Bodleian Library, University of Oxford, the British Library, and the Victoria & Albert Theatre and Performance Collections, and I am grateful to the staff at all three institutions. My thinking on the subject of opera in the 1920s has been shaped by conversations with colleagues and research students working in related fields, as well as with members of the online opera community. Such conversations have been so numerous that I must apologise for the many omissions, but I would like to single out Mark Berry, Harriet Boyd-Bennett, Jennifer Daniel, Andrew Holden, Matt Houlbrook, Steven Martin, James Nott, Jane Potter, Clair Rowden, Hugo Shirley, Laura Tunbridge, and Emma West for sharing sources and references. I am grateful to Sophie Ratcliffe for helping me to finalise the book's title and to the two anonymous readers selected by OUP, whose comments helped me to write a far better book.

I must express particular gratitude to three friends who gave their time with astonishing generosity to, variously, read the manuscript and offer feedback, help me source images, advise on contractual matters, and generally push me to reach the finishing line. Anna Maria Barry, Barbara Eichner, Paul Parker: profound thanks. Alan and Pauline Wilson and Clive and Joy Timms all offered support and encouragement from afar over a period of many years. I am extremely grateful to Andrew Timms for many things, but particularly for holding the fort at home during my period of sabbatical leave, at a time when he was starting a highly demanding new job of his own, and for expertly proofreading the final manuscript. Finally, I am grateful in all sorts of ways to the dedicatee of this book, my lovely little boy Sebastian.

Alexandra Wilson
Oxford, May 2018

NOTE ON ABBREVIATIONS

In footnotes, the following abbreviations are used for commonly referenced journals:

ILN   *The Illustrated London News*
LM   *The London Mercury*
MM   *The Musical Mirror*
MNH   *The Musical News and Herald*
MO   *Musical Opinion*
MS   *The Musical Standard*
MT   *The Musical Times*

NOTE ON OPERATIC TITLES

I have used the titles of operas as they appeared in the relevant 1920s context. Thus in situations where operas were performed and billed in the original language, I have used the original title. When operas were performed and billed in English, the English title used by the relevant company is provided.

Opera in the Jazz Age

Introduction

B ritain has always had an opera problem. The story of the peculiarly British hostility towards opera is one that spans many centuries, from the arrival of Italian opera in London in the early eighteenth century until the present day. In a long-running cultural discourse intimately connected with questions of national identity, the specifics of the debate have, of course, mutated with the passing of time. However, certain broadly con-ceived anti-operatic leitmotifs—some anti-intellectual, some economic, some suspicious of the foreign, some bound up with issues of class, and some even gendered—have remained surprisingly constant across lengthy periods.

In the present day, anti-operatic feeling manifests itself via what can feel like a concerted media campaign to construct the art form as 'elitist', an ill-informed and counter-productive cliché that actively dissuades potential audiences from engaging with it. Although the twenty-first-century obsession with so-called elitism brings new dimensions to the debate and is specific to its own time in ways there is not space to analyse here, it is in many respects merely a new and even more insidious twist upon an old prejudice. The elitism trope rests upon positing opera and popular culture as polar opposites.[1] Despite postmodernity's supposed dissolution of the boundaries between 'high' and 'low', it is clear that these distinctions remain powerfully influential in present-day British discourses about the arts in general and opera in particular.[2] Indeed, the easy

1. For further reading, see Alexandra Wilson, 'Killing Time: Contemporary Representations of Opera in British Culture', *Cambridge Opera Journal*, 19/3 (2007), 249–70.

2. As Andreas Huyssen observes, there have been many attempts over the course of the twentieth century to destabilise the high/low opposition, but most have failed, leading to the conclusion that 'perhaps neither of the two combatants can do without the other, that their much heralded mutual exclusiveness is really a sign of their secret interdependence'. Andreas Huyssen, *After the Great Divide: Modernism, Mass Culture, Postmodernism* (Basingstoke: Macmillan, 1988), p. 16.

pigeonholing of opera as elitist is symptomatic of a growing impulse to classify and to stereotype in ever more crude terms, whether in culture or in other aspects of life.[3] If we are to understand or even to combat cultural stereotypes that have powerful social implications today, it is important to interrogate their historical roots—to understand how they were created and how they were sustained. In order to illuminate the complex British relationship with opera, this book shines a spotlight on to a significant corner of the debate: the moment around a century ago when cultural hierarchies were being strictly codified.

A hard-fought battle took place during the 1920s about whether various forms of culture were 'highbrow', 'lowbrow', or that newly invented thing, 'middlebrow'. The period after the First World War, which saw the emergence of the suburban middle classes in the sense that we mean the term today— together with the expansion of the mass culture industry and a modern type of celebrity—would establish ways of thinking about cultural hierarchies that have had lasting implications. Here I ask where opera was perceived to sit on the highbrow–lowbrow spectrum, and the answer is by no means as straightforward as a present-day reader might presume. This book analyses the lively and impassioned discussions that surrounded opera during the 1920s, conducted in the pages of the press and also via memoirs, programmes, biographies, books about opera both academic and popular, novels, short stories, films, and satirical cartoons. I examine how the art form's historically contested cultural status was further complicated by new interactions with popular culture and conceptions of celebrity. Modern methods of dissemination such as gramophone recordings and broadcasting—technologies of reproduction that were closely bound up with early twentieth-century mass culture—contributed to opera's ambivalent positioning within the new cultural categories. A rather niche area of investigation it might ostensibly seem, but the 1920s opera debate was an arena in which a set of broader hang-ups in the national psyche were played out with full force.

THE BATTLE OF THE BROWS

As Andreas Huyssen observed in the 1980s, the modern mass culture industry began to emerge from the mid-nineteenth century, leading over time to what he calls a 'Great Divide': a seemingly irreconcilable separation between high art and popular culture.[4] This was a process that took

---

3. As Brown and Grover argue, 'The urge to define has had a recent resurgence, especially in America'. Erica Brown and Mary Grover (Eds.), *Middlebrow Literary Cultures: The Battle of the Brows, 1920–1960* (Basingstoke: Palgrave Macmillan, 2012), p. 2.

4. Huyssen, *After the Great Divide*, p. 18.

place over a prolonged period but gained traction at historical moments when the 'high' seemed to be under particular threat from the 'low'. One such key moment was the period following the First World War. Changes in technology, and the new audiences such developments brought with them, prompted a widespread fear in intellectuals of a civilisation in crisis.[5] As pre-War social strata began to blur, amid an expansion of mass culture, and the marketplace became an increasingly important determinant of success, former cultural elites strove to defend their position of authority by developing a stricter codification of high and low culture.[6] The deepening divide that was emerging between the extremes of high and low during this period—the Modernist avant garde on the one hand and an expanding mass entertainment industry on the other—also contributed to the impulse to draw up hierarchies.

A new vocabulary was developed to discuss the new cultural categories. The phrenological term 'highbrow' had been invented around 1880 and 'lowbrow' was in common usage by 1910, although both words changed their meaning somewhat in the interwar years in correspondence with American usage.[7] The word 'middlebrow', meanwhile, was only formally used from the mid-1920s, but there was already at the start of the decade a hazy sense of a third category between the high and the low. The satirical column 'Charivaria' in *Punch* reported on 23 December 1925: 'The BBC claim to have discovered a new type, the "middlebrow". It consists of people who are hoping that some day they will get used to the stuff they ought to like'.[8] The new buzzword did not initially have negative connotations.[9]

5. On the interwar years as an 'age of anxiety, doubt or fear', see Richard Overy, *The Morbid Age: Britain and the Crisis of Civilization* (London: Penguin Books, 2009), p. 2.

6. D. L. LeMahieu writes: 'By making the market-place the most important arbiter of success, the mass media circumvented the authority of traditional cultural élites'. D. L. LeMahieu, *A Culture for Democracy: Mass Communication and the Cultivated Mind in Britain Between the Wars* (Oxford: Clarendon Press, 1988), p. 7.

7. These dates have been widely cited. See, for example, Derek Scott, *Sounds of the Metropolis: The 19th-Century Popular Music Revolution in London, New York, Paris and Vienna* (New York: Oxford University Press, 2008), p. 86. On the changing meaning of the terms 'highbrow' and 'lowbrow' on the threshold of the 1920s, in line with American usage, see Stefan Collini, *Absent Minds: Intellectuals in Britain* (Oxford and New York: Oxford University Press, 2006), p. 110.

8. *Punch*, 23 December 1925, 673. Cited in Kate Macdonald, 'Introduction: Identifying the Middlebrow, the Masculine and Mr Miniver', in Kate Macdonald (Ed.), *The Masculine Middlebrow, 1880–1950: What Mr Miniver Read* (Basingstoke: Palgrave Macmillan, 2011), pp. 1–23, p. 7. Although the term 'middlebrow' is widely agreed to have first been used explicitly only in 1925, Lawrence Napper identifies 1924 as a decisive turning point: 'a year of heated debate over the increasingly apparent division of British culture into "high", "middle" and "lowbrows"'. Lawrence Napper, *British Cinema and Middlebrow Culture in the Interwar Years* (Exeter: University of Exeter Press, 2009), p. 31.

9. Macdonald, *The Masculine Middlebrow*, p. 7.

However, when employed in the hands of the highbrows to describe an array of different types of cultural activity it came to be loaded, emanating a distaste for the middle classes, for the feminine and the domestic, and for supposed mediocrity, social aspiration, and cultural naïveté.[10] Intense debates about highbrow, middlebrow, and lowbrow culture took place in Britain during this decade, in what has often been called the 'battle of the brows'. As Lawrence Napper wryly puts it, these were 'all terms that could be (and were) imbued with venomous intent'.[11]

Labels are, on the face of it, a helpful way of organising things. There is no doubt, however, that the new categories were semantically ambiguous, employed to mean different things by different people in different contexts. For example, not every music critic who used the term highbrow even meant the same thing. Furthermore, such labels were socially divisive and the incessant discussion of them in the contemporary media ran the risk of putting some people off culture altogether.[12] In the words of John Quinlan in the cultural review *VOX* in 1929, 'The general apathy of Everyman towards art is largely due to the artificial estrangement between "highbrow" and "lowbrow". One confines art to a clique; the other affects to despise it altogether'.[13] And yet there was no getting away from the terms, however hard one might try. All forms of art underwent what we might call a process of cultural repositioning in Britain during the 1920s.[14] There was an intense desire to assign culture to neat boxes, and this applied to music as much as to other areas of life, even if lone voices sometimes baulked at it.[15] The novelist and playwright J. B. Priestley observed in 1927 that 'Some people may want to cry out against this "brow" business altogether ... but protest now is useless, for it will be many a long day before these brows leave us'.[16]

---

10. Brown and Grover (Eds.), *Middlebrow Literary Cultures*, pp. 1, 4.

11. Napper, *British Cinema and Middlebrow Culture*, p. 37.

12. Stefan Collini writes that the new terms 'presumed a division into antagonistic social groups. From the outset, the language of "brows" ran together levels of intellectual attainment, types of cultural interest or activities, attitudes towards presumed inferiors or superiors, and social class'. Collini, *Absent Minds*, p. 110.

13. John Quinlan, 'Can Radio Justify Itself?', *VOX: The Radio Critic and Broadcast Review*, 1/3 (23 November 1929), 82.

14. There were even attempts to regularise dance steps during this period in order to avoid American influences. See James Nott, *Going to the Palais: A Social and Cultural History of Dancing and Dance Halls in Britain, 1918–1960* (Oxford: Oxford University Press, 2015), pp. 225–7.

15. R. W. S. Mendl, for instance, wrote: 'It has often been pointed out that it is impossible to divide music up into categories by hard and fast boundaries. We cannot draw a rigid line between programme music, absolute music, and emotional music'. R. W. S. Mendl, *From a Music Lover's Armchair* (London: Philip Allan and Co., 1926), p. 135.

16. J. B. Priestley, 'High, Low, Broad', in *Open House. A Book of Essays* (London: William Heinemann Ltd., 1927), pp. 162–167, p. 162. Priestley later recalled that in the 1910s, 'there wasn't any consciousness of brows' but that from the early 1920s the reading public was divided up and writing began to be assessed in terms of its potential audience. Cited in John Baxendale,

The battle of the brows was, of course, closely bound up in aesthetic terms with the Modernist movement, which, in Huyssen's words, 'constituted itself through a conscious strategy of exclusion, an anxiety of contamination by its other'.[17] Literature was relatively easy to categorise according to the brows. Napper argues that the market for books split during the interwar period, with the high and low extremes breaking away from the centre and a distinctive, albeit varied, middlebrow emerging.[18] The same applied to the visual arts: experimental, avant-garde paintings and sculptures were clearly distinguishable from artworks that continued the nineteenth-century realist tradition.[19] There were, of course, Modernist operas too, which were received in the British context as unequivocally highbrow.

More broadly, however, the relationship of opera as an art form to the new categories was a thorny one. This was an art form that defied straightforward pigeonholing, not only in purely aesthetic terms but also commercially and socially. Furthermore, members of the musical establishment—the cultural gatekeepers who were in the business of assigning labels—adopted a variety of complicated attitudes towards opera. There were critics of a Modernist mindset who attempted to defend 'serious' music against the challenges issued by the mass media, but opera didn't usually come within their purview, except as an object of sneering contempt. On the other hand there were critics we might label middlebrow who accepted opera's flirtings with mass culture past and present without qualms. In between there were critics who demanded that opera be taken seriously as an art form yet eschewed the snobbery of the most prejudiced highbrows. These figures went to considerable lengths to make the case for opera for all, yet even they occasionally flinched at opera's encounters with cinema or recoiled when it appeared alongside popular ballads on the programmes of celebrity concerts.

Opera occupied a very peculiar position, then: for some sectors of the popular press it was *too* highbrow, yet in the eyes of some members of the serious musical establishment it was categorically not highbrow *enough*, something that may seem surprising to present-day readers. Opera couldn't really be called lowbrow, but whether it was middlebrow was a moot point. British operatic life underwent considerable change in our period, reflecting profound social, economic, and cultural changes in the aftermath of world war. This, coupled with the new impulse to categorise forms of culture, meant that the operatic sphere became something of a battleground in the

Priestley's England: J. B. Priestley and English Culture (Manchester: Manchester University Press, 2007), p. 15.

17. Huyssen, *After the Great Divide*, vii.
18. Napper, *British Cinema and Middlebrow Culture*, p. 30.
19. Huyssen, *After the Great Divide*, ix.

1920s, caught between the desires of a socially minded group of musicians who fought hard to make opera 'for the people' and various hostile factions both inside and outside the musical establishment who voiced prejudices against opera that ranged from intellectual snobbery to crude xenophobia. This corresponds with a broader pattern D. L. LeMahieu observes when he argues that interwar artists and intellectuals responded in a variety of ways to the new commercial world, some retreating into self-conscious isolation from it, others engaging in polemics against it, others embracing new technologies and seeking to uplift national tastes.[20]

Discussion about the relationship of literature to interwar debates about high and low culture has been extensive, and literary scholars have, since the 1990s, made concerted efforts to render middlebrow novels—previously dismissed as unworthy of study—a legitimate field of investigation.[21] Musicology tends to lag behind other disciplines, but there has been a recent surge of interest in the ways in which the term middlebrow has been, or might be, applied to a variety of musical repertoires both classical and popular.[22] Nevertheless, this is the first study to analyse the complex place of opera in the interwar battle of the brows.[23] Opera's refusal to be pinned down has broader implications, revealing as it does the fault lines in the supposedly definitive new system of categorisation. It fundamentally undermines Huyssen's simplistic and now much-critiqued binary of the Great Divide, which consigned everything that wasn't unequivocally highbrow to an undifferentiated category called 'mass culture', largely neglecting the more complicated, more nuanced, and arguably more interesting category of the middlebrow.[24]

This book undertakes a detailed, micro-historical reading of the operatic life of the 1920s, following the example of other recent cultural histories that have examined particular decades or even individual years.[25] This closely focused historical approach allows for a detailed consideration

20. LeMahieu, *A Culture for Democracy*, pp. 2–3.

21. See, for instance, Erica Brown, *Middlebrow Literary Cultures: The Battle of the Brows, 1920–1960* (Basingstoke: Palgrave Macmillan, 2012); Collini, *Absent Minds*; Sean Latham, *Am I a Snob? Modernism and the Novel* (Cornell: Cornell University Press, 2003); Macdonald (Ed.), *The Masculine Middlebrow*.

22. See, for instance, the interdisciplinary 'Music and the Middlebrow' project, ongoing at the time of writing: http://www.musicandthemiddlebrow.org/ (accessed 17 October 2017).

23. For a discussion about opera and the middlebrow in a later period, see Christopher Chowrimootoo, 'Bourgeois Opera: *Death in Venice* and the Aesthetics of Sublimation', *Cambridge Opera Journal*, 22/2 (2010), 175–216.

24. Macdonald, 'Introduction', *The Masculine Middlebrow*, pp. 4–5.

25. Examples include Hans Ulrich Gumbrecht, *In 1926: Living at the Edge of Time* (Cambridge, MA and London: Harvard University Press, 1997) and Hugh MacDonald, *Music in 1853: The Biography of a Year* (Woodbridge: Boydell, 2012).

of a pivotal historical and aesthetic moment. However, it is not possible from the operatic perspective to consider the 1920s entirely in a vacuum. In order to understand the debates that took place during that decade, it is imperative to appreciate how opera's cultural status had changed across the course of the previous century. What follows, therefore, is a brief historical sketch that places the discussions of the 1920s in context.

HISTORICAL CONTEXTS

Let us travel back in time by a hundred years or so from the 1920s. In Georgian Britain the opera house was indisputably a meeting place for the wealthy: a venue to which one went to see and to be seen, and in which the audience was as much a part of the spectacle as was the action unfolding on-stage. The aristocracy not only financed and managed opera in London in the late eighteenth and early nineteenth centuries but used the art form as a way of negotiating its own identity. Opera was, one could reasonably argue, a resolutely elite form of entertainment, although we must distinguish elite from elitist, the latter being a much later term with different connotations. However, as Jennifer Hall-Witt has demonstrated, British opera-going was gradually transformed across the course of the nineteenth century from a social event to an aesthetic experience: audiences began to behave better, a more serious culture of listening began to develop, and opera attendance slowly began to diversify.[26]

By the late Victorian era, opera-going had become a genuinely popular and populist activity, a status it would retain throughout the Edwardian era. This is not to say that opera at Covent Garden had become radically more accessible to ordinary people; rather, opera was being performed more and more regularly beyond the West End, usually in English, to a socially mixed audience. A large number of touring opera companies, of which the Carl Rosa and Moody Manners Companies were the most famous, performed in towns and cities up and down the land, week in week out throughout the year, some even touring several different troupes simultaneously.[27] In his detailed study of British opera culture between 1875 and 1914, Paul Rodmell argues that this was 'a period of great diversity: from . . . expensive Italian operas in the West End of London to modest touring troupes playing in

26. Jennifer Hall-Witt, *Fashionable Acts: Opera and Elite Culture in London, 1780–1880* (Lebanon, NH: University of New Hampshire Press, 2007).

27. For an extensive list of touring opera companies active in late nineteenth- and early twentieth-century Britain, see Steven Edward Martin, 'The British "Operatic Machine": Investigations into the Institutional History of English Opera, c. 1875–1939', unpublished PhD dissertation, University of Bristol, 2010, Appendix 1, pp. 255–72.

towns from Penzance to Aberdeen and Limerick to Norwich, opera came within reach of a greater proportion of the population than either before or since'.[28] There is no question that so many companies could have stayed in business had their regional audience been limited to a narrow upper-class elite, and the companies were remarkably successful in attracting listeners from across the social spectrum.

As Jonathan Rose has demonstrated, there was an early twentieth-century working-class intelligentsia that, motivated by an ethos of self-improvement, was keenly interested in all kinds of 'high culture': mining communities gave a warm welcome to touring opera companies, for example, and 'opera permeated even the slums of Manchester'.[29] Furthermore, the boundaries between opera and other sorts of popular entertainment were at this time porous. Excerpts of operatic music became widely known to all classes through brass band arrangements, music hall performances, and interpolations of arias into pantomimes.[30]

There was some continuity in British operatic culture between the pre-War and post-War periods: Rodmell argues that 'the structures established in the late nineteenth century continued in use for many years after 1918, just as the ideological and aesthetic issues raised in the Victorian years continued to be debated'.[31] However, attitudes towards opera began to change after the War, partly in response to changes in operatic practices themselves and partly in response to a range of wider social, economic and cultural factors. There was a palpable sense that both opera as a creative art form and the culture of opera-going were at a turning point and potentially a moment of crisis: numerous cultural pessimists proclaimed the imminent death of the art form.[32] The problem was, to some extent at least, an international one, caused by a reduction in the number of new operas being composed, economic difficulties, and new funding models for opera houses, as well as a wider variety of leisure activities such as spectator sport, musicals, and cinema drawing audiences away from opera.[33] Mascagni, giving the Italian

28. Paul Rodmell, *Opera in the British Isles, 1875–1918* (Farnham and Burlington VT.: Ashgate, 2013), p. 5.

29. Jonathan Rose, *The Intellectual Life of the British Working Classes*, 2nd edn (New Haven: Yale University Press, 2010), pp. 198–9, p. 201.

30. For further reading, see Dave Russell, *Popular Music in England, 1840–1914: A Social History*, 2nd edn (Manchester and New York: Manchester University Press, 1997), Rose, *The Intellectual Life of the British Working Classes*, pp. 197, 201, and Dagmar Kift, *The Victorian Music Hall: Culture, Class and Conflict* (Cambridge: Cambridge University Press, 1996), pp. 28, 54.

31. Rodmell, *Opera in the British Isles*, p. 337.

32. Gerald E. H. Abraham, for instance, speculated in 1923 about whether there would even be such a thing as opera a decade thence. Gerald E. H. Abraham, 'The Aesthetic Future of Opera', *Musical News and Herald*, 65/1643 (22 September 1923), 226.

33. See Susan Rutherford, *The Prima Donna and Opera, 1815–1930* (Cambridge: Cambridge University Press, 2006), p. 4 and Russell, *Popular Music in England*, pp. 294–5.

perspective, told a British music journal in 1929 that 'The crisis of the opera and theatre is today in the front rank of discussion' and blamed the wireless, cinemas, and an 'excessive love of sport and jazz' for the fact that it was hard to get anybody to support opera, whereas in the past it was the norm for people to go to hear the same opera three or four times.[34]

Relatively speaking, however, as numerous contemporary reports affirmed, there was in fact still a rich operatic life in Italy, with dedicated opera houses in even the smallest of towns, and the same could be said for Germany. In Britain, by contrast, operas were only performed at Covent Garden for a few months a year and the fact that there was not even a permanent opera company in London was considered a matter of national shame by many in the musical establishment.[35] The reliance upon touring companies, rather than permanent local companies, also meant that the picture was more challenging than in continental Europe. During the 1920s, the touring companies fell on hard times and their number began to decline. It would be exaggerating matters to say that they disappeared altogether: there was still a good deal of opera being put on, in a rather ad hoc fashion. But in comparison to the vibrant years of the Edwardian era, opportunities for people to encounter live operatic music in the regions on a regular basis were starting to dwindle.[36]

A key argument throughout the book is the idea of opera as 'a thing apart'. It was this sense of apartness, opera's supposed removal from everyday life, which, for many commentators, lay at the root of opera's problems in Britain. This perception was in many ways overstated, yet the fact that live opera receded from view to some extent—at least in provincial theatres—undoubtedly contributed to later assumptions that opera was something for a social elite, as would the invention in the 1930s of country house opera that came with the foundation of Glyndebourne.[37] There was still plenty of so-called popular opera being performed in 1920s Britain, whether complete or in part in a wide variety of different contexts, but there was a growing problem of perception: the operatic institution that remained most visible in 1920s press reports was Covent Garden. Yet even operatic

34. Pietro Mascagni, 'Wanted—A New Wagner. Present-Day Intellectual Degeneracy', *The Musical Mirror*, 9/4 (April 1929), 89.

35. Britain's 'operatic problem'—its failure to produce successful native composers—had been the subject of much discussion since the 1870s. For further reading on the historical contexts for this debate, see Rodmell, *Opera in the British Isles*, pp. 185–220.

36. Russell, *Popular Music in England*, pp. 81, 230.

37. Looking back from the late 1940s, Percy Colson, a critic from the interwar period and Nellie Melba's biographer, wrote: 'To motor down to Glyndebourne on a warm summer evening, dine in the excellent restaurant . . . and listen to Mozart, was delightful. But it was expensive—music for the millionaire, not for the million'. Percy Colson, *Those Uneasy Years. 1914–1939: A Medley* (London: Sampson Low, Marston & Co., 1948), p. 84.

culture in its most glittering manifestations had become greatly impoverished after the War, and the artistic weaknesses of opera at Covent Garden during the first half of the decade would harden prejudices against it.

There are some parallels here with the slightly earlier transformation in opera's socio-cultural signification that had taken place in the United States. As Lawrence Levine and others have shown, opera had been extremely popular in the USA during the early and mid-nineteenth century, but was increasingly segregated by the end of the century from other forms of entertainment and performed less frequently in English.[38] Operatic music also began to disappear in the early twentieth century from the performing repertory of the numerous American bands, whereas it had hitherto been central to that repertory, making operatic excerpts extremely well known among people who had never entered a theatre.[39] America's musical elites participated in the wider construction of rigid artistic categories, consciously repositioning opera as an 'elevated' form of art that demanded hard work of the listener and was the preserve of the upper classes.[40]

Despite superficial similarities with the process Levine observes in America in terms of live opera losing some of its former status as popular entertainment, opera's repositioning in Britain during the 1920s was more complicated.[41] Ideas about opera's perceived status at this time were highly contradictory and fraught with anxieties about cultural authority. It was no longer quite so readily accepted as popular entertainment but on the other hand it was also not accepted as high art, being repeatedly characterised by the musical intelligentsia as an inferior, bastardised art form. Furthermore, opera did not turn its back upon popular culture (nor did it in the United States, in truth, as exemplified by the many songs of the ragtime era that made reference to opera).[42] As I shall demonstrate, the relationship

38. Lawrence W. Levine, *Highbrow/Lowbrow: The Emergence of Cultural Hierarchy in America* (Cambridge, MA: Harvard University Press, 1988). George Martin has documented the thriving operatic culture in nineteenth-century San Francisco in *Verdi at the Golden Gate: Opera and San Francisco in the Gold Rush Years* (Berkeley, Los Angeles, and Oxford: University of California Press, 1993).

39. For further reading, see George W. Martin, *Opera at the Bandstand: Then and Now* (Plymouth: Scarecrow Press, 2014).

40. For further reading, see Paul DiMaggio, 'Cultural Boundaries and Structural Change: The Extension of the High Culture Model to Theater, Opera, and the Dance, 1900–1940', in Michèle Lamont and Marcel Fournier (Eds.), *Cultivating Differences: Symbolic Boundaries and the Making of Inequality* (Chicago and London: University of Chicago Press, 1992), pp. 21–55, p. 22.

41. Jon Burrows argues that the intermingling of different types of entertainment in Britain during the 1920s and the juxtaposition of high and low was actually the reverse of the pattern traced by Levine in the United States, whereby the general and the eclectic gave way to the exclusive and the specific. Jon Burrows, *Legitimate Cinema: Theatre Stars in Silent British Films, 1908–1918* (Exeter: University of Exeter Press, 2003), p. 104.

42. These songs have been discussed extensively in Larry Hamberlin, *Tin Pan Opera: Operatic Novelty Songs in the Ragtime Era* (Oxford and New York: Oxford University Press, 2011).

between opera and popular culture in 1920s Britain was different from before the War but it was a closer one than has been previously recognised. Opera interacted in new and fruitful ways with precisely the forms of entertainment that might appear to have threatened its popularity, including films, popular music, and middlebrow novels.

WHY OPERA?

British perceptions of opera between the wars were, then, paradoxical to say the least, and the art form's position in both the battle of the brows and in contemporary class politics was considerably more thorny than one might initially assume. 'Elite' culture (meaning culture that was consumed by the social elite) and 'highbrow' culture were by no means one and the same thing. It is clear that for some intellectuals and members of the musical establishment, opera was something that a civilised nation ought to support, and various interesting strategies for promoting it were attempted during this period. On the other hand, some self-styled highbrows felt that opera was an inferior and frivolous art form that ought not to be encouraged.

But why did opera matter so much? For all the misgivings about it that one encounters during this period, it was evidently not something that could simply be ignored. Rather, opera was considered significant enough to be discussed almost everywhere: highly politicised discussions about its cultural status took place in Parliament, at Downing Street, at public meetings and private salons, in pamphlets and lectures, and above all in the pages of the press. The critic A. P. Hatton, who wrote for *Musical Opinion* under the pseudonym 'Figaro', argued in 1928 that 'The trouble with opera is that it is so rarely news'.[43] He was remarking here upon a rather static repertory, with few premieres of new operas that might have made the front pages. In broader terms, however, it would seem from our perspective that an astonishing number of column inches were devoted to opera during the 1920s, in daily papers of all types, and in general magazines as well as in more specialised publications. Opera had not, then, retreated from so-called everyday life.

The ongoing public interest in opera—and its potential to be considered middlebrow—is demonstrated by the fact that opera singers and other musicians were profiled in popular fiction magazines aimed at the middle classes such as *The Strand Magazine*, where excerpts from their memoirs appeared alongside stories by the likes of such writers as Sir Arthur Conan

43. Figaro, 'The Operatic World', *Musical Opinion*, 51/612 (September 1928), 1159–60, 1159.

Doyle and P. G. Wodehouse.[44] Celebrity singers gazed out from the pages of the tabloid press and figures from the world of opera, whether singers or impresarios, were regular protagonists in the popular fiction of the day. It is particularly striking that the best-selling novel of the decade, Margaret Kennedy's *The Constant Nymph*—subsequently adapted as a highly popular play with Noël Coward as the romantic lead—should have been concerned with the family of an avant-garde British opera composer exiled in Europe.[45] The book itself, indeed, grappled with the question of where high art sat in the new cultural marketplace, as well as with desire and Bohemianism.[46]

Opera undoubtedly unleashed very strong feelings, whether in the public arena or in private conversations. As the author, lecturer, and broadcaster Basil Maine wrote, 'Opera is a most dangerous subject for discussion. Many a friendship has been wrecked by the primitive emotions which are roused whenever the topic is raised. Few people are constitutionally able to take part in any examination of the subject without giving vent to the most violent prejudices'.[47] The key to opera's perceived importance during the 1920s—and to its controversial status—lies in the fact that much of the vexation surrounding it was underpinned by identity politics: questions of national identity and peculiarly British questions of class. Opera was, of course, primarily an imported art form and there had been much chauvinistically inspired hostility to it in Britain over the previous two centuries, with the art form often being caricatured as simultaneously foreign and feminised.[48] These debates remained alive and well in the 1920s; indeed they intensified in some respects, partly as a result of a growing realisation that efforts dating back to the late nineteenth century to establish an internationally successful school of English operatic composition were proving unsuccessful.

---

44. See, for instance, the serialisation of Luisa Tetrazzini's *My Life of Song* in 1921 and the reminiscences of tenor Ben Davies in June 1924. For further reading on *The Strand Magazine*, see Mike Ashley, *The Age of the Storytellers: British Popular Fiction Magazines 1880–1950* (London: The British Library and Oak Knoll Press, 2006).

45. Margaret Kennedy, *The Constant Nymph* (London: Vintage, 2014); the novel was first published by William Heinemann in 1924. On the play, which was staged at the New Theatre in 1926, see J. C. Trewin, *The Gay Twenties: A Decade of the Theatre* (London: MacDonald, 1958), p. 89.

46. Napper, *British Cinema and Middlebrow Culture*, p. 31.

47. Basil Maine, 'Is Opera a Luxury, a Habit, or Just Absurd?', *Musical News and Herald*, 73/1833 (1 November 1928), 280.

48. For further reading, see Corissa Gould, 'Aspiring to Manliness: Edward Elgar and the Pressures of Hegemonic Masculinity', in Ian Biddle and Kirsten Gibson (Eds.), *Masculinity and Western Musical Practice* (Farnham: Ashgate, 2005), pp. 161–81; Annemarie McAllister, *John Bull's Italian Snakes and Ladders: English Attitudes to Italy in the Mid-Nineteenth Century* (Newcastle upon Tyne: Cambridge Scholars, 2007); and Deborah Rohr, *The Careers of British Musicians: 1750–1850* (Cambridge: Cambridge University Press, 2001).

Furthermore, with the rupture of the First World War and the decline of the older social order came a broader need to define a distinctive cultural identity for the nation. Opera's place within the discussion was, once again, far from straightforward. Debates raged about whether a taste for opera existed at all in Britain, and whether the British temperament was constitutionally suited to the art form. Yet whilst opera was still widely posited as something alien, it raised questions about how the British wished to present themselves culturally to the rest of the world. Some writers were at ease with the fact that nations simply had different (and not necessarily superior) tastes: where Italy had opera houses, Britain had variety theatres and golf links.[49] However, a thriving operatic culture was regarded by some musicians and politicians to be a hallmark of civilisation and a nation in good health. Many members of the musical establishment palpably had an inferiority complex about Britain's failure to compete operatically with other leading nations: not only old cultural rivals such as Germany but also an important new competitor, the United States.[50] Even writers who expressed personal reservations about opera were prepared to admit that the lack of a permanent national opera house had led to 'an inestimable impoverishment of our musical life'.[51]

Musicologists and historians have tended to regard the British interwar period as something of an operatic wasteland, sandwiched between the glory days of the Edwardian era and the emergence of a properly subsidised operatic establishment after the Second World War, which paved the way for the high standards of production and performance of the late twentieth century and early twenty-first.[52] (The belated emergence of a British opera composer capable of commanding international recognition—Benjamin Britten—was another key turning point in the country's operatic fortunes after the Second World War.) The post-1918 operatic landscape was certainly a very different one from the one that audiences had known prior to the First World War, and in terms of what was being put on in theatres

49. Percy Colson, 'Opera. A Suggestion', in R. Sydney Glover (Ed.), *Apollo: A Journal of the Arts, Vol 1 January to June 1925* (Nendeln, Liechtenstein: Kraus Reprint, 1976), pp. 42–3, p. 42. On the Italian taste for melodrama, see Colson, 'Musical New and Notes', in Ibid., pp. 308–9, p. 308.

50. As Richard Capell, a critic who wrote for mainstream newspapers such as *The Daily Mail*, summed up: 'The paradox is that opera has never become a native of the British Isles, and yet the need of it is felt as a factor of civilisation'. Cited in Henry Russell, *The Passing Show* (London: Thornton Butterworth Ltd., 1926), p. 272.

51. Richard Capell, *Opera* (London: Ernest Benn, Ltd., 1930), p. 10.

52. In his social history of interwar Britain, Pugh writes that 'the 1920s and 1930s were not noted for opera' and that 'opera was struggling to establish a major national presence in Britain' during this period. Martin Pugh, *'We Danced All Night': A Social History of Britain Between the Wars* (London: Vintage, 2009), pp. 326, 343.

the picture was indeed rather bleak, at least for the first half of the 1920s. Opera companies came and went, productions were frequently cancelled, performance standards were often risibly low, and one botched funding scheme was proposed after another to put opera on a surer footing. But it is precisely the sense of an operatic 'crisis' that makes it interesting, since it played into the vexation over how opera ought to be categorised. This was a vital moment of taking stock of opera's place in British society and defining its relationship to the nation's post-War cultural identity.

CRITICAL PARAMETERS

It is well beyond the scope of this book, given its micro-historical approach, to trace the entire history of developing operatic attitudes from the 1920s to the present, and there is a separate project to be undertaken pinpointing the precise moment at which, and mechanisms by which, the elitism trope began to emerge. However, I shall reflect throughout this book on the ways in which the debates of the 1920s prefigure and inform those that we are still having about opera today. Many of the critical tropes about opera that emerged during the 1920s would crop up again and again across the duration of the twentieth century and beyond, not only in British discourse but also more globally. Even though some features of the 1920s debate traced here were peculiarly British (discussions, for example, about singing in English or about cultural protectionism), others shaped broader attitudes towards opera's cultural function that now impinge upon popular perceptions of the genre internationally. Anxieties about the relationship between opera and more recent forms of technological media, about declining audiences and the need to attract new ones, about problematic notions of celebrity, and about accessibility are global ones. Most specifically, the question of opera's place in the 'brows' certainly remains relevant. The terminology has changed, but the nagging question of how to pigeonhole opera—what to *do* with it—persists, and here we can trace a direct connection to the anxieties about cultural categorisation that began to emerge in the 1920s.

It is necessary to define some further parameters. This book does not attempt to provide an exhaustive survey of which operas were being performed where during the 1920s.[53] It is not so much a study of operatic practices, or indeed operatic policies (although these matters are discussed), but of operatic mentalities: my principal concern is with matters of taste,

---

53. For a catalogue of what was on at London theatres throughout the decade, see J. P. Wearing, *The London Stage 1920–1929: A Calendar of Productions, Performers, and Personnel*, 2nd edn (Lanham, Boulder, NY, Toronto, Plymouth: Rowman and Littlefield, 2014).

prejudice, stereotype formation, and cultural categorisation.[54] I focus not so much on operatic works (beyond the discussion of the 1920s repertory in Chapter 5) as on opera as a protean genre, its performers, audiences, and critics. I examine opera not only inside but outside the opera house, considering encounters between opera and popular culture as well as opera on stage. While professional operatic performance in interwar Britain was beset by financial problems and at times shambolic, opera found innovative and intriguing ways of making its presence felt within culture more broadly. The book therefore investigates the socially constructed nature of cultural hierarchies, their relationship to national identities, and their long-term implications.

Sharp-eyed readers will note that, in terms of repertoire, I pay relatively little attention to opera by British composers: this is emphatically not a study of English opera. Nor is it a study of Gilbert and Sullivan-type operetta, which was considered a separate genre and rarely discussed in contemporary debates about opera. Although the 'national opera debate' (rooted in the late nineteenth century and still ongoing in the 1920s)—which refers specifically to the promotion of an 'English' school of opera composition, the translation of foreign operas into English, and the promotion of British singers—impinges at times on my analysis, these questions have already been discussed extensively elsewhere.[55] Furthermore, although sizeable numbers of British operas continued to be composed during the 1920s, the works in question largely failed to survive or even to make much of an impact during their own time: most were put on only a handful of times and quickly abandoned.[56] My principal concern here, rather, is with the way in

54. An extremely thorough account of the repertory and casts at Covent Garden throughout the period can be found in Harold Rosenthal, *Two Centuries of Opera at Covent Garden* (London: Putnam, 1958). Steven Martin considers the practicalities and economics of putting on opera in the interwar period in his PhD dissertation (Martin, 'The British "Operatic Machine"').

55. Rodmell, *Opera in the British Isles*; Martin, 'The British "Operatic Machine"'; John Lucas, *Thomas Beecham: An Obsession with Music* (Woodbridge: The Boydell Press, 2008); Eric Walter White, *The Rise of English Opera* (London: John Lehmann, 1951); Irene Morra, *Twentieth-Century British Authors and the Rise of Opera in Britain* (Aldershot: Ashgate, 2007); Meirion Hughes and Robert Stradling, *The English Musical Renaissance, 1840–1940: Constructing a National Music*, 2nd edn (Manchester: Manchester University Press, 2001); and Russell Burdekin, 'The Failure to Establish English Opera in the Nineteenth Century', unpublished MA dissertation, Oxford Brookes University, 2015. The oft-expressed grand aspiration to construct a 'national' opera house in London for the performance of English operas was to be frustrated during the interwar period. However, analogous debates about the use of the vernacular and the promotion of British singers would underpin the founding principles of English National Opera much further down the line. For further reading, see Susie Gilbert, *Opera for Everybody: The Story of English National Opera* (London: Faber and Faber, 2009).

56. Edward J. Dent wrote in 1928 'The history of English Opera has been for the most part the record of three centuries of failure'. Edward J. Dent, *Foundations of English Opera: A Study of Musical Drama in England During the Seventeenth Century* (London: Cambridge University

which nationalistically inflected stereotypes and notions of cultural value developed around what we would now regard as the core foreign repertoire, something that was still in the process of being established in the 1920s.

Given the wide-ranging scope of the study—the way in which it discusses political, social, economic, and intellectual concerns as well as a variety of artistic ones—my approach is inevitably an interdisciplinary one. I am interested here in the way in which opera participated in broader cultural discourses. Thus, I draw upon the extensive work on interwar culture in general and on cultural categorisation specifically that has been undertaken by scholars working in Literature, History, Art History, and Film Studies, all areas in which there has been a recent upsurge of interest in the previously disparaged middlebrow.[57] In turn, I hope that this book will provide a useful resource for scholars in other disciplines who are interested in questions of cultural distinction, class identities, and taste formation, providing a fresh perspective upon the familiar topic of the 'battle of the brows'. Opera, and indeed classical music more generally, is almost never mentioned in studies of the brows, nor in broader historical surveys of the interwar period.[58]

My methodology is a combination of cultural-historical analysis and re-ception studies, drawing upon a broad range of textual and iconographic sources in order to document how commentators of the 1920s received opera of earlier eras and of the present. The source material for this period is immensely rich. Above all, the press has proved vital: daily newspapers, gen-eral cultural reviews, and a range of music journals with different agendas and aimed at different readerships provide an array of perspectives upon the interwar opera problem. There are many different 'voices' in this study, although a number of key figures will emerge again and again as we delve deeper into the operatic polemics of the decade. The broadsheet papers saw themselves as having a mission to guide readers through the best of con-temporary culture, with *The Sunday Times* and *The Observer* being the most serious.[59] Papers like *The Daily Mail* and *The Daily Express* were important

Press, 1928), p. 1. For a year-by-year list of English operas of this period, see Eric Walter White, *A Register of First Performances of English Operas and Semi-Operas from the 16th Century to 1980* (London: The Society for Theatre Research, 1983).

57. See Brown and Grover (Eds.), *Middlebrow Literary Cultures*, Nicola Humble, *The Feminine Middlebrow Novel, 1920s to 1950s: Class, Domesticity, and Bohemianism* (Oxford: Oxford University Press, 2001), and Napper, *British Cinema and Middlebrow Culture*.

58. A rare exception to this rule is Martin Pugh's acknowledgement that Nellie Melba's land-mark broadcast of 1920 should be seen as 'a partial corrective to the received view that interwar Britain suffered from a deep gulf between "high" culture and "popular" culture'. Pugh, *'We Danced All Night'*, p. 326.

59. Graves and Hodge write that *The Times* 'held an unchallenged position as the best-informed and most independent journal in England' (p. 45), while *The Telegraph* was the businessman's paper. Robert Graves and Alan Hodge, *The Long Weekend: A Social History of*

vehicles of middle-class and middlebrow attitudes and contain more operatic commentary than one might expect.[60] And, as noted above, opera news was also reported in tabloid newspapers such as *The Daily Mirror*. Here the focus was largely upon operatic celebrity 'human interest stories', with a particular emphasis upon pay, fashion, and diva antics, but rather surprisingly the paper also announced what was to be performed in the Covent Garden 'season', reported on performances of particular note, and reviewed new opera recordings.[61]

There were also numerous magazines devoted to music. Some of these were the voices of the musical establishment, such as *The Musical Times*, which often pursued a strikingly anti-operatic line. Others such as *The Musical Mirror* were essentially popular magazines with a musical focus, and there were further periodicals with a specialist musical slant. Notably, two magazines were established during the 1920s by parties which had an explicit interest in expanding the audience for opera. The first, simply entitled *Opera* (later *Opera and the Ballet*), was the organ of the British National Opera Company and published in 1923 and 1924 (monthly at first, later quarterly). The second was *MILO*, the magazine of Thomas Beecham's Imperial League of Opera, which ran for three issues at the end of 1929. Despite their short-lived runs, both had grand ambitions and are important historical documents in terms of illustrating the terms in which opera was promoted at two different points during the decade. Both were overtly political organs that made the case for the performance, public support, and funding of opera, although they went about their mission in rather different ways. There was also widespread commentary about musical matters in general cultural magazines, such as *The Illustrated London News* (*ILN*), *The Athenaeum*, and the fine arts journal *Apollo*.

Writers commenting upon music during the 1920s may strike the present-day reader as breathtakingly rude at times, and yet their invective was very often stylishly crafted: criticism that was biting, incisive, and witty was most certainly something that reviewers cultivated.[62] For instance, W. J. Turner of the *ILN* was particularly well known for his plain speaking: according to his contemporary Basil Maine, 'there is nothing which delights

---

Great Britain, 1918–1939 (London: The Folio Society, 2009; first published Faber and Faber, 1940), p. 46.

60. Brown and Grover (Eds.), *Middlebrow Literary Cultures*, pp. 56–7.

61. See, for instance, a report that 'The performance [of *Samson and Delilah*] gripped a full house in spite of numerous disturbing late arrivals and tedious intervals'. Anon., 'Covent Garden Opera: Performance of "Samson and Delilah" Grips a Full House', *The Daily Mirror*, 23 May 1928, 30.

62. Rodmell notes that 'adverse press comment on all aspects of operatic performances became much more common in the 1880s'. Rodmell, *Opera in the British Isles*, p. 16.

him more than to practise the blunt art of irritation' and his words were 'sledge-hammer blows'.[63] Visceral metaphors abounded: critics regularly drew analogies between opera and illness, opera and the body, opera and diet, opera and manliness (or, conversely, effeminacy). Such rhetoric is further evidence of the extent to which opera was perceived to matter: however much it might be loathed by the critic in question, it went right to the heart, and the stomach, of debates about the nation's cultural identity. It is certainly true that there was much infighting among critics, and indeed between rival opera companies, and this did not always help opera's cause in Britain. But it would be overstating matters to suggest that operatic rhetoric during the 1920s was nothing more than an incessant catalogue of negative commentary, with antipathetic highbrows and middlebrows at loggerheads with one another. The situation is far more complex: some critics cannot, themselves, be easily labelled or categorised.

The book is organised thematically rather than chronologically for the most part. Chapter 1, however, offers a loose chronological sketch of the decade as part of a general overview of its operatic culture, providing important contexts for the more analytical chapters to follow by discussing the financial, artistic, and practical challenges that beset opera. I discuss the principal companies performing opera during the 1920s, the financial difficulties they encountered, and the 'feast or famine' approach to operatic performance that typified the decade.

Subsequent chapters consider debates about opera's vexed position in the battle of the brows from a number of perspectives. Chapter 2 'anatomises' the various different audiences for opera in order to address the question of whether opera-going was considered to be an elite or a popular activity during the 1920s, a discussion that incorporates debates about class, money, exclusivity, and audience diversity that have had enduring implications for opera in Britain. Chapter 3 continues to examine the audience for opera but focuses in detail upon two key 1920s archetypes: the 'highbrow' and his opposite number, an emblematic figure commonly known as the 'man in the street'. I analyse what the term highbrow was understood to mean in 1920s musical discourse, who the key highbrow critics were (even if few would have identified openly with the term), and the reasons why they considered opera to be something for people with inferior artistic tastes. The middlebrow tastes of the man in the street, meanwhile, included opera in small doses alongside an array of different types of entertainment.

63. Basil Maine, *Behold These Daniels: Being Studies of Contemporary Music Critics* (London: H. & W. Brown, 1928), pp. 66, 67.

The extent to which contemporary commentators believed that such tastes ought to be improved will also be scrutinised.

In Chapter 4 I consider the question of 'cultural purity' and its significance within debates about the brows. Formal purity was something that was highly prized by highbrow commentators, whilst its absence was seen as a defining characteristic of the middlebrow. Opera was problematic because it was an artistic hybrid in itself—an amalgam of multiple different art forms—and because the boundaries between it and other forms of entertainment were hazy. There had been long-standing historical debates about opera's supposedly 'impure' artistic status, compounded in the nineteenth century by Romantic notions of the superiority of 'absolute music', but they reached a particular point of intensity during the 1920s when the need to categorise works of art came to be regarded as so fundamental. At the same time, this was a decade when different types of popular culture began to work together symbiotically, and when a variety of new forms of entertainment media began to converge.[64] Despite the fact that this was a moment when classical music and popular music were starting to move further apart in the public consciousness than they had been in the second half of the nineteenth century, there were still plentiful connections between the two. Opera was also interacting with a wider range of types of popular culture in ways that highbrow commentators found troubling: here I examine the permeable boundaries between opera and jazz, film, and popular novels, and discuss the reasons why the term 'best-seller' was particularly problematic when applied to operas or operatic recordings.

Chapter 5 examines the operatic repertoire of 1920s Britain and how different types of opera could be classified in different ways. Certain types of opera, notably early operas and adventurous recent works, were regarded as acceptable by the most highbrow commentators. However, such figures chastised much of the core repertoire for blurring the boundaries between high and low and for disturbing notions of cultural purity. Nineteenth-century and early twentieth-century Italian operas came in for particular condemnation, but other national schools were not immune from criticism, as witnessed by the negative reception of certain recent works by Richard Strauss. I also examine the intriguing case of Wagner, who straddled the highbrow–middlebrow divide in unexpected ways within the

---

64. Double explains that variety halls faced a crisis during the 1920s when threatened by the popularity of the revue, radio, and cinema, but survived by finding creative ways of working co-operatively with these new forms of entertainment. Oliver Double, *Britain Had Talent: A History of Variety Theatre* (Basingstoke: Palgrave Macmillan, 2012), pp. 47, 55. See also Jon Burrows, *Legitimate Cinema: Theatre Stars in Silent British Films, 1908–1918* (Exeter: University of Exeter Press, 2003), p. 96.

British context. As well as considering core issues of twentieth-century British operatic canon formation, this chapter analyses how racial essentialism was very much to the fore in 1920s discussions about artistic taste, with the consequence that foreign opera was often written off as entirely incompatible with the British character.

Chapter 6 analyses the way in which the figure of the operatic celebrity jeopardised opera's acceptance as high art. Public discussions about star singers dated back centuries, of course, but the perception that the prima donna was losing some of her social prominence by the 1920s encouraged even greater mockery of a long-caricatured figure. Aware of their declining status, singers attempted to claw back prestige by exploiting the new publicity mechanisms of the era and aping the behaviour of the new media darlings: film stars and high-profile sportsmen and women. With a particular focus upon Luisa Tetrazzini, Nellie Melba, Amelita Galli-Curci, Maria Jeritza, and Rosa Ponselle, I consider the ways in which star singers worked within the cultural marketplace in a manner that disturbed notions of high art and the work concept. Particularly disparaged, on artistic, economic, and nationalistic grounds, were those who specialised in 'celebrity concerts' rather than stage performances. Such concerts prompted a pronounced degree of cultural protectionism and concerns about what we might see as an anticipation of the 'classical crossover' phenomenon.[65] But even those star singers who sang on the operatic stage and were praised for their musical performances were sometimes seen to be undermining opera's serious artistic credentials by allowing their onstage and offstage personae to blur.

Chapter 7, finally, examines how the strategies to expand the audience for opera in the 1920s played into contemporary debates about national identities, and considers the relationship between these identities and the highbrow–middlebrow conversation. Although, as noted above, the battle of the brows would have later implications for international discourses about opera, there was also something distinctively British about it: as Harold Nicolson argued in the early 1930s, there were at that time no equivalents for the words highbrow and lowbrow in any other language.[66] I am not concerned here with Britishness alone, however, but rather with the way in which such conceptions played into a broader panoply of identity

---

65. In the twenty-first century, 'classical crossover' has become a genre in itself. I am referring here not so much to opera singers performing in or recording musicals (for example, the 1994 Deutsche Grammophon *West Side Story* with Kiri Te Kanawa and José Carreras) as to singers with classical training who perform orchestrated pop songs, hymns, and show tunes, who are marketed in a manner akin to pop stars.

66. Nicolson made this point in a broadcast entitled 'To A Low-Brow', which was a rebuttal of J. B. Priestley's 'To a High-Brow' broadcast of 1932. Stefan Collini, *Absent Minds: Intellectuals in Britain* (Oxford and New York: Oxford University Press, 2006), p. 118.

politics. I analyse how opera propagandists exploited contemporary rhetoric about sport, empire, and masculinity in order to make opera 'manly' and to foster a type of ideal citizenship among young people. I focus in detail upon the aforementioned specialist opera magazines, *Opera* and *MILO*, placing them within a nexus of wider debates. This chapter, therefore, brings together an important intersection between identity formation, propaganda, and the politics of taste. Refreshingly, the sources reveal that there was a genuine desire during the 1920s to introduce ordinary people to opera rather than to tell them it was 'not for them'. Ultimately, then, there are positive things that we, in the present moment, can learn from the operatic debates of the 1920s.

CHAPTER 1

✧

Contexts

The year: 1923. The opera: *Faust*. The star: Nellie Melba, reigning operatic queen of the *fin de siècle*, now in the early stages of what was to be a protracted farewell to the lyric stage. The occasion might appear to have been an historically momentous one, and yet it was, in the words of Melba's biographer Percy Colson, 'the saddest evening I ever spent at Covent Garden.'[1] Not only had the glamour of pre-War opera-going evaporated but Melba's golden-age co-stars were dead and her matronly appearance and diminished vocal powers in the ultimate operatic warhorse made Colson want to weep. The theatre seemed to be 'full of ghosts'.[2]

Debates about opera in the 1920s became caught up in a broader sense of mourning for a pre-War world that was perceived to have disappeared forever. The mood of the moment was captured retrospectively by Evelyn Waugh in *Brideshead Revisited* (1945). As his Oxford college servant, Lunt, bemoans the introduction of dancing in Eights Week, the narrator Charles Ryder observes: 'For this was 1923 and for Lunt, as for thousands of others, things could never be the same as they had been in 1914'.[3] Operatic discourses of the early 1920s were dogged by pessimism and nostalgia, particularly from an older generation of commentators intent upon harking back to what they perceived to be a 'golden age' that had begun at Covent Garden in the 1890s. Opinion varied as to how long it had lasted. According to former *Sunday Times* critic Herman Klein, by now the grand old man of opera criticism, the rot had begun to set in as early as 1902, which had

---

1. Percy Colson, *Melba: An Unconventional Biography* (London: Grayson and Grayson, 1932), p. 238.
2. Ibid., p. 239.
3. Evelyn Waugh, *Brideshead Revisited* (London: Penguin Classics, 2000), p. 24.

ushered in what he called with a Wagnerian flourish an '*Operdämmerung*' ('operatic twilight').[4]

Metaphors of illness were used to describe the state of British operatic culture throughout the decade, and for some commentators the art form was already as good as dead.[5] Such comments about the death of opera have, of course, been a recurring refrain throughout history—and sound particularly loudly in the present day—but in the interwar period they were coloured by a specifically medicalised language that was prevalent in general discourse during what has often been characterised as an age of anxiety. One critic wrote on the cusp of the 1920s that opera in Britain was not 'suffering from some little functional ailment' but was 'diseased, and diseased to such an extent that only the surgeon's knife can raise in us any hope of a cure'.[6] The strong impression one forms from this sort of commentary is of an art form perceived to be out of step with the times, and yet ironically the language used to characterise it as such was itself outmoded, dripping with late nineteenth-century metaphors of decay.

Where later chapters in this book look at operatic culture in its broader manifestations, this one focuses upon opera in the theatre, providing a contextual backdrop for subsequent discussions about opera's complicated cultural status by outlining the challenges that beset operatic culture in Britain during the 1920s. Some of these were economic, some artistic, some attitudinal. The chapter introduces the key companies and venues of the British operatic scene, considers such issues as performance standards, rehearsal culture, and staging practices, and examines the challenges posed to opera's success by its practical limitations and threats from rival forms of entertainment. It is necessary to be aware of these various transformations in British operatic culture and their underlying causes if one is to understand opera's positioning within the battle of the brows.

Although operatic activity during the period was varied, colourful, and accessible to mixed audiences, many branches of the operatic sector were experiencing practical difficulties. Society support for glamorous international opera was on the decline and Covent Garden Theatre itself faced

---

4. Herman Klein, *The Golden Age of Opera* (London: George Routledge and Sons, Ltd., 1933), pp. 242, 243, 251. Klein had been music critic of *The Sunday Times* from 1881–1901 and was subsequently critic for *The New York Herald* and (after returning to London in 1917) *The Saturday Review* (Nigel Scaife, 'British Music Criticism in a New Era: Studies in Critical Thought, 1894–1945', unpublished DPhil thesis, University of Oxford, 1994, p. 24).

5. 'One is almost forced to the conclusion that the correct diagnosis of the state of British operatic enterprise today is that it is dead, but struggling to rise, phoenix-like, from its own ashes'. Figaro, 'The Operatic World', *MO*, 46/541 (October 1922), 33.

6. William Beeson, 'Tradition and the Opera', *MT*, 61/924 (1 February 1920), 122. On medicalised discourse, see Overy, *The Morbid Age*, p. 4.

an uncertain future; the touring opera companies, meanwhile, had fallen on hard times, with some folding during this decade. There was a great sense of ambition for opera during the 1920s, but it was repeatedly thwarted by precarious finances. Yet the picture was by no means entirely gloomy: opera continued to be performed to large, socially mixed audiences and, in spite of the partial decline of the all-important touring companies, there was much optimism that public interest in the art form was growing. By the later years of the decade, there were some tentative expressions of hope that the ailing patient might finally be on the mend, even if it was prone to recurrent relapses. As one journalist quipped, 'The truth is that opera is neither alien, nor exotic, nor even senile: it is merely old-fashioned, badly dressed, mustily housed, and out of condition'.[7] Opera might have lost vibrancy, become institutionalised, and be out of synch with the times, but many of the problems it faced were not in fact fatal and could be resolved.

Furthermore, the retrospective glorification of the pre-War era from the perspective of the 1920s should be taken with a pinch of salt. There was much talk of contemporary singers being inferior to the great stars of the past, but this was merely—as some 1920s commentators themselves recognised—a recurring operatic refrain that had been heard repeatedly over the generations, just as it is still regularly heard today.[8] Indeed, the nostalgia for an earlier golden age expressed by the interwar cultural pessimists was often not really about the music at all: what they were really mourning was the glamour of pre-War Covent Garden. As a commentator for *The Telegraph* wrote: 'gone the beauties, gone the dandies, gone the sparkling tiaras, the glittering stomachers, the smiles of royalty, the visits from box to box, the State occasions'.[9] Opera's shifting social status and the unease that this prompted in some writers is, as we shall see, an important factor in the vexed debates concerning its cultural categorisation.

7. Anon., 'Can Opera Survive the Dole?', *MNH*, 71/1807 (27 November 1926), 465–6, 465. The critic Figaro wrote in 1926 that 'Opera in its convalescence since the war has hardly been capable of doing more than sit up, propped with pillows, and perhaps it is the doctors who are keeping it there with their incessant dirge. Presently opera will get out of bed, kick the doctors through the door and the medicine table through the window'. Figaro, 'The Operatic World', *MO*, 49/581 (February 1926), 471–2, 471.

8. 'Let us soberly conclude this truth—a fixed belief that the stars of one's youth glittered more brilliantly than any other star, and that the melodies of youth will outlast in charm and sweetness all other melody, is inherent in all generations since Adam'. The Old Stager, 'Memory Corner', *The Daily Telegraph*, 3 July 1929, n.p. [V&A Theatre and Performance Collections, production box: Covent Garden Theatre, 1929].

9. Ibid. *The Sphere* reported in 1910 that 'To visit Covent Garden Opera House in the season is to know life at its most magnetic point'. Anon., 'At the Fall of the Curtain', *The Sphere*, 42/546 (9 July 1910), 42–3.

THE POST-WAR OPERATIC LANDSCAPE

It might seem inevitable that the War should have taken some sort of toll upon British musical life. In fact, musical activity had been surprisingly vibrant during the first two years of the conflict, and there was to some extent a prevailing spirit of 'business as usual', with companies keen to stay on the road both for the sake of performers' livelihoods and to boost national morale.[10] Rodmell argues that 'London enjoyed some of its longest seasons and the number of active touring companies was as great as during the Edwardian decade'.[11] However, there were inevitable difficulties—not least the loss of many male musicians to the front—and operatic culture was indisputably in a worse condition by 1918 than it had been in 1914.[12]

By the end of the War there were casualties among those touring companies which had thrived in the Edwardian era. Particularly notable was the disbanding in 1916 of the Moody-Manners Company, which placed a rather pitiful advert in the theatrical journal *The Era* in 1920 offering its 'services and effects gratis to any legitimate attempt to found a National Opera Company'.[13] The Beecham Company was one of the most important touring companies in the immediate aftermath of the War but would cease operations at the end of 1920. Touring companies remained a highly significant part of the 1920s operatic landscape, however, all of them less lofty and cosmopolitan than Covent Garden and more inclusive of audience members from across the class spectrum. Some popped up for merely a matter of months before disbanding, whilst others continued to thrive against a backdrop of difficult circumstances. A particularly active company during this decade was the Carl Rosa Company, which put on a broad range of popular foreign operas alongside British operas old and new.[14]

In 1922, however, a new and important touring company formed: the British National Opera Company (BNOC). The BNOC scooped up many of the singers from Beecham's troupe and bought the company's entire assets for £15,000.[15] It toured extensively, performed operas in English, and aspired to reach wide audiences by selling tickets at low prices. There was a groundswell of regional support for the company and its future success was regarded as vital to the long-term operatic health of the nation. Regional

10. Herman Klein, *Musicians and Mummers* (London, NY, Toronto and Melbourne: Cassell and Company, 1925), p. 324.

11. Rodmell, *Opera in the British Isles*, p. 122.

12. Ibid., p. 175.

13. *The Era*, 83/4256 (14 April 1920), 3.

14. Martin, 'The British Operatic "Machine"', pp. 146, 149; Rosenthal, *Two Centuries of Opera at Covent Garden*, p. 412.

15. Anon., 'British National Opera', *The Financial Times*, 29 September 1921, 6.

committees in large provincial cities raised funds and local choirs were used to supplement the chorus, a practice that had been fairly routine with the pre-War touring companies.[16] However, the BNOC—aspiring to become a truly national company with a permanent base in London—regarded itself as a cut above the average touring company and distanced itself from its rivals by performing a more ambitious repertory, launching its own magazine and putting on a programme of educational activities.[17] The company also formed a very close and significant relationship with the BBC and was a key player in 1920s discussions about the democratisation of opera, even if it would, itself, ultimately not survive the decade and would eventually be in the position of having to sell off its own effects.[18]

Surveying the state of touring opera in 1923, 'Figaro' of *Musical Opinion* could only point to the Carl Rosa and the BNOC, plus the O'Mara Company and another provincial company whose name he could not even recall, beyond which 'the outlook is next door to tragic'.[19] Compared to the number of touring companies operating before the War, this was a drastic decline. Nevertheless, the touring companies continued to do valiant work in disseminating and democratising opera throughout Britain, with particular support in the north. By 1924 the BNOC had an astonishing thirty-three works in its repertory, nine of them hitherto unknown to British audiences, and was reportedly turning away thousands of people when it visited cities such as Glasgow and Liverpool, where interest in opera was particularly strong.[20] For an operatic culture supposedly in crisis and whose repertory was supposedly in stagnation (as we shall see in Chapter 5), this seems a rather impressive state of affairs.

Numerous accounts from the 1920s testify to the fact that standards of performance had fallen since the War, although it is clear that they rose again as the decade progressed. Thomas Beecham spoke pessimistically in 1923 of the altered circumstances for opera in Britain, lamenting the fact that musical standards were infinitely lower than they had been two decades previously.[21] Staging practices had become ossified: a critic in 1920 drew a comparison between a performance he had just seen of *Faust* and one he had seen fifteen years earlier: 'The same old stage setting was used and

16. Martin, 'The British Operatic "Machine"', 152.

17. Ibid., p. 157.

18. Anon., 'A Toreador for 4S. 7D.: Stage Bargain Sale', unattributed press clipping, 19 October 1929 [V&A Theatre and Performance Collections, production box: Covent Garden Theatre, 1929].

19. Figaro, 'The Operatic World', *MO*, 46/552 (September 1923), 1128–9, 1128.

20. Figaro, 'The Operatic World', *MO*, 47/556 (January 1924), 366–8.

21. Anon., 'Sir T. Beecham's Views: Pessimistic Outlook on Future of Opera and British Musical Conditions in General', *MM*, 3/5 (May 1923), 139.

there was the same old incompetent chorus. Tradition grasps opera today in its bony claws, and dresses and stages it with commonplace tawdryness, slavish in its adherence to the hoary past'.[22]

Critics made frequent reference to rough-and-ready performances by the touring companies and to the habit of 'making do'.[23] In low-budget touring productions, singers were cast according to approximate vocal suitability with little concern for age or physical appearance: reports abounded of overweight Madam Butterflies sobbing over ten- or even fourteen-year-old children masquerading as toddlers, or 'mature and ungainly' Marguerites being seduced by elderly Fausts.[24] Productions were thrown on to the stage in a haphazard manner, with inadequate rehearsal time, leading critics to bemoan a peculiarly British culture of amateurism.[25]

In 1922, at the time of the launch of the BNOC, Landon Ronald wrote of witnessing a great improvement in the standard of British operatic singers— although as Principal of the Guildhall School he had a vested interest in saying so.[26] The critics, however, were often more cutting. Describing a heavy cold from which he was suffering, Ernest Newman, music critic of *The Sunday Times*, wrote to his wife Vera telling her that he was 'barking like a Carl Rosa tenor'.[27] Flippancy aside, Newman pointed to weaknesses in the training on offer to British singers, who were not being taught to specialise and were singing all music—whether it be by Wagner, Puccini, Debussy, or Elgar—with exactly the same oral inflections.[28]

Whatever the standard of contemporary singing may have been, it is evident that audiences enjoyed the performances by the touring companies and that they looked forward to hearing and seeing particular singers. Local newspaper critics in some of the large cities where the BNOC performed tended to give their shows glowing reviews, although this is unsurprising

22. William Beeson, 'Tradition and the Opera', *MT*, 61/924 (1 February 1920), 122.

23. W. J. Turner, for instance, wrote in 1924: 'We are contaminated, corrupted through and through, I am afraid, with the ideal of the makeshift. "Do what you can and hope for the best" is the motto of our English musicians'. W. J. Turner, 'The World of Music', *ILN*, 24 May 1924, n.p.

24. Gilbert Forsyth, 'Can British Composers Write Popular Opera?', *MM*, 7/1 (January 1927), 5/12, 5; Harold Rosenthal, *Two Centuries of Opera at Covent Garden* (London: Putnam, 1958), p. 407; Edwin Evans, 'Lyric Drama of Tomorrow', in R. Sydney Glover (Ed.), *Apollo: A Journal of the Arts, Vol 1 January to June 1925* (Nendeln, Liechtenstein: Kraus Reprint, 1976), pp. 93–5, p. 95.

25. See, for example, Percy Colson, 'Opera. A Suggestion', in Glover (Ed.), *Apollo: A Journal of the Arts, Vol 1*, pp. 42–3 and Percy Colson, 'Musical New and Notes', in Glover (Ed.), *Apollo: A Journal of the Arts, Vol 1*, pp. 308–9.

26. Ronald, *Variations on a Personal Theme*, p. 164.

27. Vera Newman, *Ernest Newman: A Memoir By His Wife* (London: Putnam, 1963), p. 29.

28. Ernest Newman, 'Specialisation in Singing', *The Sunday Times*, 4 June 1922, cited in Newman, *From The World of Music: Essays from The Sunday Times* (London: John Calder, 1956), pp. 42–5, p. 43.

since they often sat on the company's regional committees.[29] The attitude of the London press towards the touring companies, on the other hand, was more varied. Some critics—to the disgust of others—made special allowances for poor performances, simply in order to encourage the endeavour of English opera.[30] Nevertheless, it did not feel to the touring companies themselves as if they were receiving any special favours.[31]

Covent Garden, meanwhile, had closed during the War in order to be used as a furniture store.[32] It reopened with its first 'Grand Season' in the summer of 1919 and a second followed in 1920, and some foreign singers performed, including Melba, Emmy Destinn, and Gilda Dalla Rizza.[33] On the whole, however, the casts were not as starry as those before the War. Both seasons, by the Grand Opera Syndicate, were propped up by Thomas Beecham but ended in financial disaster, meaning that there would be no Grand Opera seasons thereafter until the summer of 1924.[34] The opera house was rented out during the intervening years to the Carl Rosa and the BNOC, but such residencies were often short—typically between three and seven weeks—leaving lengthy periods of the year with no performances at all.[35] (Compare this to the situation prior to the War, when there had typically been a core season that ran from September to June. [36]) Indeed, opera had become something of a novelty at the opera house: more often than not the theatre was playing host to revues, film screenings, charity balls, pantomimes, or even boxing matches, effectively becoming something akin to an upmarket variety hall, with a consequent shedding of much of its pre-War prestige.[37] (Similarly, today's opera aficionados often express concern about the London Coliseum—home of English National Opera—being used for semi-staged musicals as a means of income generation.)

29. Martin, 'The Operatic "Machine"', 153.

30. W. J. Turner expressed exasperation that some of his contemporaries such as Percy Scholes were 'passing lightly' over the faults of the BNOC in the name of patriotism, arguing that giving them an easy ride was more of a hindrance than a help. W. J. Turner, 'The World of Music, *ILN*, 24 May 1924, n.p.

31. The view of Frederic Austen, Director of the BNOC was that 'Some critics give us a fair field, but others would rather kill than cure'. G.A.P., 'The B.N.O.C. and its Critics: Frederic Austin's Report', *MNH*, 67/1685 (12 July 1924), 29.

32. Richard Northcott, 'A Musical History of Covent Garden Theatre', Royal Opera, Covent Garden, *Stories of the Operas and the Singers*, Official Souvenir, Season 1919, 69–84, 78.

33. For a full breakdown of seasons, repertory and casts throughout the 1920s, see Harold Rosenthal, *Two Centuries of Opera at Covent Garden* (London: Putnam, 1958), pp. 764–78.

34. Ibid., p. 391.

35. The Carl Rosa ran seasons at Covent Garden in the autumn–winter of 1921, 1922, and 1923. The BNOC were in residence in spring and winter 1922, May–June 1923 and January–February 1924.

36. Rodmell, *Opera in the British Isles*, p. 145.

37. Rosenthal, *Two Centuries of Opera at Covent Garden*, p. 411.

There was certainly a widely shared view among benevolent critics that companies such as the BNOC should not be judged by the standards of the international seasons of the pre-War era, where the world's foremost singers had been brought to London at colossal expense.[38] Again there is a wistfulness here for a vanished era. But in fact the international seasons had not always, themselves, been completely fault free, and nor were they through the 1920s. At the beginning of the decade, performance standards at Covent Garden were considered by critics to be well below the standard one might expect to see abroad, with singers who were below par, scenery that was shabby and wearing out, and costumes that were cast-offs from older productions.[39] And yet there was no realistic expectation during this period—as there most certainly would be today—that each new production *should* have new scenery, something that would have been regarded as an extravagance.

Dyneley Hussey characterised the average Covent Garden production as one 'in which singers from half-a-dozen different foreign opera-houses act in different styles and even sing in different languages before antiquated scenery, that was in some instances originally painted for a different opera.'[40] Hussey was referring here to the fairly routine practice of polyglot performance, in which one or several singers sang in a different language from that in which the opera as a whole was being performed. This typically happened when a star singer was hired to sing in an English-language performance: such singers were usually reluctant to relearn a role in English.[41] For instance, when Melba sang in *La bohème* with the BNOC in 1923—a considerable coup for the company even though the star was nearing retirement—she was quoted as saying that she preferred opera in English, but sang her role in Italian nevertheless.[42] And the Scottish tenor Joseph Hislop, who had established a successful career in Scandinavia, sang the role of Pinkerton in *Madama Butterfly* in Swedish at Covent Garden in 1920.[43] Polyglot performances were presumably accepted by audiences up

38. Anon., 'The Press and the Opera', *MNH*, 62/1573 (20 May 1922), 625.

39. See, for instance, Francis E. Barrett, 'Opera in London', *MT*, 61/927 (1 May 1920), 317–20, 319; H. J. K., 'Covent Garden', *MT* (1 August 1924), 746; Philip Page, 'Realism in Opera', *LM*, 18/105 (July 1928), 290–7, 294.

40. Dyneley Hussey, *Eurydice, or the Nature of Opera* (London and NY: Kegan Paul, Trench, Trubner and Co. Ltd./E. P. Dutton & Co., 1929), pp. 71–2.

41. Rodmell notes that polyglot performances were comparatively routine in the late 1890s, choruses often singing in a different language from the soloists. Rodmell, *Opera in the British Isles*, p. 89.

42. Anon., 'Dame Nellie Melba. "English the most Beautiful Language"', *Opera*, 1/2 (February 1923), 8. It was noted elsewhere that even when Melba sang English, she sang it 'like a foreigner'. Anon., 'Some Singers of the Month', *MT*, 63/958 (1 December 1922), 875.

43. Harold Rosenthal, *Two Centuries of Opera at Covent Garden* (London: Putnam, 1958), p. 407.

to a point but critics recognised that the practice was far from ideal. *The Musical Standard* appealed: 'For decades we bore with German and Italian opera, but now in any case let us have it *all* in one language. Let us understand *all* or nothing'.[44]

Covent Garden theatre itself—desperately in need of refurbishment onstage and behind the scenes as well as in the auditorium—had antiquated stage machinery, scenery and lighting.[45] Any scenes of a spectacular nature were therefore staged in a Heath Robinson manner. These problems were particularly acutely felt when it came to the performance of Wagner's works. The British inability to do scenic justice to this repertory was something that had troubled critics for decades and there was little improvement in the 1920s.[46] Scenically complex episodes such as Mime's death scene and the dragon in *Siegfried* took place offstage, leading one critic to observe that 'At Covent Garden a great many things are supposed to be just around the corner'.[47] Scenery modelled on the original Bayreuth production was still in use at the opera house in the late 1920s and becoming progressively shabbier: what critics regarded as an otherwise near-perfect production of *The Ring* in 1929 (with a very high standard of singing from a cast led by Friedrich Schorr) was marred by antiquated scenery.[48]

In 1924 there would be a return to something resembling the international seasons of old. The Grand Opera Syndicate put on a summer season between early May and late July, denying the BNOC its usual lease, with several weeks of German operas (Wagner and Strauss works, including two complete cycles of the *Ring*, all conducted by Bruno Walter), followed by an Italian season.[49] This was followed by seasons along similar lines in 1925, 1926, and 1927 funded by the patronage of the Courtauld family; 'grand opera seasons' under Colonel Blois, who had acted as managing director of the Courtauld syndicate, followed in the final summers of the decade.[50]

44. Anon., 'The Sublime and the Ridiculous', *MS*, 22/413 (14 July 1923), 5.

45. Percy Colson, 'The Covent Garden Opera Season', *Apollo*, 3/15 (March 1926), 171–2, 172.

46. Rodmell notes that 'a passionate interest in seeing [Wagner's] works faithfully and professionally produced became a running thread' in critical commentary of the Grand Opera Syndicate at Covent Garden in the years around the turn of the century. Rodmell, *Opera in the British Isles*, p. 85.

47. Anon., 'Stagecraft of the Ring', *The Times*, 19 May 1928, 12.

48. Anon., 'Covent Garden Opera: *Das Rheingold*', *The Times*, 24 April 1929, n.p.

49. See prospectus 'Royal Opera: Covent Garden. Grand Opera Season 1924', in V&A Theatre and Performance Collections, production box: Covent Garden, 1924.

50. The Courtauld family had made its fortune after developing a way of making artificial silk. The three Courtauld brothers, Samuel, Stephen, and Jack, financed opera at Covent Garden at the behest of Samuel's wife, even though their personal interests were more in art and racing. Colson, *Those Uneasy Years*, p. 96.

Covent Garden's repertory during the later 1920s was certainly more adventurous: *L'heure espagnole*, *Gianni Schicchi*, and *Falstaff* were among the works performed in 1926, while the 1927 season included the long-neglected *Fidelio*, the ever-popular *Ring*, a highly successful *Rosenkavalier*, and the much-anticipated premiere of *Turandot*.[51]

Artists of international calibre began to return in the later 1920s, both to the stage and to the pit, and lavish praise was heaped upon a new generation of singers, including Maria Jeritza, Lotte Lehmann, Elisabeth Schumann, Frida Leider, and Maria Olczewska.[52] The need for unfavourable comparisons with great singers of the past was diminishing. In artistic terms, London was once again on the verge of being able to rival New York, regarded from the British perspective, at least, as the operatic capital of the world during the 1920s.[53]

Yet the constant changing of the lessees of Covent Garden during this period led to a far greater sense of instability than before the War.[54] And throughout the decade there was also a discernible sense that the theatre itself (see Figure 1.1) was on its last legs.[55] It was a shabby relic of an earlier, now unfashionable age: an 'old, grey building, surrounded by slums and vegetable stalls', as *Opera* described it, with winding corridors and a dated Victorian foyer with heavy curtains, decorative carpets, and large aspidistras in pots.[56] The auditorium and backstage areas were also in need of refurbishment and the organisation of the seating was incompatible with what many critics held up as a new democratic age of opera-going.[57] The auditorium still maintained its Victorian structure, with many tiers of boxes (although there were experimental seasons

51. Figaro, 'The Operatic World', *MO*, 49/587 (August 1926), 1081–3, 1081; Figaro, 'The Operatic World', *MO*, 50/595 (April 1927), 677–8, 677.

52. H. E. Wortham, 'Music of the Month', in R. Sydney Glover (Ed.), *Apollo: A Journal of the Arts, Vol 5 January to June 1927* (Nendeln, Liechtenstein: Kraus Reprint, 1976), pp. 272–4, p. 273.

53. 'We get a finer variety of first class singers than any other capital city except New York'. Figaro, 'The Operatic World', *MO*, 51/611 (August 1928), 1061–2, 1061. Rosa Ponselle, who came to London in 1929, was fought over by managers on both sides of the Atlantic. See Mary Jane Phillips-Matz, *Rosa Ponselle: American Diva* (Boston: Northeastern University Press, 1997), p. 238.

54. Rosenthal, *Two Centuries of Opera at Covent Garden*, p. 391.

55. Edward J. Dent went so far as to say in 1921 that 'Covent Garden has collapsed: we need say no more about it'. Edward J. Dent, 'The World of Music', *ILN*, 23 July 1921, 114.

56. 'Editorial', *Opera*, 1/5 (May 1923), 5. A photograph of the foyer can be seen in Richard Northcott, 'A Musical History of Covent Garden Theatre', in *Stories of the Operas and the Singers*, Official Souvenir, Royal Opera, Covent Garden Season 1919, 69–84, 75.

57. 'The Covent Garden opera house was built for a social world that has greatly changed, and it is totally unsuited as a theatre to present conditions'. W. J. Turner, 'The World of Music: The Opera Season', *ILN*, 29 April 1922, 630.

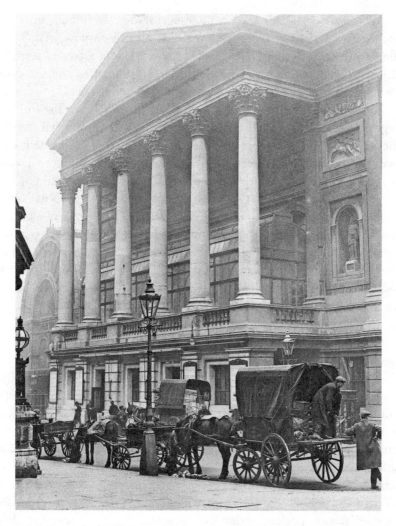

Figure 1.1 Covent Garden Theatre in London, 1927. © SZ Photo/Knorr & Hirth/Bridgeman Images.

when some were replaced by rows of seats), for which the theatre was struggling to find subscribers either from the aristocracy or the *nouveaux riches*.[58]

58. *The Times* reported that in the mid-1920s the pit-tier boxes had been replaced by two rows of guinea seats. The author of the article believed, however, that the only commercially viable option was to return to boxes and to find a full complement of subscribers for them. Anon., 'The Grand Opera Season: Plans for Covent Garden Performances', *The Times*, 8 January 1927, 8. Turner argued in 1927 that the number of medium-priced seats was 'ridiculously small' and that the theatre's financial problems could be solved only if it were reconfigured on the can-tilever system along the lines of the Palladium, Coliseum, or Drury Lane. W. J. Turner, 'The World of Music: Opera Present and To Come', *ILN*, 22 January 1927, 146–7, 146.

Agnes Savill, a doctor and opera evangelist, described the approach to the theatre in 1923 in evocative terms that recall Henry Mayhew's mid-nineteenth-century social tract *London Labour and the London Poor*: 'Past the closed cabbage and fruit stalls, and the huge emptied wooden cases, through the long dark tortuous streets—at last we were safely settled in the warm bright atmosphere of the Covent Garden stalls'.[59] But the fruit and vegetable stalls were actually a threat to the theatre. The group that acquired the lease of the opera house and surrounding area in 1928 made it clear that they intended to knock the building down by 1930 in order to develop the site for commercial purposes and to make way for the expanding fruit and vegetable market.[60] Rather than being regarded as a proposed act of architectural and cultural vandalism, the prospect of losing Covent Garden was not necessarily considered a matter for regret. Music critics repeatedly complained that it was 'one of the worst-sited of opera houses' and expressed their desire for a new national theatre that would be more 'centrally located'.[61] (It is not clear where they perceived the 'centre' of London to be.) Various complicated negotiations and deals took place, however, and the theatre was finally given a reprieve in the mid-1930s.

Covent Garden was not, of course, the end of the story for opera in London. Numerous other venues staged operas during the 1920s, with the Old Vic being particularly significant. There were endless discussions throughout the decade about London's need for a permanent opera house, but Percy Scholes (then music critic for *The Observer* but also a critic and lecturer who did much to democratise opera) wrote in 1921: 'We have in London a permanent opera house; it lies south of the river in an unfashionable quarter and year after year quietly goes on with its job'.[62] The Old Vic was a very important home for popular opera under its conductor Charles Corri: opera in English was presented alongside Shakespeare plays and lectures by learned speakers, and special performances were put on for school children. Tickets were cheaply priced and nobody wore evening dress. The audience was initially solidly working class, although there was some change in the social demographic of the theatre as the decade went on, with some loss of the original audience to other attractions such as cinema, and an incursion of middle-class listeners.[63] The operation ran on a shoestring, with constant appeals for funding: the theatre was in a shabby state prior

59. Agnes Savill, *Music, Health and Character* (London: John Lane, The Bodley Head, 1923), p. 72.

60. See Rosenthal, *Two Centuries of Opera at Covent Garden*, p. 392.

61. Figaro, 'The Operatic World', *MO*, 52/617 (February 1929), 431–2, 431.

62. Percy A. Scholes, 'The Season Opens', *The Observer*, 2 October 1921, 10.

63. Gilbert, *Opera for Everybody*, p. 39.

to extensive remodelling at the end of the decade, and production stand-ards were amateurish.[64] Yet the Old Vic commanded the respect and sup-port of well known musical figures such as Thomas Beecham, Nellie Melba, and Henry Wood, all of whom assisted with fund-raising endeavours. The company also received the backing of prominent academics such as Edward Dent, Fellow of King's College, Cambridge, whose clear and comprehen-sible translation of *The Magic Flute* was produced at the Old Vic every year between 1920 and 1939.[65]

Many other one-off operatic ventures came and went in London throughout the decade. Often, performances took place in multi-purpose venues, undermining the idea of opera as some sort of lavish or pretentious art form far removed from other contemporary forms of entertainment. The Fairbairn-Miln Company, for example, a modest and short-lived rival to the Old Vic Company, performed a twelve-week season in 1920 at the Surrey Theatre on Blackfriars Road, a theatre that was by this time prin-cipally being used as a cinema.[66] And Rutland Boughton's Celtic-themed *The Immortal Hour* enjoyed long-running success at the Regent Theatre in the Euston Road, a former music hall.[67] The London Coliseum—now the home of English National Opera—was during this period used primarily for variety shows and musical theatre. However, the BNOC visited in 1927 to perform a week of operatic extracts (the second act of *The Marriage of Figaro*; parts of *Cavalleria rusticana*), the fragmented format presumably being chosen to suit an audience used to watching variety performances.[68]

Semi-staged operas were sometimes presented at the Albert Hall, al-though it was generally deemed to be a less than suitable location for opera, with uncomfortable and distant seats in the upper galleries where people were 'herded like sheep'.[69] Productions by students from the conservatoires and amateur troupes, meanwhile, were staged regularly at the New Scala

64. Ibid., pp. 23, 29, 34.

65. Ibid., pp. 23, 31.

66. This troupe provided popular opera priced between 1s. and 5s., its repertory including popular favourites such as *Maritana*, *Faust*, and the *Cavalleria rusticana/Pagliacci* double bill, but also *Don Giovanni* and *The Valkyrie*, all in English. In contrast to the polite applause at Covent Garden, audience members in different parts of the house competed to see which could applaud with greatest warmth and make the most noise after a well-sung aria. Anon., 'Music and Drama', *The Manchester Guardian*, 6 March 1920, 8; Anon., 'The Valkyrie at the Surrey', *The Observer*, 14 March 1920, 20.

67. The opera was staged 216 times between October 1922 and April 1923 and revived from November 1923 for 160 performances. The opera was subsequently staged at the Kingsway Theatre in 1926. Michael Hurd, *Rutland Boughton and the Glastonbury Festivals* (Croydon: The Rutland Boughton Memorial Trust, 2014), p. 146.

68. Anon., 'Opera at the Coliseum', *The Daily Mail*, 10 May 1927, 8.

69. W. J. Turner, 'The World of Music: Opera at the Albert Hall, and Elsewhere', *ILN*, 29 October 1927, 772.

Theatre on Charlotte Street, near Tottenham Court Road, and a summer season of light opera was produced at the Court Theatre near Sloane Square in 1928, conducted by Adrian Boult.[70] There were also numerous operatic performances in suburban London, at theatres with their own distinctive local audiences. Critics often observed that the audience for opera in Hampstead, for instance, would not travel to hear opera in Lewisham and vice versa, and grumbled that London's opera problem was as much geographical as psychological. And yet there is evidence that this was not entirely true: for example, Southwark residents formed the backbone of the Old Vic audience, but there is evidence that people also travelled to the theatre from as far away as Golders Green, Hampstead, and Hammersmith.[71]

Beyond London, in addition to the regular performances by the touring companies, there were sporadic opera festivals, most notably the Glastonbury Festival (1914–26), established in Somerset by the composer Rutland Boughton, with support from the local shoe manufacturing firm, Clarks. This festival was modelled on Bayreuth, with the purpose of producing operas based upon British legend.[72] One-off seasons of opera were also put on sporadically, such as the Bristol British Opera season of 1926. However, many of the regional opera companies were short lived, collapsing within a short time of being established. A rather unusual venture was the Oxford University Opera Club, which combined scholarship and performance in its revivals of operas not performed since the seventeenth century. And in the autumn of 1929, Covent Garden launched its own touring company with an initial season in Halifax, although it seemed unclear of its place in the operatic marketplace. Figaro reported that 'Apparently they are just out to give good popular opera in the best possible way. They are neither appealing to highbrows, nor are they making a bold bid for popularity and applause by professing adherence to any such democratic, and perhaps unfortunate, slogan as "Twopence-a-week-opera for all" '.[73]

As already observed, members of the musical establishment called repeatedly throughout the decade for the establishment of a 'national opera house', ideally one with a training school for singers attached.[74] The

70. W. J. Turner, 'The World of Music: Opera at the Court and at CG', *ILN*, 9 June 1928, 1066.

71. Gilbert, *Opera for Everybody*, p. 29.

72. Between 1914 and 1922, the Festival had staged 266 operatic performances, as well as concerts and ballets, and put on an extensive educational programme. Rutland Boughton, *The Glastonbury Festival Movement* (London: Somerset Folk Press, 1922), p. 20.

73. Figaro, 'The Operatic World', *MO*, 53/625 (October 1929), 23–4, 24.

74. Ethel Smyth proposed a slightly different plan, whereby a students' opera house, fed by the three London conservatoires, would be established in a London suburb. The students would be trained in enunciation, moving, acting, and dancing, and their repertoire would consist of works by composers such as Handel, Mozart, Gluck, and Purcell, with 'grand opera and

performances would be in English, the performers would be British and the prices would be cheap. Above all, there would be opportunities to give exposure to the works of British composers, to which Covent Garden had long been resistant. There had been previous attempts at setting up such a theatre, such as the new opera house on the Victoria Embankment planned by James Mapleson in 1875 and Oscar Hammerstein's short-lived London Opera House, opened on the Kingsway in 1911, but all had thus far foundered.[75]

Proposals were regularly mooted for opera houses that would hold 3,000, 4,000, or even 10,000 people: commentators speculated that if the seats were priced modestly, such theatres would be full every night of the year, such was the supposed growing demand for 'people's opera'.[76] In 1928, for instance, the *ILN* reported a new plan that seemed to offer the answer to London's operatic problems. A theatre could be built on the site of the Foundling Hospital in Bloomsbury, with the main hospital building preserved as an imposing frontispiece.[77] The extensive grounds, meanwhile, would allow ample room to provide parking for 1,000 cars. Interestingly, parking was regarded as a key consideration: the number of cars on the road in the West End was considered to be at breaking point, even at this early stage in the history of motoring.[78] The fact that it loomed large, despite London's extensive and efficient public transport network, reveals that the *ILN* would appear to have envisaged a continuing model of high-society glamorous opera-going (only the wealthy owned cars in this period). In any case, the Bloomsbury project never got off the ground, and the Foundling Hospital was in due course demolished.

touring absolutely forbidden'. Ethel Smyth, 'An Iron Thesis on Opera', *LM*, 17/98 (December 1927), 157–68, 163.

75. On Mapleson's and Hammerstein's opera houses, see Rodmell, *Opera in the British Isles*, pp. 25–7 and 106–8. Rodmell writes that 'In the Edwardian years, the establishment of a national opera became, for many, the panacea for Britain's "operatic problem"'. Ibid., p. 207.

76. W. J. Turner, 'The World of Music: Opera at the Albert Hall, and Elsewhere', *ILN*, 29 October 1927, 772; W. J. Turner, 'The World of Music: Opera Present and To Come', *ILN*, 22 January 1927, 146.

77. W. J. Turner, 'The World of Music: Sir Thomas Beecham's Opera Scheme', *ILN*, 16 November 1927, 976. The hospital itself had moved out to the countryside and various other plans had been mooted for the site, including—ironically—the relocation of Covent Garden market.

78. Pugh estimates that the number of cars in Britain increased from 132,000 in 1914 to 1,056,000 by 1930 (Pugh, *'We Danced All Night'*, p. 243).

PRIVATIONS

Finances, of course, were what prevented most of the grander operatic ambitions of the decade from coming to fruition. Putting on opera was always
expensive: W. J. Turner wrote in the *ILN* that 'There is not in the world a
costlier form of amusement, unless it be keeping a racing stable'.[79] (During
the interwar period, horseracing was uneconomic and verging on unviable,
despite its popularity, due to rising costs.[80]) But specific financial difficulties following the War undoubtedly affected audiences' ability to support
opera as well as theatres' ability to put it on. Opera companies struggled
from 1916 after the introduction of the entertainments tax, a tax that was
levied on gross box-office receipts rather than profits, which had to be paid
even if a production made a loss: ultimately it would be this tax, together
with other bills, which would cause the BNOC to founder.[81] Furthermore,
although it would be an exaggeration to suggest that the aristocracy had
ceased to attend the opera, there was much talk of it no longer having as
much spare money to patronise the opera as it had during the Edwardian
era.[82] This group had been hit by large rises in income tax and 'super tax'
since the War, while death duties were leading to the break-up of the estates
of the landed gentry.[83] Unfortunately, the decline of traditional aristocratic
patronage of opera in Britain was not immediately replaced by other forms
of support, either public or private. And although the problem was largely
financial, it was also attitudinal: Herman Klein concluded in 1922 that
Britons had 'lost the habit' for opera before the War and probably wouldn't
be able to afford to resume the habit even if they wanted to.[84]

Opera struggled to re-establish itself at Covent Garden after the War
but by 1925 there had been a marked improvement in bookings.[85] Even
when productions at Covent Garden sold out, however, they still did not
always make a profit; the seasons of the interwar period, in fact, made losses

79. W. J. Turner, 'The World of Music', *ILN*, 25 July 1925, 182/188, 188.

80. Mike Huggins, *Horseracing and the British, 1919–1930* (Manchester: Manchester
University Press, 2003), pp. 19–20, 186.

81. Maggie B. Gale, *West End Women: Women and the London Stage, 1918–1962* (London and
New York: Routledge, 1996), p. 45; Martin, 'The British "Operatic Machine"', 194.

82. As the singer Robert Radford wrote in 1923, 'Money has changed hands—the old aristocracy are feeling the pinch terribly, and the person who subscribed to the Grand Opera because
it was the thing to do, cannot now afford it'. Robert Radford, 'The Future of Opera in England',
Opera, 1/1 (January 1923), 6–8, 6.

83. Clive Barker, 'Theatre and Society: The Edwardian Legacy, The First World War and the
Inter-War Years', in Clive Barker and Maggie B. Gale (Eds.), *British Theatre Between the Wars,
1918–1939* (Cambridge: Cambridge University Press, 2000), pp. 4–37, p. 23.

84. Herman Klein, 'Our Lost Operatic Lead', *MT*, 63/947 (1 January 1922), 20–1.

85. Bookings were up 30 per cent on the previous year for German opera and 80 per cent for
Italian. Figaro, 'The Operatic World', *MO*, 49/579 (December 1925), 247–8, 248.

varying from a thousand to ten thousand pounds.[86] These losses became progressively smaller as the years progressed, halving each successive year between 1925 and 1927, which the London Opera Syndicate cited as evidence of growing public demand.[87] But losses there still were, despite the venture being propped up by the Courtauld Family, and the money made was still not enough to put the undertaking on a secure financial basis. An article in *The Musical Times* of 1925 went so far as to claim that opera was bankrupt as far as London was concerned and that sooner or later it would cease to exist as an activity.[88]

Some commentators blanched at the expense of producing opera and recommended a new spirit of financial prudence. The BNOC itself sometimes voiced this message in unashamedly politicised terms via the mouthpiece of its house magazine, *Opera*. In 1924, for instance, J. H. Clynes—the son of J. R. Clynes, Leader of the Labour Party and the House of Commons—wrote an article appealing for a 'Reformation movement' in opera, which would involve the simplification of props, costumes, and lighting schemes, and the cutting of star artists' fees.[89] (Clynes senior—a former textile worker—was at this time agitating for an operatic subsidy, knowing that it would appeal to many of his constituents who enjoyed opera.[90]) Other writers for *Opera* criticised the cost of lavish pre-War productions at Covent Garden that had only been put on a handful of times.[91] Yet on the other hand it was widely acknowledged that economies were more problematic in opera than in other forms of theatre, since audiences expected opera to provide escapist spectacle and a reprieve from the drabness of day-to-day life.[92]

In post-War Britain money was in short supply for lavish set designs, costumes, or even rehearsal time, and this led to bad habits and lazy attitudes. British singers of the 1920s had a reputation for learning their parts in automaton-like fashion, being reluctant to learn new translations, and

86. Rosenthal, *Two Centuries of Opera at Covent Garden*, p. 395.

87. London Opera Syndicate Season Brochure for 1927 [V&A Theatre and Performance Collections, production box: Covent Garden Theatre, 1927].

88. Anon., 'The Bankruptcy of Opera', *MT*, 66/990 (1 August 1925), 697–8, 697.

89. J. H. Clynes, 'Opera for the Masses', *Opera*, 2/3 (March 1924), 6–7, 7.

90. Rose, *The Intellectual Life of the British Working Classes*, p. 201.

91. For instance, Beecham had put on three performances of *Iris* in his last season at Covent Garden in a production that was reputed to have cost three times as much as any musical comedy in London and was unlikely to be revived. Oliver Bernard, 'Staging Grand Opera', *Opera*, 1/1 (January 1923), 10–11, 11.

92. Edward J. Dent argued in 1921 that 'If [a man's] own normal life is drab, he wants the theatre to give him gorgeousness. Some men want gorgeous women, some gorgeous scenery, others gorgeous emotion, gorgeous singing, or a gorgeous orchestra'. Edward J. Dent, 'The World of Music', *ILN*, 23 July 1921, 114.

refusing to waste time analysing the motivations of a character.[93] This 'spirit of routine' had, however, a practical purpose: it allowed singers to step into the role for any company that might hire them, and to perform with little or no rehearsal, which was a fact of contemporary theatrical life. At the Old Vic, for instance, operas were put on after a single orchestral rehearsal and a single rehearsal for soloists and principals: orchestra and singers met for the first time during the actual performance.[94] The chorus were enthusiastic amateurs and the orchestra a scratch band; costumes and sets were routinely recycled from opera to opera.[95] Given the low budgets of the touring companies, it is inevitable that standards of staging should have been low, although audience expectations were often similarly low. A performance during which only a few things went wrong was generally considered to have been a success.[96]

DISTRACTIONS

Money and interest were also being siphoned off by other forms of entertainment during this period. Interwar Britons benefited from increased leisure time and more leisure opportunities: there was a boom in holidays, sport, motoring, and a wide variety of forms of entertainment.[97] As we shall see in subsequent chapters, audiences for opera remained sizeable during the 1920s; likewise, opera found interesting ways of interacting with popular culture. Nevertheless, these alternative forms of entertainment prompted considerable anxiety on the part of many of those who were trying to promote opera.[98]

Cinema was the principal threat—not only in Britain but even in more thriving operatic nations, including Italy, where opera was characterised in *The Musical News and Herald* as an old lady 'in high dudgeon' at having been abandoned 'for the fresher charms of Miss Cinema newly arrived from

93. Dent, 'Music: The Naturalization of Opera in England', *LM*, 1/6 (April 1920), 763–5, 763.
94. Gilbert, *Opera for Everybody*, p. 36.
95. Ibid., pp. 32, 36.
96. The stage management of the BNOC's 1922 summer season, for example, was praised by the *ILN* for being 'well above the average standard' yet the picture created by the report sounds farcical: in *The Valkyrie* some doors revealing the woods in the spring opened too soon during Sieglinde and Siegmund's duet and a large rock dropped to the ground in the second act, whilst in *Siegfried* Wotan's spear did not shatter but remained intact. W. J. Turner, 'The World of Music', *ILN* (3 June 1922), 822.
97. Pugh, 'We Danced All Night', pp. 216–17.
98. The *Musical Standard* asserted in 1929 that 'Entertainment enters everyone's lives these days—there is the wireless, or the cinema, or the hosts of theatres and dance palaces: the public is in the mood for entertainment, but it must not be expensive or too exclusive, for there are so many counter-attractions'. Anon., 'Operas and Hopes', *MS*, 33/557 (26 January 1929), 21.

America'.[99] Second only to cinema as the new inter-generational, cross-class craze of the decade was social dancing, which took place not only in the growing number of dance halls, but in town halls, public swimming baths, and department stores.[100] Although dancing was predominantly a lower middle-class and working-class activity by the mid-1920s, it had a more glamorous manifestation in the charity balls and tea dances that were held at Covent Garden.[101]

A lesser, although still significant threat was posed to opera by rival types of theatrical entertainment. The decade witnessed a marked growth in enthusiasm for ballet, with Anna Pavlova in particular drawing large audiences and Diaghilev's Ballets Russes attracting intense media attention. Ballet was, it should be noted, considerably more progressive than opera during this period. Although a distinct audience was developing for dance—including 'Bright Young Things' who, in the words of John Collier and Iain Lang, 'made a homosexual ritual of the Russian ballet'—it did encroach to some extent upon the audience for opera and was reported at the beginning of the decade to be 'cast[ing] opera into the shade'.[102] Drama in London flourished during the 1920s and there was big money to be made from theatres by speculators, to the ire of W. J. Turner who argued that the proprietors of *The Daily Mail* would never be allowed to run public libraries.[103] These were optimistic years for British drama in terms of experimental approaches and a relaxation of Victorian dramatic conventions—which is not to say there were not also plenty of theatrical flops.[104] In comparison, the operatic repertory seemed stuck in a rut.

Later in the decade musical theatre started to draw audiences away in earnest from operas being put on by touring companies in the provinces. Manchester, for instance, had had a reputation for fine opera that 'stood second to none in the Empire' during the War—productions there supposedly being up to continental standards of professionalism—and had

99. Anon., 'Can Opera Survive the Dole?', *MNH*, 71/1807 (27 November 1926), 465–6, 465.

100. For further reading, see Nott, *Going to the Palais*.

101. Charity balls—typically organised in aid of local hospitals—were usually fancy dress occasions, with prizes for the best costumes. They featured demonstrations of the latest dances and songs and were attended by society members or famous actors and variety stars. (See unattributed and untitled clippings from the *Dancing Times*, November–December 1925: V&A Theatre and Performance Collections, production box: Covent Garden Theatre, 1925.)

102. John Collier and Iain Lang, *Just the Other Day: An Informal History of Great Britain since the War* (London: Hamish Hamilton, 1932), p. 169; J. T. Grein, 'The World of the Theatre', *ILN*, 4223 (27 March 1920), 510.

103. Richard J. Hand and Michael Wilson, *London's Grand Guignol and the Theatre of Horror* (Exeter: University of Exeter Press, 2007), p. 9; W. J. Turner, *Variations on the Theme of Music* (London: Heinemann, 1924), p. 78.

104. J. C. Trewin, with pictures by Raymond Mander and Joe Mitchenson, *The Gay Twenties: A Decade of the Theatre* (London: MacDonald, 1958), pp. 9, 24–8.

been a city where touring opera had done very well during the early twenties, but by 1927 the BNOC started to lose a lot of money there as theatre managers began to put on enticing pre-West End runs of popular musicals.[105] Some British opera singers were even deserting opera for the musical theatre stage themselves, prompted either by a shortage of work or a taste for a more diverse career. Marie Louise Edvina, for example, who had been a regular principal at Covent Garden from 1908, played the lead in the musical comedy *Hearts and Diamonds* at the Strand Theatre in 1926.[106] It should be noted, however, that opera's rivals also threatened one another: many music halls were converted into cinemas during the 1920s.[107]

Jazz and sport were two other significant counter-attractions to opera: this was, of course, an international problem. Mascagni, interviewed for a British music magazine, argued that interest in these two pursuits had become 'excessive', 'a mania', and 'a symptom of intellectual degeneracy'.[108] The good health of jazz versus that of opera is captured in a full-page cartoon that appeared in *The Musical Mirror* in 1926, entitled 'Opera and jazz—a study in contrasts'.[109] In the background, a lively dance is taking place, the dancers in *commedia dell'arte*-style fancy dress; in the foreground, a beggar with a hat, crutches, and an eye patch. The caption for the image reads 'Dear Friends, I am crippled and starving. (Signed) Opera'. People of all classes, meanwhile, were being drawn to participatory and spectator sport, which enjoyed a huge surge of interest during the 1920s, and the racecourse was to some extent the new site of sartorial display that the opera house had once been.[110] Sir Hugh Allen, Director of the Royal College of Music, even proposed that audiences were giving less support to music because of their enthusiasm for motorcars, although he predicted that this would be only a passing fad that would burn itself out.[111]

As Rodmell has argued, these new forms of entertainment 'started to erode the support networks the touring opera companies had built up over

105. N. C., 'The Opera Question. Our Last Chance', *The Manchester Guardian* (24 March 1928), 15; Figaro, 'The Operatic World', *MO*, 50/593 (February 1927), 469–70.

106. Michael Scott, *The Record of Singing, Vol. 2 1914–1925* (London: Duckworth, 1979), p. 56. Figaro wrote in 1929 that over a dozen first-rate English singers were now singing in musical plays. Figaro, 'The Operatic World', *MO*, 53/627 (December 1929), 219–20, 219.

107. Oliver Double, *Britain Had Talent: A History of Variety Theatre* (Basingstoke: Palgrave Macmillan, 2012), p. 37. See also Kift, *The Victorian Music Hall*, p. 58.

108. Pietro Mascagni, 'Wanted—A New Wagner. Present-Day Intellectual Degeneracy', *MM*, 9/4 (April 1929), 89.

109. Anon., 'Opera and Jazz—A Study in Contrasts', *MM*, 6/2 (February 1926), 26.

110. On fashion at the races, see Huggins, *Horseracing and the British*, pp. 47–8.

111. Anon., 'Music v. Motorcars', *MM*, 7/7 (July 1927), 165. Pugh argues that motoring maintained an upper-class glamour throughout the 1920s and was seen as a symbol of modernity, emblematic of the age. Pugh, *'We Danced All Night'*, pp. 248, 251.

decades and maintained even through the war'.[112] Many of the touring companies had fallen on hard times and for them there was never any question of, to use a contemporary expression, 'making opera pay': doing good business meant little more than covering basic expenses.[113] In 1922 the Carl Rosa Company announced that it had had to disband one of its troupes for financial reasons—it could no longer afford to cover the entertainments tax, travelling expenses, and the high costs of orchestral musicians.[114] This move not only put a hundred people out of work but meant that certain towns and cities lost their regular visits. The BNOC, meanwhile, which was established at precisely the time when the Carl Rosa was scaling back its operations, supplemented a small chorus with local singers when on tour because the costs of employing a large professional chorus were prohibitive.[115] It also toured with an orchestra of no more than sixty musicians, even when performing works by composers such as Wagner and Strauss. (For comparison, Covent Garden had employed 120 players for large-scale works prior to the War.) Some commentators predicted that operas requiring large orchestras would simply have to be abandoned.[116]

Arguments for and against public subsidy, following the European model, and/or endowments along American lines were debated in the press throughout the decade, since it was widely acknowledged that 'grand opera' (a broad term used to mean serious foreign opera) was not able to cover its costs from ticket sales alone. Opera's growing need for public subsidy, as aristocratic patronage fell away, would harden public attitudes towards the art form across the course of the twentieth century. A limited government subsidy for opera was in fact drawn up in 1930 and implemented in 1931, but during the 1920s the prospect seemed highly unlikely.[117] Thus, members of the musical establishment proposed a succession of grandiose funding schemes, most of which were dependent upon enthusiasts taking out shares. In 1924 the composer and singer Isidore De Lara launched his National Opera Scheme, which would involve asking two million people to give £1 each to raise funds to build a permanent opera house with seats that would be affordable to all classes. The newly established *Gramophone*

112. Rodmell, *Opera in the British Isles*, p. 334.

113. Anon., 'Operatic Vicissitudes', *MNH*, 62/1561 (25 February 1922), 241.

114. Anon., '100 Carl Rosa Artists Unemployed', *MM*, 2/3 (March 1922), 72.

115. Anon., 'Amateur Opera Choruses', *MM*, 2/3 (March 1922), 76.

116. The Editor, 'Is Grand Opera doomed?', *MM*, 3/3 (March 1923), 75.

117. The Government promised to subsidise the Covent Garden Opera Syndicate by £17,500 a year. The timing was poor, with two and a half million people on the dole, and the proposal was greeted by a torrent of denunciation. An article in *The Times*, for example, scoffed at opera as 'that branch of the theatrical art in which the taxpayer takes the least possible interest' 'Taxation for Opera', *The Times*, 21 November 1930, cited in *MMR* (1 January 1931), 7–8, 8. For further reading, see Chapter 5 of Martin, 'The British "Operatic Machine"'.

magazine gave the scheme its backing and appealed for funds throughout 1925, but by 1926 was hinting that it was struggling, finally admitting in early March 1927 that it had handed the money received back to the donors.[118]

Undeterred by the failure of De Lara's scheme, Thomas Beecham launched the Imperial League of Opera (ILO) in 1927, believing that the old aristocratic patronage of opera was impossible and that it was hopeless to expect support from the State. He calculated that he could attract 150,000 members around the country, each of whom he would charge 10s. a year and encourage to take out a five-year subscription. With the proceeds raised, he estimated that he would be able to mount an annual London opera season of five to six months per year, plus shorter seasons in the provinces. A new orchestra was planned, which was to have a vast new theatre as its regular base.[119] Yet despite a highly elaborate publicity campaign, Beecham's scheme also came to nothing: donors gave large sums of money in the first instance but Beecham could attract nowhere near the amounts needed and the ILO was finally wound up in the early 1930s.

TRANSNATIONAL ENVY

From the British perspective during the 1920s, everything operatic looked so much rosier overseas. Music magazines piqued readers' envy with tales of the vibrant operatic life that was supposedly to be found in the major continental cities, reflecting a broader sense of cultural *malaise* about London's post-War place in the world.[120] An article published in *The Sackbut* in 1928 tantalised readers with reports that in Germany there were about a hundred theatres putting on an exclusively operatic repertory, often presenting an annual season of ten-and-a half months.[121] Certainly the situation in Berlin

---

118. Anon., 'Trade Winds and Idle Zephyrs', *Gramophone*, 4 (March 1927), 429.

119. For a detailed discussion of the various funding schemes that were launched during the decade, see Martin, 'The British "Operatic Machine"', and on the ILO specifically, see Alexandra Wilson, 'Gender', in Helen Greenwald (Ed.), *The Oxford Handbook of Opera* (New York: Oxford University Press, 2014), pp. 774–94.

120. Writing in the early 1930s, John Collier and Iain Lang remarked that: 'Even when, after the Armistice, the blinds were drawn up, the lights switched on, and the traffic began to flow again, London was still a poor relation of its pre-War self'. John Collier and Iain Lang, *Just the Other Day: An Informal History of Great Britain since the War* (London: Hamish Hamilton, 1932), pp. 37–8.

121. Wilhelm Altmann, 'The German Operatic Repertory', trans. Whyte Monk, *The Sackbut*, 9 (December 1928), 168–70, 168. Munich alone was said to have staged 293 opera performances in 1922, comprising 64 different operas. 'Crescendo', 'Musical Munich', *Opera*, 1/2 (February 1923), 20. Figaro estimated the number of opera houses in Italy to be between 300 and 400. Figaro, 'The Operatic World', *MO*, 46/541 (October 1922), 33.

outclassed that in London by some distance, with operas (including many new works) being performed to a high standard at the Staatsoper under Erich Kleiber, the Städtische Oper under Bruno Walter, and the Kroll Oper under Otto Klemperer.[122] Even 'poor little Belgium' was managing to keep La Monnaie open for ten months a year and able to sustain a training school.[123] To some extent, this may have been a case of the grass always being greener, but many well-to-do British people, including critics, regularly attended the opera when travelling in Europe, and would have experienced the contrasting circumstances at first hand. There was, of course, a discernible note of *Schadenfreude* in the more nationalistic sectors of the British press when major European opera houses were struggling, such as in 1921 when it was reported that the Paris Opéra was being run at a serious loss, despite state subsidy.[124]

Stories also abounded about a boom in operatic production and opera-going on the other side of the Atlantic. In the early 1920s the Metropolitan Opera was thriving, and the extravagant-sounding accounts in the British press are backed up by testimonies from New York.[125] *Time*, for example, reported that during the 1922–3 season, the Met's manager Giulio Gatti-Casazza had, by instilling a regime of rigorous discipline, managed to put on 169 performances of forty different operas (an outstanding achievement by any measure), and was making an annual surplus rumoured to be as high as $200,000.[126] The money available for opera in America's leading cities— much of it raised by philanthropically minded society ladies—meant that it was possible to put on programmes featuring all the new big names in opera that would 'make the mouths of opera-starved Londoners water'.[127] The sophisticated model of opera-going that was perceived to be on the decline at Covent Garden was alive and well in the States, primarily at the Met but also at other big city opera houses. For example, *Time*'s coverage of the opening of the Chicago Opera's 1927–8 season emphasised that the event

122. Erik Levi, *Music in the Third Reich* (Basingstoke: Macmillan, 1994), pp. 1–2.

123. Mrs Albert de Belleroche, 'Permanent British Opera in London', *MT*, 67/1006 (1 December 1926), 1094–5, 1094.

124. Rollo H. Myers, 'Music in Paris', *The Nation and the Athenaeum*, 30/4 (22 October 1921), 154–6, 154.

125. In the UK stories abounded about the Met being able to sustain a six-month season of international opera each year, having subscribers running into the thousands, sold-out houses, long lists of 'standees', an excellent chorus, and an array of star singers. See, for example, Ronald, *Variations on a Personal Theme*, p. 165; Frederick Bruegger, 'The Metropolitan Opera Co's Season', *MS*, 19/378 (11 March 1922), 75–6, 75.

126. Anon., 'The Opera Business', *Time*, 1/10 (5 May 1923), 19.

127. Mary Garden reported that 'to the average American man, opera is as painful as an operation' and that the development of opera in America was being driven entirely by women. Anon., 'The End of the BBC—On Being an Operatic Nation', *MNH*, 70/1772 (13 March 1926), 241–2, 242.

was all about fashionable people being seen: 'Mrs Rockefeller McCormick clasped her ancestral necklace of giant emeralds. Mrs Samuel Insull donned a new black chiffon, all spangled with gold. John McCormack buttoned himself into a new dress shirt. Photographers gave their flashlight cameras a final inspection'.[128]

Yet beneath the superficial glamour and beyond a handful of big cultural centres, the US had its own share of operatic problems. Although opera was indeed flourishing in New York during the 1920s, financial losses were the norm elsewhere: opera was in decline in many major American cities.[129] Even in Chicago, the 1923 season deficit was in the region of $300,000, a figure that reached almost $400,000 four years later.[130] At the end of the decade, the city's multi-million-dollar new opera house, funded by Samuel Insull, head of the Edison Company, opened with catastrophic timing on 4 November 1929: the New York Stock Exchange had crashed just six days earlier.[131] The number of touring companies was falling, just as it was in the UK. Nevertheless, the question was one of perception. Stories of America as a land of operatic riches seemed painfully ironic to contemporary British observers: Herman Klein noted that 'it is not exactly pleasant to be re-minded by our American friends, as we frequently are, that in matters oper-atic (at any rate on the vocal side) we have completely "lost our standard"'.[132] Interwar British critics regarded America as a lowbrow country—one lacking both class and culture—and continental Europe as the cradle of civilisation.[133] And yet European opera was being actively threatened by a creeping Americanisation in the form of cinema, while America now also appeared to be outdoing Europe in terms of the healthy production of opera.[134] Thomas Beecham wrote: 'I have read in an American paper an opinion that England seems to be becoming more and more content with the position of nursery to other more grown-up and musically appreciative countries'.[135] Such a situation was humiliating indeed.

128. Anon., 'Chicago Opera', *Time*, 10/20 (14 November 1927), p. 28.

129. John Dizikes, *Opera in America: A Cultural History* (New Haven and London: Yale University Press, 1993), p. 413.

130. Anon., 'The Opera Business', *Time*, 1/10 (5 May 1923), 19; Anon., 'Chicago Opera', *Time*, 10/20 (14 November 1927), p. 28.

131. For further reading, see Daniel Snowman, *The Gilded Stage: A Social History of Opera* (London: Atlantic Books, 2009), pp. 270–2.

132. Herman Klein, 'Our Opera Standards', Letter to *The Times*, 6 December 1921, 6.

133. Napper, *British Cinema and Middlebrow Culture*, pp. 25–6.

134. Official British resistance to American models of cultural consumption was manifested in the foundation of the BBC as a non-profit-driven monopoly and in the Cinematograph Films Act of 1927. Ibid., pp. 24–5.

135. Anon., 'A Message from Sir Thomas Beecham', *MILO*, 1/1 (October 1929), 4–6, 6.

FEAST OR FAMINE

The British operatic situation throughout the decade might best be summed up as 'feast or famine', and at the beginning of our period famine was the norm.[136] Opera seasons were put on sporadically, even in London, and there was often little certainty about whether seasons would be staged or not: periodicals would speculate in the spring about whether there would be any opera that same summer or autumn. Indeed, as late as the October of 1920, there was conjecture about whether there would be an autumn season at Covent Garden that same month, with commentators observing that a statement that appeared in one paper one day would be contradicted in another paper the next.[137]

The Times noted pessimistically that 'it is clear that while circumstances remain what they are, and London has to take its opera in little short spasms of excitement, not much real progress can be made'.[138] One such 'spasm' came in the summer of 1924, when opera-goers could choose between watching the international season at Covent Garden, the BNOC at His Majesty's, or the Carl Rosa at the Scala Theatre on Charlotte Street: a veritable glut of opera 'to suit all tastes and all purses'. In an analogy between opera and food characteristic of contemporaneous music criticism, Dyneley Hussey likened the three seasons to the fare on offer at different restaurants. Covent Garden came out most positively in his assessment, because although it had served up 'the oldest stock dishes', it had at least ensured that they were 'properly cooked and served reasonably hot with no stint of sauce and garnish'. Hussey confessed that he would rather hear *Rigoletto, La traviata,* or 'even the glutinous sweetmeats of Puccini' than try to swallow 'worthy attempts at novelties done *à l'anglaise* in understaffed and inadequate kitchens'.[139] In between such busy seasons, however, there was a drastic slackening of operatic activity. Even in 1926, when the operatic landscape was in a healthier state than it had been at the beginning of the decade, the situation was still unpredictable. Many music critics lamented

136. Julia Chatterton complained that 'It seems that we must either be inundated with opera, so to speak, or be left starving and without a single performance to enjoy'. Julia Chatterton, 'The Operatic Triangle', MS, 23/438 (28 June 1924), 216–17, 216.

137. Figaro, 'Whispers from the Wings', MO, 44/517 (October 1920), 36; Schaunard, 'Stray Musings', MO, 44/517 (October 1920), 32–3, 33.

138. Anon., 'Close of Opera Season. A Melba Night. Wireless Listeners' Tribute', The Times, 22 January 1923, 8.

139. Dyneley Hussey, 'The Glut of Opera', The Saturday Review, 137/3582 (21 June 1924), 632–3, 633.

this unpredictable situation but some considered opera's absence a boon for other forms of musical activity.[140]

Furthermore, it was also not unusual for productions or even entire seasons that had already been promised and advertised to be cancelled.[141] In 1926 the *ILN* wrote that the London Opera Syndicate was to be congratulated on its organisation of that spring/summer's season because 'it performed its advertised programme to the letter', which was 'an achievement sufficiently rare in the opera world to attract special notice'.[142] Several foreign opera companies considered visiting Britain in the 1920s: hopes were raised that London might put on seasons by the Metropolitan Opera, the Chicago Opera, the Danish Royal Opera, and the Stockholm Opera.[143] None came to fruition: promoters were concerned about whether there was sufficient support for opera in Britain to guarantee the necessary ticket sales and believed that excessively high prices would need to be charged in order to cover costs.[144]

By the end of the decade, British operatic culture seemed in some ways to be on a firmer footing but operatic activity remained patchy. In 1927 Herman Klein characterised Covent Garden as 'still standing, but utterly useless for permanent operatic purposes', the BNOC as 'financially at its last gasp', and the Carl Rosa as 'an excellent provincial troupe but only a shadow of its former self'.[145] The Old Vic opera troupe was in deficit and losing ground to the resident drama company.[146] The future of touring opera would deteriorate in the summer of 1929 when, after seven years, it was announced that the BNOC itself was to be wound up, having suffered losses

140. See, for instance, Edwin Evans, 'The Passing of the Top E Flat' (originally published in the *MNH*), reprinted in Evans, *The Margin of Music* (London: Oxford University Press/ Humphrey Milford, 1924), pp. 34–8, p. 34.

141. There is continuity here with the late nineteenth-century practice of giving notice of premieres only a few weeks in advance and postponing them if they were not ready. Rodmell, *Opera in the British Isles*, p. 13.

142. W. J. Turner, 'The World of Music: The End of the Opera Season', *ILN*, 10 July 1926, 84.

143. As reported respectively in Figaro, 'Whispers from the Wings', *MO*, 44/517 (October 1920), 36; Figaro, 'Whispers from the Wings', *MO*, 44/519 (December 1920), 215; Symphonicus, 'Heard in the Interval', *MM*, 2/2 (February 1922), 37; Figaro (citing speculation in *The Daily Mail*), 'The Operatic World', *MO*, 44/523 (April 1921), 589; and Figaro, 'The Operatic World', *MO*, 47/555 (December 1923), 253–4, 253.

144. The Editor, 'Is Grand Opera Doomed?', *MM*, 3/3 (March 1923), 75. There was also an ugly spat between the Covent Garden management and the BNOC when the former invited the Vienna State Opera to give a season to coincide with the British Empire Exhibition at Wembley: a time when high ticket sales could be guaranteed. The Viennese company tactfully withdrew, however, after the British press voiced outrage at the fact that the BNOC would be ousted from what had, for a short time, become its regular slot. Martin, 'The British "Operatic Machine"', 164.

145. Herman Klein, 'The Great Opera Scheme', *MNH*, 72/1823 (15 December 1927), 443–4, 443.

146. Gilbert, *Opera for Everybody*, p. 40.

it could not sustain. The ILO, as we have seen, would be nothing more than yet another bright idea that failed to come to fruition. The gradual arrival at Covent Garden of more and more high-profile singers from America was cause for cautious optimism, but there was still, on the cusp of the 1930s, an axe hanging over the theatre itself.[147]

The spasmodic nature of operatic production throughout the decade undoubtedly contributed to Klein's theory that Britons were 'losing the habit' of opera-going during the 1920s. Francis E. Barrett, a regular opera columnist in the early 1920s for *The Musical Times* (and also for *The Morning Post*), put his thumb on something particularly noteworthy by observing in 1920 that opera's absence from London for months at a time 'causes it to be regarded as a thing apart and something not included in our everyday lives'.[148] This comment indicates the comparative vibrancy of operatic culture before the War as well as its subsequent deterioration. More interestingly, it crystallises an idea that is still discussed today in debates about opera's accessibility: the importance of opera being presented as something ordinary, rather than something extraordinary if it is not to be regarded as 'elite'. In some senses, opera *was* something 'ordinary' in the 1920s: as we shall see presently, office boys and factory workers listened to operatic hits on the gramophone and the wireless and genuinely whistled them in the street, and opera interacted with popular culture in many different ways. Nevertheless, the idea of opera being 'something apart' so far as the British were concerned is a nagging concept one comes back to time and again in 1920s assessments of contemporary operatic culture, and it is a vital factor in the discussions surrounding opera's place in the brows.[149]

147. In December 1929 Figaro reported rumours that the theatre—'our star and hope'—would have no more than three seasons, writing 'Something must happen before that. Something *will*. Something always has happened to save just a little opera, in the best style, for us connoisseurs at the last minute. So our optimism has orders to hang on to the last ditch at all costs!' Figaro, 'The Operatic World', *MO*, 53/627 (December 1929), 219–20, 219.

148. Francis E. Barrett, 'Opera in London', *MT*, 61/924 (1 February 1920), 103–4, 103.

149. Henry Russell, for instance, stated that opera was regarded in England 'as a sort of extravagant and superfluous theatrical enterprise' (Henry Russell, *The Passing Show*, p. 288). Edward Dent wrote in his study of early English opera that 'To the Italian, music is a means of self-expression, or rather, or self-intensification; to the Englishman music is a thing apart, a message from another world' (Dent, *Foundations of English Opera*, p. 2).

CHAPTER 2

✧

Audiences

T o our eyes, the operatic culture of 1920s Britain, with its regular performances in towns and cities up and down the land to socially mixed
audiences, seems both vibrant and laudably democratic, even if performance standards sometimes left much to be desired. However, that is not
how it was seen by the more austere members of the contemporary music
establishment, whose snobbery about the audience for opera was directed
against two targets. They looked down simultaneously on humble Bradford
or Lewisham theatre-goers, who were happy to put up with unsophisticated touring productions, and on the old social elite who prioritised the
idea of opera-going as a social experience. In this, the first of a series of
chapters examining where opera fitted into the new cultural categories,
I shall examine the different audiences for opera in 1920s Britain and where
they heard it; questions of cost, dress, and etiquette; and strategies companies used to entice new types of listener. Perceptions of who opera was
'for' contributed to discussions about whether the art form was highbrow
or middlebrow.

If different art forms needed to be classified during the 1920s, so too
did the people who produced art, wrote about it, and consumed it. There
was not, of course, one single homogeneous operatic demographic but several quite different ones, depending upon whether one considered Covent
Garden, the Old Vic, or regional theatres to which companies such as the
BNOC toured. Even within the different audiences there were sub-sections,
and within a single theatre there might be entirely different audiences for
different types of repertoire. As *The Musical News and Herald* observed in
1924: 'One of the main difficulties to be solved in connection with the

advertising of the public performance of music is that the musical public is a heterogeneous mass'.[1]

Class distinctions and prejudices remained extremely powerful in interwar Britain, and yet class membership was sometimes hard to define and becoming increasingly fluid.[2] Perceptions of class and class snobbery were undoubtedly key features in discussions of cultural categorisation. The battle of the brows emerged in part out of a concern on the part of former social elites at the emergence and increasing social clout of the suburban middle classes. However, to assume that there was a straightforward correlation between the brows and the classes would be far too simplistic, just as one would be wrong to assume that only certain sectors of society attended the opera. The operatic audience in the 1920s was certainly not exclusively upper class, just as the audience for variety shows was not exclusively working class: demographics for both types of entertainment cut across class lines. There was still an elite audience for opera at Covent Garden, made up in part of members of 'Society', a term that should not simply be taken to mean the upper classes but rather that sector of the class that associated itself with social display, augmented by some successful social climbers.[3] At theatres such as the Old Vic there was a working-class audience for opera, and the middle classes attended opera at a variety of different types of venue.

Moreover, the divisions among different types of audience were not merely class-based: there were intellectual as well as social elites and these were not the same thing. To be wealthy and well bred did not necessarily make you an intellectual: indeed, as Aldous Huxley observed, many members of the upper middle classes had a 'healthily Public-School contempt' for the highbrows.[4] Conversely, there were many members of the middle classes and even the working classes who took a committed interest in serious art of various kinds. Jonathan Rose has written extensively about the

1. Anon., 'Music and Advertising', *MNH*, 66/1675 (3 May 1924), 417.

2. As Matt Houlbrook writes, this was 'a period when advertising encouraged dreamlike fantasies of social mobility'. Matt Houlbrook, *Prince of Tricksters: The Incredible True Story of Netley Lucas, Gentleman Crook* (Chicago and London: Chicago University Press, 2016), p. 3.

3. Ross McKibbin writes: 'The image of Society was a very powerful one, in the interwar years particularly, and many of its *habitués* were indeed upper-class. But some of its members would not have been thought upper-class by those who indisputably were. Furthermore, much of the upper class, the "old" upper class especially, did not choose to "move in Society"'. Ross McKibbin, *Classes and Cultures: England 1918–1951* (Oxford: Oxford University Press, 1998, repr. 2013), p. 2.

4. Aldous Huxley, 'Foreheads Villainous Low', in *Music at Night and Other Essays* (London: Chatto and Windus, 1931), pp. 201–10, p. 203. Collini writes that highbrows were often assumed to be educated and well-spoken but that 'In reality . . . the upper and upper-middle classes were full of "lowbrows"'. Collini, *Absent Minds*, p. 110.

flourishing working-class British intelligentsia of the late nineteenth and early twentieth centuries, whose members—often manual workers—were keen cultural autodidacts. For instance, he discusses a 1918 survey of 816 Sheffield manual workers, which identified a distinctive 'intellectual group'. Among them were young people who defined their jobs as 'engineer', 'engine tenter', 'grinder', 'munitions worker', 'machinist', and 'file cutter' and who listed attending the opera and concerts among their regular interests, alongside reading, visiting museums and galleries, and amateur musical performance.[5]

The audience for opera could be separated into groups, then, but the divisions between them did not necessarily fall along predictable lines. Figaro of *Musical Opinion*, a serious critic well disposed towards opera, divided opera lovers into two non-class-based categories: 'steady-going' music-lovers, who attended particular companies' performances loyally, and people who were 'ready to follow any will-o'-the-wisp'.[6] The sheer existence of such fickle listeners within the audience for opera—who wished to attend opera as a purely social occasion and were seduced by the latest star—bolstered the highbrows' case against it.

An article published in *The Times* in 1930, meanwhile, divided the operatic public into three principal groups.[7] The first was the audience for the Covent Garden international season—claimed to be 'entirely a London public'—which wanted to hear famous singers in canonical operas by Wagner, Verdi, and Puccini, and was willing to pay high prices in order to do so. The second group, whose size was far more difficult to estimate, was scattered all over the country and attended local performances by touring troupes such as the Carl Rosa Company. This public, according to *The Times*, had a genuine if unsophisticated taste for opera so long as it was sung in English, enjoyed hearing works that it already knew, and was 'untroubled by niceties of taste and style'.

The third public that *The Times* identified had never been satisfactorily catered for. This group, some of whose members regularly encountered high standards of operatic performance abroad, was more interested than the first two categories in opera as art and was dissatisfied with the current state of operatic culture in Britain. Its members, portrayed as the intelligent, serious audience for opera, attended performances by many different companies but found none of the existing operations entirely satisfactory. Covent Garden was 'too expensive, too foreign, and too snobbish' and the

5. See Jonathan Rose, *The Intellectual Life of the British Working Classes*, 2nd edn (New Haven: Yale University Press, 2010), pp. 190–2.

6. Figaro, 'The Operatic World', *MO*, 51/603 (December 1927), 255–6, 255.

7. 'Endowed Opera: For Whose Advantage?', *The Times*, 29 November 1930, 10.

travelling companies 'too rough-and-ready in their methods and too oppor-
tunist in their choice of repertory'. The Old Vic, with its performances of
works by Mozart and modern English composers, came closest to fulfilling
the artistic ideals of this group but was hampered by its small orchestra.
What this group really wanted to see was the much-discussed hypothetical
national opera house dedicated to the serious cultivation of the art form,
where there would be well-trained British singers and an adventurous repertory including new operas and lesser-known older works.

Such categorisation provides a basic overview of the audiences for opera
during the late 1920s but *The Times* was guilty of over-generalisation and
not all audience members could be pigeonholed so neatly. Let us examine
first the audience at Covent Garden, which was not homogeneous, either
in terms of social make-up or taste. The theatre still depended upon Society
support, but the aristocracy's presence could no longer be guaranteed in
large numbers, partly due to the financial difficulties already discussed and
partly due to the fact that 'being seen' at the opera was no longer regarded as
quite so essential.[8] The blame for a change in attitude that was already setting in before the War was sometimes laid at the door of royalty, who were
still regarded as key figures in setting public taste.[9] During the nineteenth
century, Queen Victoria's presence had encouraged both more regular attendance and better decorum on the part of members of the aristocracy,
and she had played a role in 'domesticating' opera as an art form.[10] Her son
Edward VII was an even more enthusiastic opera-goer, both as Prince of
Wales and as King. Although members of the Royal Family still attended
Covent Garden with reasonable regularity during the 1920s—BNOC performances as well as the international season—critics chastised George V
for not supporting opera as devotedly as his father had done.[11] Furthermore,

---

8. The Editor of *The Musical Mirror* argued that 'apparently society has ceased to regard it as so
desirable to be "seen" at the opera, or else it no longer has the necessary wealth available to pay
for the privilege'. The Editor, 'Is Grand Opera Doomed?', 75.

9. *The Strand Magazine*, for example, attributed the popularity of *La bohème* on record to the
fact that the King and Queen were said to have a particular liking for the opera. G. M. Thomson,
'Britain's Favourite Gramophone Records', *The Strand Magazine*, 67 (January 1929), 70–7, 72.

10. Hall-Witt, *Fashionable Acts*, pp. 201, 203.

11. The King, Queen, Duke of York, and Princess Victoria giving 'the royal seal of approval'
to the BNOC in 1922 was reported in Anon., 'The World of Women', *ILN*, 10 June 1922, 872.
This column often reported the presence of the Princesses at Covent Garden and noted that
the Princess Royal, in particular was 'a real opera lover' (26 May 1923, 916). However, Richard
Northcott, archivist of the Royal Opera House, wrote in 1933: 'The death of King Edward the
Seventh robbed the Royal Opera of its best friend... The extent to which Society had followed
the personal lead of its most genial and constant patron, whether as Prince of Wales or King
of England, can only be gauged by the fact that, from the time of His Majesty's decease to the
intervention of the War, the institution had prospered less and less'. Herman Klein, *The Golden
Age of Opera* (London: George Routledge and Sons, Ltd., 1933), p. 260.

without sufficient funds for Covent Garden to hire star singers in large numbers during the early years of the decade, opera lost some of its appeal to the most elite demographic, for whom celebrity was an important attraction.[12] Finally, the upper classes were as susceptible as any other social group to the attractions of new forms of entertainment and were drawn in particular to fashionable jazz clubs.[13] The Bright Young Things, meanwhile, sought pleasure in 'slumming it', larking around in the most raucous of London music halls.[14]

And yet clichés about Covent Garden abounded and critics were often disdainful of the opera house's 'typical' audience, which they caricatured as rich, ignorant, and only interested in hearing the leading tenor and soprano hit the top notes.[15] Rival opera companies sometimes criticised the excesses of the Covent Garden Season overtly. In the first issue of *Opera* magazine, for example, bass and BNOC founder member Robert Radford issued a stinging attack on the old model of Covent Garden opera-going, painting the decline of the luxurious, cosmopolitan opera of the pre-War days as a blessing in disguise, even though he himself had performed regularly at the theatre in the first two decades of the century.[16] This model of opera was 'a privileged affair, supported by a clique', which pushed the 'real' opera lovers away and into uncomfortable seats.[17]

Of course, a very different audience attended operatic performances at Covent Garden during the periods when it was leased to the BNOC and the Carl Rosa. In April 1924, the Editor of *Opera* used 'Mr Punch' as a mouthpiece to praise the BNOC's own performances at Covent Garden and to speak approvingly of the lack of tiaras, the crowds of young people in ordinary clothes, and the better-informed modern-day audience.[18] But

12. 'The fact is that "Grand" Opera in London has never been other than a social function, and the moment its old public was not in a position to continue supporting it, and there was not enough money available to engage stars of the first magnitude, the interest in it quickly died'. Percy Colson, 'Opera. A Suggestion', in R. Sydney Glover (Ed.), *Apollo: A Journal of the Arts, Vol 1 January to June 1925* (Nendeln, Liechtenstein: Kraus Reprint, 1976), pp. 42–3, p. 42.

13. Graves and Hodge, *The Long Weekend*, p. 113; The Editor, 'Wanted: An Opera Theatre', *Opera*, 2/2 (February 1924), 6–7, 6. Mendl argues that 'Jazz music has permeated through all "strata" of society. It shows, so to speak, no respect of persons or classes, but exercises its stimulating or disturbing influence over rich and poor alike'. R. W. S. Mendl, *The Appeal of Jazz* (London: Philip Allan and Co., 1927), p. 83. By 1925, London boasted 11,000 nightclubs (Pugh, 'We Danced All Night', p. 218).

14. Collier and Lang, *Just the Other Day*, p. 162.

15. Edwin Evans wrote 'When Puccini's tortured tenor exults and shouts "Vittoria", it is a victory for the top-note party. They have heard what they came to hear'. Evans, 'The Passing of the Top E Flat', p. 37.

16. Elizabeth Forbes, 'Robert Radford', in Laura Macy (Ed.), *The Grove Book of Opera Singers* (New York: Oxford University Press, 2008), pp. 396–7.

17. Robert Radford, 'The Future of Opera in England', *Opera*, 1/1 (January 1923), 6–8, 6.

18. Anon., Editorial, *Opera*, 2/4 (April 1924), 5.

other sectors of the mainstream press betrayed a certain embarrassment at the behaviour of the new operatic demographic. *The Times* told readers that the audience for the BNOC performances did not know the expected social etiquette at Covent Garden: they were uncertain of the propriety of standing at the arrival of the King and Queen, some sitting and applauding 'as though the Royal Party were a part of the entertainment'.[19]

Although the audience demographic at Covent Garden was changing during the decade, it would certainly be overstating matters to say that Society support for opera collapsed entirely. The fact that opera-going continued to be a central feature of the fashionable summer 'season' during the later 1920s—attracting foreign royalty, significant political figures and members of the aristocracy—is evident from the annual season preview in the 'Society' pages of the *ILN*, which gave opera as high a billing as important sporting events. The advertisements placed in the souvenir brochures published for the international seasons at Covent Garden throughout the decade were unambiguously targeted at a wealthy readership, selling furs, the latest French fashions, perfume, and expensive cars.[20] *Plus ça change*, one might remark: the typical present-day Royal Opera House programme still features adverts for expensive watches and jewellery, luxury hotels, a wealth management company, and the like.[21]

Anxieties about what to wear to the opera were symptomatic of a broader concern in 1920s society about new modes of dress that blurred hitherto obvious social hierarchies. Suddenly, as historian Matt Houlbrook has observed, 'The smart domestic servant was indistinguishable from her mistress; a sharp suit and a cultivated accent could make the crook a gentleman'.[22] The official dress code at Covent Garden during the international season, as stipulated in a note that appeared in contemporary programmes, remained what it had been before 1914: evening dress was still required to be worn in the boxes, orchestral stalls, and circle seats.[23] In practice, however, the rules were starting to be relaxed. Since the War there had been an influx of *nouveau-riche* opera-goers who could afford the tickets at Covent Garden but did not see the point of changing their clothes in the evening, and tiaras were, for the most part, something high-born ladies would leave at home.[24]

19. Anon., 'Opera at Covent Garden', *The Times*, 18 February 1924, 17.

20. See, for instance, *Stories of the Operas and the Singers*, Royal Opera, Covent Garden 1926 Season Official Souvenir, British Library.

21. *La bohème* programme book, Royal Opera House, 2017–18 season.

22. Houlbrook, *Prince of Tricksters*, p. 6.

23. See, for instance, the note published in the programme for *Falstaff*, London Opera Syndicate Ltd., Season, Covent Garden, 29 June 1926.

24. Erroll Sherson, *London's Lost Theatres of the Nineteenth-Century, With Notes on Plays and Players Seen There* (London: John Lane, The Bodley Head, 1925), p. 353. Sherson predicted that

Changes in dress were the most visible manifestation of a changing social order after the War. As such, they were a source of much consternation to those who harked back nostalgically to the pre-War 'golden age', a deplorable crumbling of the status quo.[25] Nellie Melba showed herself to be an unreconstructed snob of the first order when recalling her return to Covent Garden in 1919. She wrote (or at least her ghost writer wrote with her approval): 'Can you imagine in the old days, men walking into Covent Garden on a Melba Night, or on any other night, and sitting in the stalls, in shabby tweed coats?'[26] Melba was frank about the fact that the new post-War audience prompted in her 'a sensation almost of resentment'—if they could afford stalls seats, why on earth couldn't they afford the correct clothes? So contemptuous was she of the people who had paid to see and listen to her that she declared herself to have ignored them and addressed her performance to the ghosts of aristocrats past. Astonishingly, anxieties about what to wear to the opera live on in Britain almost a century after Melba made these comments, despite wholesale shifts in attitudes towards formal dress generally and explicit attempts by some opera companies, such as English National Opera, to stress their lack of a dress code. In 2017 *The Guardian* published an article by the novelist Howard Jacobson in which he lambasted fellow male opera-goers for wearing leisure wear and trainers rather than suits.[27] (This time, however, such comments prompted widespread condemnation on social media from operatic performers as well as audience members.)

Although Society still attended Covent Garden in the 1920s, its attitude towards the function of opera was changing. Whereas in 1920 the *ILN* had referred to opera-going as 'quite as much a social institution as a musical one' and an activity that 'fills in most agreeably the gap between dinner and dancing',[28] it observed six years later that, although still an important social function, it was now attended by those who genuinely enjoyed music rather than those who wished to display diamonds.[29] The periodical's music critic, W. J. Turner, argued that there had been an extraordinary shift both in fashions—tiaras replaced by unadorned shingled heads—and attitudes

it would soon become acceptable for men in lounge suits, walking boots, and smoking pipes, and hatless, smoking women to be admitted to the stalls and boxes.

25. See, for example, the retrospective comments by Percy Colson about 'a marked carelessness in dress' typifying the post-War 'wave of disillusionment'. Colson, *Those Uneasy Years*, p. 22.

26. Nellie Melba, *Melodies and Memories* (London: Butterworth, 1925), p. 303.

27. Howard Jacobson, 'Howard Jacobson Diary', *The Guardian*, 14 October 2017, https://www.theguardian.com/books/2017/oct/14/howard-jacobson-suits-leisurewear-curse-opera-dressing-up (accessed 16 October 2017).

28. A. E. L., 'Ladies' News', *ILN*, 9 October 1920, 570.

29. Jane Ramsay-Kerr, 'The Brilliant Season: A Forecast of 1926', *ILN*, 17 April 1926, n.p.

at Covent Garden since the 1890s. The new public was more intellectual, more critical, and more willing to listen attentively, because 'If one goes to Covent Garden now, one goes exclusively to hear the music'.[30] This was surely an overstatement but there was truth in the claim that Covent Garden opera-going was losing its status as a purely social function. Box-holders were now in their seats at the rise of the curtain rather than timing their arrival to hear their favourite aria.[31] Under the patronage of the industrialist Courtauld family, aristocratic support remained important for financial reasons—the boxes and stalls had to be filled—but the purely social side of Covent Garden was of little concern to Mrs Courtauld, who was more interested in attracting genuine music enthusiasts.[32]

Nevertheless, the stereotype of the Covent Garden socialite persisted in the popular imagination. In his history of opera in England, published in 1930, Captain George Cecil satirised the tastes of the 'soulless' well-heeled male frequenters of the boxes. He quipped that their response to Caruso was: 'Caruso? Very good, I've no doubt. What they call "highbrow" singing, I believe, though I don't care for these foreign operatic fellows: they won't go in for sport'.[33] The viewpoint of these imagined Covent Garden aristocrats sums up long-standing prejudices about opera being suspect on the grounds of its foreignness and supposed antithesis to hearty British pursuits; there is even perhaps a whiff of homophobia to be detected here. At the same time, it demonstrates the paradoxes in opera's perceived cultural categorisation: for Cecil, the fact that the opera was attended by such an unthinking elite negated any claims to its being highbrow whereas for the socialite, opera's assumed highbrow status was something to be regarded with suspicion. This, again, was the nub of the problem in terms of opera's categorisation: opera was not highbrow enough for some and too highbrow for others, including even for some who actually attended the opera.

In reality, the audience at Covent Garden was more diverse than it might at first appear. The theatre would have disputed *The Times*'s claim that its audience was 'entirely a London one', publishing as it did a report in 1929 stating that there had been a recent 'extraordinarily large' influx of ticket-buyers from the provinces, and boasting that one man had come from as

30. 'The public of today which goes to opera is so much more intellectual, so much more coolly critical, observant, and experienced, that its strongest instinct is to listen attentively'. W. J. Turner, 'The World of Music: Melba and Jeritza', *ILN*, 3 July 1926, 40.

31. *The Manchester Guardian* deemed that arriving in time for curtain-up 'would have been deemed of questionable taste in the old days'. Anon., 'Our London Correspondence', *The Manchester Guardian*, 26 May 1926, 8.

32. Colson, *Those Uneasy Years*, p. 97.

33. Captain George Cecil, *The History of Opera in England* (Taunton: Barnicott and Pearce, the Wessex Press, 1930), p. 2.

far afield as John O'Groats.[34] The theatre was also by this time keen to stress the social diversity of the audience, underlining the point that the gallery audience included large numbers of ardent opera lovers from the East End. This was the 'other' audience at Covent Garden: people from humble backgrounds, uninterested in social cachet, who crowded on to the uncomfortable gallery benches in order to hear the music.

In all parts of the house, the demographic varied according to the national provenance of the opera being performed. A correspondent for *The Manchester Guardian* observed that the best-dressed audience members at Covent Garden invariably appeared on the nights when the 'poorest quality' operas were performed, quipping that 'A Wagnerian audience is almost dowdy by comparison with one attracted by Puccini'.[35] The number of Society attendees, in other words, tended to decline when German opera was on the bill, giving way to a more 'serious' type of audience member.[36] (A night during the Covent Garden German season of 1925 is shown in Figure 2.1.) The audience for German opera was also 'almost exclusively highbrow' up in the gallery, but these listeners were replaced during the Italian season by 'a vivacious mixture of Soho and the suburbs', the Soho contingent being made up largely of noisy Italians.[37] This was a demographic that was extremely knowledgeable about singers and discussed them with what Turner called 'the connoisseurship of a stableman discussing a horse'.[38]

Commentators also observed that the Covent Garden audience for performances of Wagner specifically was becoming both younger and more balanced in terms of gender, with *Apollo* noting in 1927 that the gallery was now brimming with the young women who would be the beneficiaries of the forthcoming 'Flapper Election'.[39] The term 'flapper'—hitherto merely denoting a sporting, active young woman—started to become one of reproach around 1927, precisely at the point where there became a real

34. Anon., 'Most Musical Suburbs', *The Daily Mail*, 15 June 1929 [V&A Theatre and Performance Collections, production box: Covent Garden Theatre, 1929].

35. Anon., 'Our London Correspondence', *The Manchester Guardian*, 26 May 1926, 8.

36. *Parsifal* in particular attracted people who were 'of a type distinct', in Agnes Savill's words, with 'thoughtful faces alight with intellect and character. Expressions grave and earnest, fine and sincere, with little show and no display'. Agnes Savill, *Music, Health and Character* (London: John Lane, The Bodley Head, 1923), pp. 72–3.

37. W. J. Turner, 'The World of Music: The Victorian Age Back Again', *ILN*, 27 June 1925, 1312; Dyneley Hussey, 'The Return of the Prima Donna', *The Saturday Review*, 139/3634 (20 June 1925), 669–70, 670.

38. Turner, 'The World of Music: The Victorian Age Back Again'.

39. H. E. Wortham asserted that while the stalls were full of grey hairs and bald heads, the gallery at a Wagner performance was now bursting with 'those gracious young women to whom a Conservative Gvt, trusting to the innate good sense of the female, propose to give the vote'. H. E. Wortham, 'Music of the Month', in R. Sydney Glover (Ed.), *Apollo: A Journal of the Arts, Vol 5 January to June 1927* (Nendeln, Liechtenstein: Kraus Reprint, 1976), pp. 272–4, p. 273.

Figure 2.1 Robert Heger conducting Strauss's *Elektra* at Covent Garden: drawing by Fortunino Matania, *The Sphere*, 13 June 1925. © *Illustrated London News* Limited/Mary Evans Picture Library.

prospect of young women being granted an equal vote.[40] As Maggie B. Gale has shown, there was a certain degree of paranoia in the 1920s press generally about flappers, their independence, their supposed loose morals, and their growing political power.[41] The papers regularly noted a visible increase

40. Robert Graves and Alan Hodge, *The Long Weekend: A Social History of Great Britain, 1918–1939* (London: The Folio Society, 2009; first published Faber and Faber, 1940), p. 33.

41. Maggie B. Gale, 'Errant Nymphs: Women and the Inter-War Theatre', in Clive Barker and Maggie B. Gale (Eds.), *British Theatre Between the Wars, 1918–1939* (Cambridge: Cambridge University Press, 2000), pp. 113–34, p. 121.

in the number of women in the audience for theatre in general during the 1920s—either alone or with friends—prompting some anxiety that the repertory would become 'feminised'.[42] There was also concern about the social class of these new female audience members, who were often unmarried schoolteachers and secretaries from the suburbs.[43]

For all this growing audience diversity, however, Covent Garden continued to be presented by the press as a socially exclusive place cut off from the real world, both by music critics who were hostile towards opera, or by those who were keen to see a new national opera house as an alternative to Covent Garden. In the former camp, the middlebrow *Musical Mirror* gave its readers a stereotypical perspective 'from below' of opera-going as a pursuit for the rich, writing sarcastically about chauffeurs, silk dresses, and tiaras, even though the author of the article admitted that he had not actually been present on the evening he purported to be describing.[44] In the latter camp, Herman Klein and other commentators sought to differentiate Covent Garden—which they characterised as a luxury for those who could afford it, akin to orchids, caviar, and Rolls-Royce cars—from operatic culture in the country more broadly, where there was 'genuine' appreciation for the art form.[45]

The fact that the band played on at Covent Garden during the General Strike of 1926 was greeted by mixed responses. It was welcomed by some opera-loving music critics but ridiculed by other journalists as a sign of the theatre's apparent aloofness from the realities of life for ordinary people at a time of economic depression, long-term unemployment, and hunger marches. There was a subtle nationalistic, patriotic undercurrent to this, a faint suggestion that the opera house—and perhaps by implication opera itself—was not properly British. (This was, of course, nothing new, but a refrain familiar from not only the nineteenth century but also the eighteenth.) *The Musical News and Herald* quipped:

> One of London's decorative functions, the Opera Season at Covent Garden has so little to do with a nation at grips with serious issues, that Covent Garden Opera House might almost be regarded in the same category as neutral territory, protected by international guarantees.[46]

42. Gale, 'Errant Nymphs', p. 114; Maggie B. Gale, *West End Women: Women and the London Stage, 1918–1962* (London and New York: Routledge, 1996), p. 14.

43. Gale, *West End Women*, p. 14.

44. Anon., 'Music Today: The Opera Season', *MM*, 8/6 (June 1928), 141.

45. Herman Klein, 'The Great Opera Scheme', *MNH*, 72/1823 (15 December 1927), 443–4, 443; V. Norman Lucas, 'The Tragedy of Musical England', *MNH*, 72/1816 (15 May 1927), 198–9, 198.

46. Anon., 'Opera in and out of season', *MNH*, 70/1780 (22 May 1926), 433–4, 433.

Internationalism, or cosmopolitanism, is here constructed as a threat to indigenous cultural identities, a theme one finds in much music criticism of the period, both in Britain and elsewhere.[47]

In terms of cost, tickets for the good seats at Covent Garden remained expensive and there were even reports that prices were rising.[48] Once the international seasons resumed under the Grand Opera Syndicate, ticket prices were inflated and the seating capacity increased when performers of special note were performing, such as the bass Feodor Chaliapin in 1928.[49] However, Covent Garden did make efforts to bring its ticket prices down from time to time, putting on, for instance, an additional week of performances in July 1928 'at ordinary theatre prices' and replacing some of the grand tier boxes with the seats. Such performances were packed out and enthusiastically received, but were only occasional.

Beyond the West End opera was by no means always too expensive or too exclusive but it was sometimes difficult to put this message across. As *The Times* observed in 1927, 'The most difficult part of the explainer's task is to banish the prevalent idea that opera is an extravagant luxury which no one but the idle rich can afford to enjoy'.[50] Opera was often equated in the popular imagination with Covent Garden glamour of a type that no longer really existed, and the press paid little attention to the cheap operatic performances beyond the West End and throughout the country. The touring companies such as the Carl Rosa and the BNOC made a selling point of putting on 'popular opera at popular prices', even when performing at Covent Garden during the early 1920s.[51] Although the need to pay the Old Vic's popular regular singers higher fees in order to stop them defecting

47. The supposed internationalism of Puccini's operas, for example, prompted much concern in contemporary Italy. For further reading, see Alexandra Wilson, *The Puccini Problem: Opera, Nationalism, and Modernity* (Cambridge: Cambridge University Press, 2007).

48. 'Opera is getting to be a more and more expensive diversion'. C., 'Covent Garden Opera', *MT*, 66/960 (1 August 1925), 740–2, 740. The *Musical News and Herald* observed in 1927 that prices at Covent Garden had risen to the extent that, for the most part, only the wealthy could afford them, with real enthusiasts being banished to the gods. V. Norman Lucas, 'The Tragedy of Musical England', *MNH*, 72/1816 (15 May 1927), 198–9, 198.

49. W. J. Turner, 'The World of Music', *ILN*, 30 May 1925, 1076. Anon., 'Chaliapine [*sic*] in an Angry Scene', *The Daily Express*, 23 June 1928 [V&A Theatre and Performance Collections, production box: Covent Garden Theatre, 1928].

50. Anon., 'Opera: "But" and "If". Explainers Wanted', *The Times*, 26 November 1927, 12. The *Musical Mirror* perpetuated the cliché, reporting in 1928 that opera in Britain was destined to languish, not because people didn't like it, but because it was too expensive. Anon., 'Music Today: Matters Operatic', *MM*, 8/5 (May 1928), 113.

51. The programme for the Carl Rosa four-week residency at Covent Garden in 1922 stipulated 'In view of the season being only for four weeks, it is proposed to present a popular programme at popular prices'. Prospectus, The Royal Carl Rosa Opera Company, Autumn Season, 1922 [V&A Theatre and Performance Collections, production box: Covent Garden Theatre, 1922].

to the West End led to an increase in ticket prices in 1920, these still remained accessible, with stall seats at 3s. and balcony seats at 1s. 6d.[52] Opera performances at other London theatres such as the Lyceum were sold at the same prices as any other show, and performances were packed.[53] But of course there was a tension in the 1920s, just as there has been throughout the history of public opera, between accessibility and the costs of staging a hugely expensive multi-media art form, and the laudable efforts of the touring productions to sell tickets cheaply almost certainly contributed to their ultimate collapse.

There was considerable support in the music press for the idea that, in principle, opera ought to be 'cheap', but anxiety about the fact that it might in consequence become 'nasty'.[54] As we have already seen, the number of touring companies was on the decline, and their performances were increasingly ad hoc and of variable artistic standards. Nevertheless, it is evident that great efforts were being made on the part of opera companies to take opera to working-class audiences, even in difficult circumstances. A notable example was the 1926 season of popular standards by the O'Mara company at the Alexandra Theatre on the Stoke Newington Road (now a trendy area on the up, but then an overcrowded working-class district). The Alexandra was a large-capacity theatre that occupied a whole block, if not a comfortable venue for either performers or audience members (its huge draughty auditorium was filled with tobacco smoke).[55] Astonishingly, the company would perform each opera twice, back to back, in an evening—an extraordinary feat given that the operas in question, such as *Faust* and *Rigoletto*, were hardly short and that the company had only a single cast.[56]

The fact that the company could sell two performances a night testifies to high local demand from the working-class East End audience. But this

---

52. Gilbert, *Opera for Everybody*, p. 27.

53. Ursula Greville wrote in 1929 of going several times within a month to hear opera at the Lyceum, reporting: 'And the people who say there is no popular public for opera are evidently quite wrong – for the house each time was packed. It is good to be able to get in at ordinary theatre prices'. Ursula Greville, 'Excursions', *The Sackbut*, 10/2 (September 1929), 29–31, 29.

54. A correspondent for *The Musical Mirror* wrote with regard to De Lara's funding scheme for a national opera house: 'Will it be apparent ever that a *cheap* opera-house need not be a *nasty* opera-house?'. Anon., 'Opera for All', *MM*, 23/428 (9 February 1924), 39.

55. Figaro, 'The Operatic World', *MO*, 49/580 (January 1926), 359–61, 360. Designed by Frank Matcham and first opened in 1897, this 3,000-seat theatre put on a mixed array of entertainments, was briefly renamed 'Palace Theatre of Varieties' during the Edwardian era and managed by Oswald Stoll from 1917–1921. It was later used to host boxing matches. Diana Howard, *London Theatres and Music Halls 1850–1950* (London: The Library Association, 1970), pp. 7–8.

56. The same tenor, Furness Williams, sang Faust twice on Tuesday, the Duke in *Rigoletto* twice on Wednesday, Thaddeus in *The Bohemian Girl* twice on Thursday, and Myles in *The Lily of Killarney* twice on Saturday. Ibid., 360.

quirky performance practice is also significant in terms of our consideration of cultural categorisation. The 'twice nightly' system was a practice that had been borrowed from music hall: what we see here is a striking reciprocal influence between supposedly 'higher' and 'lower' forms of entertainment.[57] It was a practice that had been wheeled out across the Moss/Stoll empire of music halls from the late 1890s, allowing the management to pack in double the number of audience members without necessarily paying the performers twice.[58] That opera should be borrowing practices from music hall might at first sight seem odd, but ought not to surprise us too much within the context of a venue such as the Alexandra, a multi-purpose theatre usually used for variety acts during this period. As noted in the introduction, there was a tradition throughout the Victorian era of operatic arias and duets being performed in music halls and being enjoyed by audiences alongside a wide range of other types of act.

At the Old Vic, meanwhile, Lilian Baylis was determined that the opera should explicitly not be 'fashionable' and was successful in creating a genuine sense of community and loyalty among a primarily working-class audience.[59] Baylis eschewed the star system. Using a regular repertory cast meant that audiences felt that they knew the performers personally and this fostered considerable loyalty to the troupe: when the theatre reopened with *Carmen* in 1928 after renovations, *The Times* reported that 'old friends filled the principal parts'.[60] The atmosphere at the Old Vic was evidently one of fun. *The Observer*, reporting on an earlier performance of *Carmen* (1921), wrote that 'The spirit of enjoyment was in everybody: principals, orchestra, and chorus', and the audience, which greeted each favourite performer with cheers, showed themselves to be 'in good heart likewise, willing and anxious to be pleased'.[61] The niceties of conventional operatic etiquette were ignored—applause bubbled up continuously, reportedly 'to the annoyance of the highbrows who object to clapping till the music is over'—but such was the audience's enthusiasm that most critics could forgive it.[62]

57. The influence worked both ways. Many music halls had been restructured in the later nineteenth century to resemble theatres, with fixed seating and the removal of food and alcohol from the auditorium. See Kift, *The Victorian Music Hall*, pp. 22, 28.

58. Double, *Britain Had Talent*, p. 43.

59. Gilbert, *Opera for Everybody*, pp. 21, 26.

60. Anon., 'Reopening of the Old Vic', *The Times*, 7 February 1928 [V&A Theatre and Performance Collections, production box: Old Vic Theatre, 1928].

61. W. R. A., 'Carmen at the Old Vic', *The Observer*, 2 October 1921, 11.

62. H. E. W., 'Mozart at the "Old Vic."', *MT*, 65/972 (1 February 1924), 164. Edward Dent, for example, argued that 'there is no audience to equal it for quick intelligence and responsiveness to both tragedy and comedy'. Edward J. Dent, 'Music: The Naturalization of Opera in England', *LM*, 1/6 (April 1920), 763–5, 764.

The Old Vic company adopted imaginative strategies in order to foster a close relationship with its audience, for example by publishing *The Old Vic. Magazine*, which was billed as 'The link between friends on both sides of the curtain'.[63] (Such gestures prefigured the modern system of opera company 'Friends', whereby an annual donation is exchanged for a range of perks.) Similarly, the BNOC, which was run on co-operative lines, used its magazine *Opera* to make it clear that it wished to make audiences feel a part of the BNOC 'family'.[64] Such publications were clearly established in order to drive ticket sales and yet they also testify to a genuinely laudable desire to enthuse a broad audience. Readers were repeatedly invited to send feedback and to engage directly with the magazines. A note in the back cover of the first issue of *Opera* stated the magazine's democratic aims: 'This is YOUR magazine and yours the right to criticise it . . . We are trying to make *Opera* something different—a co-operative affair, that is why the Editor will appreciate your views and opinions'.[65] It published stories about how the company operated and about backstage comings and goings, alongside articles by or interviews with singers and managers.

In effect, *Opera* sought to break down the fourth wall, the editor expressing his desire for it to be 'a link by means of which those on both sides of the orchestra may be kept in closer touch'.[66] The magazine ran a number of schemes to allow readers a sort of vicarious participation in the world of the company.[67] Readers were offered the opportunity to enter competitions to win tickets, either by submitting reviews or by guessing the bestselling operas from the previous season. They could also purchase packs of postcards of BNOC singers performing in recent productions. As Michela Ronzani has observed, late nineteenth- and early twentieth-century operatic postcards fulfilled a number of different functions: as a means of long-distance communication, as souvenirs, as collector pieces, and also crucially as a source of income generation and advertisement.[68] In March 1924 it

63. See, for instance, the advert for the magazine in the programme for *Lohengrin*, 10 January 1920 [V&A Theatre and Performance Collections, production box: Old Vic Theatre, 1920].

64. All BNOC performers were shareholders in the company and had a say in company policy. Martin, 'The British "Operatic Machine"', pp. 150–1.

65. *Opera*, 1/1 (January 1923), 24. *Opera* was accessibly priced at sixpence from booksellers or 6s. and 6d. for a subscription. Anon., Editorial, *Opera*, 2/4 (April 1924), n.p.

66. Anon., 'Editorial', *Opera*, 1/1 (January 1923), 5.

67. On how Hollywood used similar techniques—making fans see consumption as a form of participation—see Samantha Barbas, *Movie Crazy: Fans, Stars, and the Cult of Celebrity* (New York and Basingstoke: Palgrave, 2001), p. 5.

68. Michela Ronzani, 'Creating Success and Forming Imaginaries: The Innovative Publicity Campaign for Puccini's *La bohème*', in Christina Bashford and Roberta Montemorra Marvin (Eds.), *The Idea of Art Music in a Commercial World, 1800–1930* (Woodbridge: The Boydell Press, 2016), pp. 39–59, p. 51.

was announced that *Opera* readers could choose between two sets of post-cards, depicting the casts of the recent productions of *The Mastersingers* or of Rutland Boughton's *Alkestis*.[69] The cards were sepia photographs on high quality deckle-edged paper, taken by 'the well known photographic artist SASHA', and the advertisement claimed them to be 'the finest stage photographs extant'.[70] Presumably in a bid to drum up interest, the April issue announced that the magazine had been unable to fulfil all orders for the cards, such was the demand for them, but that there was now a limited supply back in stock.[71]

References in *Opera* to a 'cooperative' suggest that the magazine, and indeed the BNOC itself, sought to present itself as being 'for the people', the antithesis of the elite model of opera-going that still prevailed for the most part during the international season. Nevertheless, some commentators attacked the popular opera companies for their efforts in taking opera to more humble audiences. Cecil—satiriser of Covent Garden socialites—was equally snooty about the Old Vic, characterising it as doing nothing more than keeping locals out of the gin house.[72] He also turned his tongue upon other pedlars of 'popular opera', accusing them of lowering rather than raising tastes and of a lack of respectability. He attacked the J. W. Turner Company in particular for putting on an endless programme of 'lamentable' operas by Balfe and Wallace, as well as for shoddy performance standards in a flea-infested Shoreditch theatre (the manager appointed himself principal tenor).[73] While some commentators, as we saw in the previous chapter, applauded such companies for their efforts to popularise opera, the intellectual elite derided them, suspicious that their efforts were driven by purely commercial motivations.[74] Even Dent, ostensibly supportive of popular opera, argued that touring troupes tended to be complacent about artistic

---

69. The BNOC gave the London premiere of *Alkestis* at Covent Garden in January 1924, conducted by the composer. A tour to Birmingham, Leeds, Bradford, Manchester, Glasgow, and Edinburgh followed, before the work returned to London for performances at His Majesty's Theatre in July. Despite this run of performances, the opera was not a commercial success. Hurd, *Rutland Boughton and the Glastonbury Festivals*, p. 168.

70. Back inside cover, *Opera*, 2/3 (March 1924).

71. Back inside cover, *Opera*, 2/4 (April 1924).

72. Cecil, *The History of Opera in England*, p. 38. Cecil also recalled Oscar Hammerstein's failed London Opera House of 1911, which, thanks to its informal dress code and invitation to patrons to 'make yourself at home', attracted 'rough-looking customers' wearing work clothes and 'vulgar, whiskey-swilling ruffians' smoking pipes in the foyer.

73. Cecil, *The History of Opera in England*, pp. 3–4.

74. Cecil made withering remarks about the Carl Rosa, which 'doubtless will carry on business till Doomsday' and about Moody Manners taking operas 'to the uttermost ends of Great Britain'. Cecil, *The History of Opera in England*, pp. 9, 14.

standards—their casts wearied by 'the eternal *Faust* and *Cavalleria*'—so long as ticket receipts were high.[75]

The worlds of Society and popular opera, seemingly so far removed from one another, occasionally converged. In 1928, for instance, Queen Mary watched a performance of *Pagliacci* at the Excelsior Kino, a cinema (and former swimming baths) in Bethnal Green, leased by Oxford House. The remit of Oxford House was both to educate and to entertain: it had been established by Keble College, Oxford in 1884 for the educational, social, and religious benefit of the poor of the East End. The purpose of such Anglican 'Settlements' was to bring rich and poor together in purposeful endeavour. Films were the main entertainment on offer but operas were staged on one night a month, sometimes alongside the cinematic fare: Queen Mary watched a film called *Chang* in conjunction with Leoncavallo's opera performed by the Oxford House Choral Society.[76]

Finally, of course, the 1920s audience for opera as conceived in the broadest sense included people from across the social spectrum who heard performances of operatic excerpts in a range of different non-theatrical spaces. To cite just one example among many, the Lyon's Corner House chain of London restaurants arranged a series of performances in 1923 by the Carl Rosa Company on the third floor of its Coventry Street branch: 30–40-minute performances were given three times daily on a specially constructed stage. Such an endeavour was of mutual benefit: the Lyon's Company presumably sought to draw in new customers, the Carl Rosa to attract new audience members.

The Lyon's Corner Houses were large establishments, each housing three or four 'super restaurants' across the equivalent number of floors, and the Coventry Street branch boasted facilities including a food hall, shoe-shining parlour, theatre booking office, and telephone bureau.[77] The Corner Houses were grand in architecture and suggestive of luxury hotels—or, for that matter, theatres—with their marble, gilt, and red plush. Their menus, on the other hand, were cheap and unpretentious.[78] They attracted a mixed, unpretentious clientele including a large contingent from the respectable working class: clerks, typists, civil servants, shop girls, and families from the suburbs. But two specific, rather more cosmopolitan groups were drawn to them in large numbers. The first was the London Jewish community, and

75. Edward J. Dent, 'The World of Music', *ILN*, 23 July 1921, 114.

76. Photographs of Queen Mary's visit may be found at www.eastend-memories.org/excelsior/excelsior_2.htm (accessed 20 January 2016).

77. Judith R. Walkowitz, *Nights Out: Life in Cosmopolitan London* (New Haven and London: Yale University Press, 2012), pp. 195, 198.

78. On decor, see Collier and Lang, *Just the Other Day*, p. 163.

particularly Soho Jews, who regarded the Lyon's Corner Houses as their 'special place' (the company had been set up by Jewish entrepreneurs).[79] The second was homosexual men, with the Coventry Street branch becoming the 'absolute Mecca of the gay scene' in 1920s Britain.[80] Live musical performances by jazz bands, accordionists, and gypsy violinists were the bread and butter of the Corner Houses.[81] A performance of operatic excerpts was sufficiently unusual to lead *The Financial Times* to write 'Whether grand opera represents the ideal accompaniment to a meal may be open to doubt, but the experiment deserves to succeed on account of its boldness, if for no other reason'.[82]

It is clear, then, that irrespective of efforts on certain sceptical parts of the press to reinforce stereotypes about opera being 'elite', opera continued to play to sizeable socially mixed audiences. Indeed, the fact that operatic activities were reported in tabloid newspapers such as *The Daily Mirror* is indicative of an interest in opera that crossed the social spectrum. There was in fact much discussion during the 1920s of the audience for opera having both grown and diversified further in social make-up since the War, in spite of the many counter-attractions that threatened to lure away audiences.[83] Some of those making this case, however, had an obvious vested interest in saying so. Propagandists for the BNOC boasted in 1925 for instance that the company's success in the north and its forthcoming season at Covent Garden 'means that the cause of opera in these hard times is triumphing over sport, the motor, the cabaret, films, gramophones and broadcasting'.[84]

In fact, despite being regarded in some quarters as a threat to live opera-going, new technologies such as gramophones and (later in the decade) broadcasting were, in conjunction with the music appreciation movement, playing an active role in stimulating interest in and 'democratising' opera. Herman Klein believed that there had been a great forward movement 'in the intellectual calibre and musical culture of concert audiences all over the country' thanks to radio, gramophone records, and advances in music criticism, and that 'To those who have watched it carefully this growth has been

79. Walkowitz, *Nights Out*, pp. 194–5.

80. Matt Houlbrook, *Queer London: Perils and Pleasures in the Sexual Metropolis, 1918–1957* (Chicago and London: The University of Chicago Press, 2005), p. 85. See also Walkowitz, *Nights Out*, pp. 203–7.

81. Walkowitz, *Nights Out*, p. 198.

82. Anon., 'Grand Opera at Lyons', *The Financial Times*, 25 October 1923, 8.

83. *Opera* published an article by J. H. Clynes in which he argued that the movement for popular opera was irresistible, 'in spite of horse-racing and jazz-music'. J. H. Clynes, 'Opera for the Masses', *Opera*, 2/3 (March 1924), 6–7, 7.

84. Figaro, 'The Operatic World', *MO*, 49/579 (December 1925), 247–8, 248.

quite astonishing; and it has pervaded every class of society'.[85] There were other contributing factors as well that were specific to the historical moment: for example, many servicemen had been introduced to opera as the only source of ready entertainment when stationed in France, Italy, and on the Rhine.[86]

Those with a vested interest in promoting opera, whether opera companies or critics, often spoke of a 'vast, potential, and untapped opera-loving public' waiting to be cultivated.[87] Francis E. Barrett wrote a regular column in *The Musical Times* during the early 1920s entitled 'Opera in London'; his articles typically demonstrate a benevolence towards the art form not always shown by the journal's editor and some other contributors. Barrett repeatedly expressed his confidence that there was a large public that would enjoy opera if only it had the opportunity to encounter it, and expressed his enthusiasm for various schemes to put on 'opera for the people', such as the fourteen-month lease of the Surrey Theatre taken by the Fairbairn Opera Company in 1920. There was, however, much work to be done in introducing audiences to core repertoire.[88]

Despite the many such optimistic comments about a surge of interest in opera, there were also many naysayers, who dismissed such claims as wishful thinking. The untapped audience for opera was then, just as now, arguably something of a mythical beast. Numerous column inches were devoted to the question of whether Britain was an inherently operatic nation at all. Any critic or conductor who declared that the average British man in the street was a shrewd judge of music was, in one commentator's words, 'repeating a gigantic and palpable falsehood'.[89] According to Cecil, the British public was ignorant and provincial, never travelling beyond the British seaside and preferring tennis, golf, and cards to more cultural pursuits, caring nothing for what happened outside 'their own twopenny-halfpenny, narrow world'.[90] There were, in other words, certain sectors of society that simply weren't interested in opera, and it wasn't the cost of tickets that was putting them off. Those sceptical about opera's supposed

85. Klein, *Musicians and Mummers*, p. 326. *The Times* wrote in 1923: 'It is conceivable that this development of wireless may be the thing which will ultimately restore opera as a permanent institution in London'. Anon., 'Close of Opera Season. A Melba Night. Wireless Listeners' Tribute', *The Times*, 22 January 1923, 8.

86. Figaro, 'The Operatic World', *MO*, 50/593 (February 1927), 469–70, 469.

87. Figaro, 'The Operatic World', *MO*, 52/619 (April 1929), 623–4, 623.

88. 'There are still vast numbers of the people who do not know the "standard" works as well as they ought to do, and there is a great deal of educative work to be gone through before we can be said to have an opera-going public'. Francis E. Barrett, 'Opera in London', *MT*, 61/924 (1 February 1920), 103–4, 103.

89. George Coulter, 'An Open Letter to Dame Clara Butt', *MM*, 8/9 (September 1928), 229.

90. Cecil, *The History of Opera in England*, p. 29.

wide appeal observed that most people appeared to have plenty of disposable money to spend on cinema and popular theatre, and even 'quite poor people' seemed to have plenty to spend on greyhound racing and were prepared to travel from one end of London to the other in order to enjoy it.[91]

At the very least, commentators urged, it was important not to get carried away with wild prophecies: to understand that an intense thirst on the part of a small devoted public was not a steady and widespread demand for opera on the part of the public as a whole.[92] Cecil Hann of *The Spectator*, for instance, believed that 'our present meagre supply of opera more than meets the existing demand', and was far from being 'the form of musical art which appeals most easily and effectively to the masses of the people' as the BNOC liked to claim.[93] And yet, there are frequent reports in the 1920s press of packed houses and people being turned away, whether from Covent Garden, other theatres in London, or from theatres in regional cities such as Manchester, where the musical culture was particularly strong and socially mixed.[94] Figaro was cheered by the frequency with which he met people who complained that they had been unable to get seats at Covent Garden, while there were reports of hundreds of people being turned away from the BNOC's performances, whether at Golders Green or the Lewisham Hippodrome.[95] More than 400 people were reported to have been refused entry to the Amphitheatre alone when Maria Jeritza sang at Covent Garden as Tosca.[96]

The idea that Britons might be becoming a nation of operatic enthusiasts such as could be found in Italy or Germany was almost certainly wishful thinking. However, the audience for opera was still reasonably large during the 1920s and there was undoubtedly great public curiosity about it. Opera was neither too expensive nor too grand, even if certain sectors of the population remained deeply suspicious of it for reasons bound up in complicated ways with a sense of national identity. The opera demographic in this period was certainly diverse, cutting across the class spectrum in what might

91. W. H. Kerridge, 'Music and the People', *The Sackbut*, 9 (December 1928), 171–4, 171–2. On the 1920s working-class 'greyhound boom' and the threat it posed even to cinemas, dance halls, and billiard clubs, see Collier and Lang, *Just the Other Day*, pp. 114–16 and Pugh, '*We Danced All Night*', pp. 298–9.

92. Filson Young, 'Music in a Life VII – Opera in England', in R. Sydney Glover (Ed.), *Apollo: A Journal of the Arts, Vol 3 January to June 1926* (Nendeln, Liechtenstein: Kraus Reprint, 1976), pp. 70–3, p. 70.

93. Cecil Hann, 'Opera – If You Will', *The Spectator*, 19 December 1925, 8.

94. On Manchester, see Rose, *The Intellectual Life of the British Working Classes*, p. 201.

95. Figaro, 'The Operatic World', *MO*, 50/599 (August 1927), 1063–4, 1063; Figaro, 'The Operatic World', *MO*, 50/593 (February 1927), 469–70, 469; Figaro, 'The Operatic World', *MO*, 52/619 (April 1929), 623–4, 623.

96. Anon., 'Madame Jeritza's Triumph', *The Daily Mirror*, 17 June 1925, 2.

seem today to be unexpected ways. And although one comes across distinct undercurrents of snobbery from highbrow critics of the 1920s about members of the opera audience—whether stupid aristocrats of popular cliché or ordinary people who didn't know the required etiquette—this was counterbalanced by a sincere desire on the part of many members of the musical establishment to get people of all types listening to opera. The diversity of examples presented in this chapter undermines any notion that opera was the preserve of a particular social group in the early twentieth century. Operatic culture clearly traversed class identities in complex ways during the 1920s. However, it is refreshing to discover that contemptuous references to opera being an 'elitist' art form were never heard in the discourse of this period; such loaded rhetoric would not emerge for many decades to come. This is not to say, however, that there were not intellectual critics who attempted to protect certain forms of high culture against the threat of mass culture. It is to the figure of the highbrow—and his complex attitudes towards opera—that we now turn.

CHAPTER 3

⌒

Brows

British intellectuals of the 1920s were profoundly concerned about the growth of mass culture and its effects upon both so-called high art and social hierarchies. Within such a climate, they increasingly felt that their cultural authority and ability to regulate taste were under threat.[1] At the same time, they became figures of fun, increasingly ridiculed by the middle-brow and popular press. Brown and Grover argue that 'hostility to the highbrow preceded and was more generally pervasive than hostility to the middlebrow', although the two groups were certainly locked in battle with each other.[2] In 1927 Leonard Woolf, publisher, member of the Bloomsbury Group (much derided for its supposed snobbery), and husband of Virginia Woolf, published a short book entitled *Hunting the Highbrow*, which opened with the declaration that 'The highbrow is an extremely unpopular person... When I open a paper or listen-in I am continually told that we are all much better fellows—more honest, and clean, and happy, and wise, and English—for being lowbrows'.[3]

Woolf's point about Englishness is particularly significant: the pillorying of the highbrow as ridiculous was part of an attempt to form a post-War national identity that was healthy, hearty, sporting, and anti-intellectual. Stefan Collini notes that intellectualism had verged upon becoming fashionable around 1910 but that the term 'highbrow', as employed in the 1920s, was

---

1. See, for instance, the way in which F. R. Leavis lamented the 'sinister' developments of mass production, standardisation, and a blurring of cultural boundaries, and asserted the rights of the elite to regulate culture, arguing that 'In any period it is upon a very small minority that the discerning appreciation of art and literature depends'. F. R. Leavis, *Mass Civilisation and Minority Culture* (Cambridge: The Minority Press, 1930), p. 3.

2. Brown and Grover, *Middlebrow Literary Cultures*, p. 5.

3. Leonard Woolf, *Hunting the Highbrow* (London: The Hogarth Press, 1927), p. 5.

indisputably pejorative.[4] As such, it was not a label many cultural commentators of the day would have adopted to describe themselves, for identifying as a highbrow was to put oneself in a lonely position.[5] Indeed, in some circles being a philistine was considered a veritable virtue: Aldous Huxley observed in 1931 that while, some time ago, the stupid and unintelligent had aspired to become intelligent and cultured, it was now the fashion for intelligent and cultured people to 'do their best to feign stupidity'.[6] This public swing against intellectualism was, Huxley argued, the result of a growing culture of mass consumption: it was in the interests of industrial producers to discourage people from sitting quietly in their rooms with their own thoughts or perhaps a book, and thus newspaper propaganda portrayed such people as 'miserable, ridiculous, and even rather immoral'.[7] The peculiarly English strand of anti-intellectualism that was intensifying around this time would undoubtedly colour later twentieth-century public attitudes towards opera.

In the first part of this chapter I shall analyse the complex attitudes held about opera by the anxious music intellectuals of the 1920s. The views of highbrow critics merit detailed attention because these figures were important voices in contemporary musical debates, acting as gatekeepers with responsibility for setting the new terms of reference. In the second half of the chapter, I turn to examining the tastes and attitudes of an emblematic figure who was set up in 1920s musical discourse as the highbrow's opposite number: the so-called man in the street. This protagonist in the 1920s opera debate is interesting for the way in which he enjoyed opera alongside a wide range of other forms of entertainment, embodying the new eclectic middlebrow taste. Both the highbrow and the man in the street were, to some extent, figures of the imagination: variously caricatured, maligned, and celebrated by the contemporary press. But understanding the position of these two key players in the debate is important because it helps us to consider the ways in which perceptions of public taste contributed to discussions about opera's cultural categorisation.

---

4. Collini, *Absent Minds*, p. 110.

5. As Leavis observed, the cultured minority 'is made conscious, not merely of an uncongenial, but of a hostile environment'. F. R. Leavis, *Mass Civilisation and Minority Culture*, p. 25.

6. Huxley, 'Foreheads Villainous Low', pp. 201–2.

7. Ibid., p. 208.

THE MUSICAL HIGHBROW

The battle of the brows was as intense in the sphere of music as in any other field of art. The term highbrow was employed liberally in the 1920s press and in different ways: either to mean something quite specific (a particular genre of music or a critic) or as a loose term of abuse.[8] In his thoughtful study of jazz and its place within wider musical contexts (1927), R. W. S. Mendl protested against crude aesthetic labels, arguing that it was impossible for music itself to be highbrow and that the term signalled nothing more than the speaker's personal lack of enthusiasm for it.[9] Indeed, perhaps the term highbrow should be considered a synonym for 'good' or 'exemplary'. Drawing a comparison with the ostensibly more populist field of sport, Mendl argued that:

> To describe a musical production as 'highbrow' has no more meaning than to use the word of Hobbs' batting, Carpentier's boxing, or anything else which is good of its kind in the opinion of the majority of those people who have studied the subject.[10]

The reference to sport here is not merely casual. As will become clear over the coming chapters, classical music and sport were routinely measured against one another in debates about British identity, sometimes as polar opposites (often with the implication that 'real Britons' preferred sport) but sometimes as fields that had a surprising amount in common.

Mendl taps into both facets of the sport–music debate here. He uses the reference to sport in order to ridicule the idea of a musical performance being 'highbrow', but he also demonstrates that music and sport are not so far removed as many would imagine. He continues the sporting analogy when discussing people as well as works, arguing that there could be 'sports-highbrows' (or indeed 'food-highbrows') just as easily as musical highbrows. The crucial point Mendl makes here is the importance of distinguishing between taste and prejudice. He argues that 'A man does not deserve to be condemned as a highbrow just because he takes delight in the classics of art, but only if he looks down upon the poor souls who have not attained to his own high level of taste'.[11] Being a 1920s highbrow

---

8. In terms of repertory, the term 'highbrow' was often associated with new music, particularly the works of Stravinsky and Les Six, which enjoyed a brief post-War vogue. This fashion is discussed pejoratively ('keyless, tuneless, formless agglomerations of chaotic sounds') in Klein, *Musicians and Mummers*, p. 325.

9. Mendl, *The Appeal of Jazz*, p. 104.

10. Ibid., p. 105.

11. Ibid., p. 104.

in the pejorative sense, therefore, had nothing to do with enjoying Bach or Shakespeare; rather, it had everything to do with being a snob.

This was the core of the highbrow issue: it meant being condescending to others, and in some cases feigning tastes in order to set oneself apart. The 1933 edition of *The Oxford English Dictionary*, indeed, defined a highbrow as 'a person of superior intellectual attainments or interests; always with derisive implication of conscious superiority to ordinary human standards'.[12] The problem was that the rest of the population, aggrieved at being talked down to, was then prone to becoming inclined to set its mind stubbornly against any activity associated with the highbrows, running the risk of cutting off its nose to spite its own face. Lionel R. McColvin, author of a 1926 book about art and taste, put his finger on the nub of the argument, writing that:

> too many of those who appreciate, or pretend to appreciate, the best are apt to set themselves apart and to insist that there is an unbridgeable gulf between their art and that of the common herd. The average man hates this highbrow snobbery and hates, too, everything they are supposed to care for, since it is tarred with the same brush.[13]

This does not really apply to opera in the 1920s, since few of the most ascetic highbrows cared for it. Nevertheless, one can see how this mindset was a factor in the emergence of a self-defeating elitism rhetoric later in the century.

The archetypal highbrow music critic was satirised in the popular press as being recognisable for his distinctive appearance (domed forehead, pimpled face, horn-rimmed spectacles), as well as for his leaning towards certain inaccessible types of music.[14] In reality, however, it is not entirely straightforward to assign labels to the music critics of the 1920s, particularly when it comes to their views on opera. The picture was complex: some were avowed highbrows and proud of it, but generally speaking, critics rarely identified themselves explicitly as highbrows or middlebrows and some exhibited attitudes that were a mixture of both stances. There were also different types of highbrow, ranging from the out-and-out snob of popular cliché to the advocate of serious music who embraced the word highbrow in a more positive way and whose attitudes were not caught up with ideas of social exclusivity. For members of this latter group, highbrowism was

---

12. Collini, *Absent Minds*, p. 112.

13. Lionel R. McColvin, *Euterpe, or the Future of Art* (London and New York: Kegan Paul and E. P. Dutton, 1926), p. 38.

14. Coulter, 'An Open Letter to Dame Clara Butt', 229.

not incompatible with notions of cultural 'uplift': their ideal was highbrow music for all.

Music journals of this period found subtle ways of signalling their place within the new cultural categories. There was a great deal of infighting among critics of this period about what constituted good taste, and it is striking that many publications ostensibly devoted to music displayed a pronounced hostility towards particular types of repertoire. Indeed, it is noteworthy that the most negative voices speaking out against opera tended to come from within the specialist music press rather than from the general press. They were a force against which those attempting to make the case for opera had to fight, at the same time as trying to convince the public at large.

Music magazines that attempted to speak to the middlebrow often de-nounced what they called 'academic' music, by which they meant chamber music and serious orchestral music. As *The Musical News and Herald* pro-claimed, 'A good waltz will always outlive a dull symphony'.[15] Some popular music magazines, such as *The Musical Mirror*, were also prone to mocking opera for being too highbrow, albeit in a fairly affectionate manner. Conversely—and intriguingly, for our purposes—there were certain peri-odicals that attacked opera, with some venom, for not being highbrow enough. In an article entitled 'Opera: A Vindication', Cecil Gray—a mu-sical highbrow who believed in the idea of a cultural 'aristocracy' yet who was also, unusually, a champion of Italian opera—wrote that: 'It would be idle to deny . . . that there exists at the present time a strong and influential body of enlightened opinion which is definitely hostile to opera, particu-larly among musicians themselves'.[16] Occasionally, publications managed to combine both standpoints: the hostility of *The Musical Standard* towards opera was a mixture of aesthetic snobbery from above and money-minded suspicion from below.

There was much disparagement of opera's status as an art form from pub-lications that considered themselves to be primarily concerned with more serious types of music, such as *The Musical Times* (*MT*), whose primary ambition at this time was to promote church music, and whose views on opera are worth examining in detail.[17] The *MT* more or less explicitly billed itself as highbrow with the frank declaration in 1924 that 'This journal is not

15. Anon., 'Highbrows', *MNH*, 64/1615 (10 March 1923), 225.

16. Cecil Gray, 'Opera: A Vindication', *MILO*, 1/1 (October 1929), 8–12, 8. On Gray, see Scaife, 'British Music Criticism in a New Era', pp. 35 and 227–39.

17. Other church music figures who spoke out against operatic culture included Sir Richard Terry, whose campaign against operatic stars we shall encounter in Chapter 6. Terry was or-ganist and Director of Music at Westminster Cathedral until 1924, where he placed a strong emphasis upon promoting Renaissance polyphony.

read by the kind of folk who like rubbish'.[18] There were some pro-operatic voices on the *MT*'s staff, notably the aforementioned Francis E. Barrett. More broadly, however, the journal's editor Harvey Grace (1874–1944), a church organist and the author of a book on Bach's organ works, steered the journal on a deliberately anti-operatic course.[19] He regularly wrote outrageously dismissive articles about opera and other types of so-called 'popular music' under the pen name 'Feste', after the fool in Shakespeare's *Twelfth Night*.

Under Grace's editorship, the *MT* regularly insulted the audience for opera. The idea that opera was something for less intelligent people and that the truly cultured appreciated 'higher' forms of art was one that would become something of a leitmotif in the journal, one of whose contributors argued that opera was 'only completely satisfactory to undeveloped artistic tastes'.[20] Grace himself disparagingly observed: 'It has been said that the operatic public is the least musical of all, and hard though the saying be one cannot but feel that it is true, seeing the absurdities and inconsistencies that opera-goers will swallow'.[21] He was referring in this particular case to recent polyglot performances at Covent Garden but continued to assert this argument about the audience for opera over a period of some years, later declaring that the opera public is 'not on the same level of musical intelligence as those who attend orchestral and chamber concerts'.[22]

In 1925, Grace wrote a lengthy diatribe about opera, attacking it as musically and dramatically weak, too expensive, and (in response to calls for subsidy) 'the very last form of enterprise with claims on the state' since it would—unlike libraries, playing fields, and public parks—only benefit a minority.[23] Resentment about the use of public money to subsidise specialist art forms such as opera would, of course, rumble on throughout the twentieth century and beyond—witness the furore in the 1990s over the allocation of over £78m in lottery funding towards the refurbishment of the Royal Opera House. The difference is that while hostility towards opera today may have increased in the general press, it has surely diminished in the specialist music press, since the pressures to defend all types of classical music against charges of elitism have become acute.

Many opera propagandists of the 1920s proposed that opera ought to be valued not only on its own merits but as an effective medium for introducing

18. 'Feste', 'Ad Libitum', *MT*, 65/976 (1 June 1924), 504–6, 504.

19. Harvey Grace, *The Organ Works of Bach* (London: Novello, 1923).

20. Arthur L. Salmon, 'The Artistic Values in Opera', *MT*, 61/930 (1 August 1920), 519–20, 520.

21. 'Feste', 'Ad Libitum', *MT*, 64/965 (1 July 1923), 465–8, 466.

22. 'Feste', 'Ad Libitum', *MT*, 66/990 (1 August 1925), 698–701, 699.

23. Ibid., 698.

listeners to a wider range of types of classical music. The BNOC's magazine *Opera*, for instance, asserted that 'opera is the best introduction to art', while the opera convert and evangelist Agnes Savill proposed that opera provided an enjoyable way for the beginner to acquire a taste for music: they might at first just watch the acting, coming to appreciate the music later.[24] Earnest meetings about the democratisation of opera were also held in the drawing rooms of Chelsea: Lady Hoskyns hosted a discussion entitled 'Why Opera is Needed' under the auspices of the British Confederation of the Arts at her home in Sloane Gardens in July 1929.[25] H. C. Colles of *The Times* argued at the meeting that opera could provide an elementary education in the arts for those who were at present 'grovelling in the cinemas.'[26]

Such well-intentioned (if to our ears patronising) comments about diverting people towards a more 'improving' form of art stand in direct opposition to Grace's disparaging remarks about opera actually having a good deal in common with lowbrow entertainment. And since opera was itself veritably lowbrow, Grace proposed, it was in fact useless as a tool by which to convert musical novices to 'good' music. He noted that people often uttered the expression ' "Get the man in the street into the opera house, and he is half-way to Queen's Hall".'[27] (The Queen's Hall was the home of symphony concerts and vocal recitals, and attracted a well-to-do, cosmopolitan audience.) Grace's pithy response to this assumption was: 'Only half-way though, and likely to stay there'. Such a listener, incapable of recognising the 'genuine article', would mistakenly believe himself, upon attending the opera, to be 'at an important artistic function'. The real musician, Grace snapped, knew better, recognising opera to be 'merely a superior and very expensive kind of variety show': similar rhetorical tropes about music hall and variety clustered around star singers, as we shall see in Chapter 6.

Individual members of the musical establishment argued about whether the highbrow was a force for good or ill within the world of music. The various voices who spoke out against highbrows approached the issue from a range of slightly different stances. Herman Klein, by this time an elder statesman of music criticism and an opponent of Modernism, posited the musical highbrow as a dangerous figure because of the influence he could exert both upon susceptible young composers and listeners, subverting

24. E. G. J., 'The Truth about British Opera: An Incident at Wembley', *Opera and the Ballet*, 2/7 (July 1924), 6–7, 7; Agnes Savill, 'Opera and the People', *The English Review* (September 1928), 327–31, 327.

25. Anon., 'British Opera: National Effort Required', *The Times*, 24 July 1929, 12.

26. 'British Opera: National Effort Required', *The Times*, 24 July 1929, 12.

27. Laura Tunbridge, 'Singing Translations: The Politics of Listening Between the Wars', *Representations*, 23/1 (summer 2013), 53–86, 57.

accepted norms of taste.[28] The contralto Clara Butt, meanwhile, adopted a crowd-pleasing angle, arguing that highbrows were simply putting a dampener on musical enjoyment: 'There are a number of musical snobs who consider that because a song is popular it cannot be good. Were I to have a concert merely for the musical "scientists" it would have to be at a small hall; there are so few of them.'[29] As a concert and recording artist, Butt had, of course, much to gain from being seen to endear herself to the largest possible audience. Indeed, she took pride in irritating the 'musical snobs' by singing 'the songs the people like instead of the songs they *ought* to like' (namely *Lieder*).[30] The term scientist is a significant one, constructing serious music as 'difficult' and antithetical to lighter repertoires that Butt posited as speaking from the heart.[31]

Ethel Smyth is an interesting case, as a composer of serious music who nevertheless positioned herself in opposition to the highbrow. Smyth contrasted attitudes in Germany and Italy, 'where opera is taken naturally and simply because it is indigenous to the soil', with those in Britain, where a highbrow mentality had imposed a stuffy 'oratorio-like solemnity' upon musical life.[32] Recounting an exchange with an unidentified conductor who had taken her work *The Boatswain's Mate* too seriously, Smyth remarked that 'if people confuse opera with divine service there is nothing more to be said', adding 'Here we have the result of highbrowism'. This puritanical, humourless attitude, Smyth argued, was attributable to the background of many of the commentators writing about music. She lamented the fact that the English musical establishment was so closely entwined with the Church (as we have already seen in the case of Harvey Grace) and with Oxford and Cambridge. Observing the fact that 'the highbrow is essentially a University product', Smyth wrote 'To be frank, this influence seems to me wholly deplorable. What we need in our musical outlook is oxygen, and I cannot bear to see the freshness and innocence of would-be cultivated amateurs smiled or sneered away by these pretentious graduates in the school of Professor Stodge'.[33]

The highbrow musical establishment was, in Smyth's view, setting itself apart from the majority of opera-goers. Critics were actively putting operatic

28. Klein, *Musicians and Mummers*, p. 324.

29. Symphonicus, 'Heard in the Interval', *MM*, 4/8 (August 1924), 143.

30. This story was reported in Coulter, 'An Open Letter to Dame Clara Butt', 229.

31. A similar debate took place in late nineteenth-century and early twentieth-century Italy, where German music was regularly disparaged by dilettante music critics as 'scientific'. For further reading, see Wilson, *The Puccini Problem*.

32. Ethel Smyth, 'On Non-Grand Opera and Solemnity', *The Midland Musician*, 1/3 (March 1926), 87–8, 88.

33. Smyth, 'An Iron Thesis on Opera', 165.

novices off attempting to enjoy the art form by telling them that the works they enjoyed were poor or old-fashioned (Smyth cites the rather surprising example of *Fidelio*), thus depriving them of music that could serve as a pain-soothing balm.[34] Mocking the tastes of those who enjoyed popular music in the hope of encouraging them to explore art music was also counter-productive. Mendl railed against the musical snobs who characterised jazz as detestable and worthless, arguing: 'Could anything be more calculated to keep the musically uneducated man away from other forms of music? No wonder that he looks upon musicians generally as a lot of eccentric freaks whom he does not profess or wish to understand, and the musical connois-seurs as a body of stuffy, academically-minded highbrows!'[35]

We can see, then, that highbrow had become a term of abuse in the 1920s, a silencing reprimand, rather akin to the way in which the word elitist might be used today. According to W. J. Turner, 'The word "highbrow" is one of those usefully vague words which can be stuck on to anything or anybody one dislikes. If you suspect a man of knowing more than you yourself do on any subject, fling the epithet "highbrow" at him and his superiority is at once undermined.'[36] But Turner advocated that critics should reclaim the term as a compliment—indeed, the highest of compliments. Conceived more positively, the label might be used to describe a writer who had confi-dence in his own convictions and did not feel the need to adjust his stance to mirror what he supposed might be the view of the majority.[37]

Turner was an outspoken poet and member of Ottoline Morrell's Garsington Circle whose views on opera, although more intuitive than aca-demic, were often insightful.[38] His attitude towards the musical public, how-ever, show a marked and overtly snobbish disdain for middlebrow tastes, and he actively condemned the efforts of the music appreciation lobby.[39] Working on the principle that everything of value in the world—whether concepts of morality, honour, and justice, or works of art—had been cre-ated by an elite, he proposed that 'The public does not know what is good, it does not even care to know ... it is lazy, stupid, indifferent, apathetic and incapable of sustained desire, effort or discipline.'[40] Turner's view here cor-responds with the typical highbrow stance of the day, as exhibited particu-larly strongly in the Modernist mindset, which hinged on the idea that both

34. Ethel Smyth, 'Catchwords and the Beloved Ignorantsia', *LM*, 17/97 (November 1927), 37–51, 44.

35. Mendl, *The Appeal of Jazz*, p. 108.

36. W. J. Turner, *Variations on the Theme of Music* (London: Heinemann, 1924), p. 82.

37. Ibid., pp. 85–6.

38. Scaife, 'British Music Criticism in a New Era', pp. 40, 288.

39. Ibid., p. 298.

40. Ibid., p. 89.

the creation and the appreciation of great art required special, rare talents, and training.[41] At the same time, Turner refused to 'write down' to the ordinary man, arguing that what we would now refer to as 'dumbing down' was contemptuous and insulting. [42]

Some music critics were keen to distance themselves from the highbrow tag and clearly felt affronted to be labelled thus when they considered themselves to be simply speaking common sense about opera's weaknesses. An anonymous writer for the largely anti-operatic *Musical Times* argued that:

> A musician need not be derided as a highbrow or a purist if jealousy for his art makes him resent the lavish expenditure of money, effort, and applause on works wherein music that is merely conventional or weak is tolerated and even acclaimed because of its association with a successful drama, or owing to its performance by star singers.[43]

As we have seen above, a certain type of 'highbrowism' went hand in hand with the attitude that opera was beyond the pale. However, to equate highbrowism systematically with a hostile attitude towards opera would be to oversimplify matters. Virginia Woolf—the archetypal self-proclaimed highbrow voice of the decade—confessed that her youth had largely been spent at Covent Garden in the years before the War, although her passion for it was, by the early 1920s, starting to cool.[44]

Some critics who were openly anti-democratic in their attitudes towards music in general and disdainful of the tastes of the masses were simultaneously—and seemingly paradoxically—enthusiastic about opera, such as Kaikhosru Sorabji, who was enthusiastic about the works of Verdi and Puccini, if not the excesses of prima donna-dom, as we shall see in due course.[45] And there were also other serious, if less overtly highbrow, music critics who were enthusiastic about opera, who took it very seriously, and who wanted to see it well performed, such as Figaro of *Musical Opinion*. Some of these critics were keen to engage a wider public, while sacrificing

---

41. LeMahieu, *A Culture for Democracy*, p. 120.

42. Turner, *Variations on the Theme of Music*, p. 88.

43. Anon., Review of Dyneley Hussey, *Eurydice, or the Nature of Opera*, MT, 70/1038 (1 August 1929), 720.

44. In a letter of 1923, she told a friend that she had found a recent performance of *Tristan und Isolde* boring, although in her younger days she had thought it 'the most beautiful thing in the world'. Virginia Woolf, letter of 8 July 1923 to Barbara Bagenal, in Nigel Nicolson (Ed.), *A Change of Perspective: The Letters of Virginia Woolf, 1923–1928* (London: Chatto & Windus, 1977), p. 56. In the same year, Woolf describes attending the BNOC's staged performance of Bach's *Phoebus and Pan* at Covent Garden in 1923, wearing 'attenuated evening dress' because she was accompanying a friend who 'takes stalls'. Virginia Woolf, letter of 18 May 1923 to Roger Fry, in Nicolson (Ed.), *A Change of Perspective*, p. 39.

45. Scaife, 'British Music Criticism in a New Era', p. 251.

nothing in terms of high artistic expectations and standards. Agnes Savill, writing in 1923, listed Ernest Newman of *The Sunday Times*, Percy Scholes of *The Observer*, Robin Legge of *The Daily Telegraph*, and H. C. Colles of *The Times* as critics who were making concerted efforts to introduce musical works to readers who did not understand musical terminology (even if Colles had a reputation as a rather severe intellectual).[46]

Music critics did not all share the same vision of their role. As Nigel Scaife has observed in his study of early twentieth-century music critics, some, such as Ernest Newman, firmly believed that there was a single, objective assessment of the merits of a musical work, whereas 'subjectivists'—particularly those writing for *The Manchester Guardian*—saw themselves as simply putting forward a personal perspective in such a way as to engage and interest the reader.[47] Some critics identified as professionals, others as (in Scaife's words) 'reporters, reviewers and belletristic "chatterers" on musical subjects who neither intended nor were expected to provide critical thought about music'.[48] Some had professional musical training; others—such as Neville Cardus of *The Manchester Guardian*, who was also a cricket correspondent—had no such musical education and wrote in a non-technical manner.[49]

The example of Percy Scholes illustrates how difficult it was to pigeon-hole critics. He wrote to Compton Mackenzie in 1923 about their shared dislike of 'this confounded high priest business', writing: 'I think what you call "the little London clique" cannot understand that the music critic of a serious London paper may be none the less competent in that job, although he does write books on music for the man in the street, and even for that man's children'.[50] Scholes, a former extension lecturer for the Universities of Manchester, London, Oxford, and Cambridge turned critic for *The Observer* (1920–7) and the BBC (1923–8),[51] made a concerted effort to take music to a wider audience. His book *Everybody's Guide to Broadcast Music* was aimed uncompromisingly at musical beginners. Brief introductions to selected operas included a pronunciation guide: 'Pronounce "Fee-*day*-lee-oh"'; 'Pronounce name of composer

---

46. Savill, *Music, Health and Character*, 133. Newman's writings on opera in *The Sunday Times* in the 1920s were largely devoted to what he saw as the failure of opera in Britain, whose cause he attributed to the weaknesses of English singers. Paul Watt, 'Critics', in Helen Greenwald (Ed.), *The Oxford Handbook of Opera* (New York: Oxford University Press, 2014), pp. 881–98, p. 893.

47. Scaife, 'British Music Criticism in a New Era', pp. 8–9, 136.

48. Ibid., p. 10.

49. Ibid., p. 29.

50. Compton Mackenzie, *My Life and Times: Octave Six 1923–30* (London: Chatto and Windus, 1967), p. 20.

51. Scaife, 'British Music Criticism in a New Era', p. 33.

"*Bee*-zay".[52] On the other hand, Scholes acknowledged that he was some-times seen as a highbrow and certainly demonstrated a certain aversion to the wider aesthetic tastes of the middlebrow, criticising 'nasty, pinchbeck jewellery on their bodies, and sentimental pictures on their walls, and shallow novels on their tables'.[53] Nevertheless, Scholes was firmly of the opinion that good taste—in music, as in other matters—was within the grasp of everyone, and that taste could only go up, not down.[54]

THE MAN IN THE STREET

The so-called 'man in the street' was of course the archetypical lover of sentimental pictures and shallow novels. This everyman figure was often mocked by the highbrow critics and simultaneously lauded by the popular press for his 'plain speaking' and 'uncontaminated' view of music. His inter-ests were regularly discussed in the contemporary music press; indeed, he became a near-mythical figure. While some commentators were disdainful of his tastes, others applauded him for his no-nonsense attitude and lack of pretensions. Certain sectors of the musical establishment took an earnest, benevolent attitude towards him, considering him to be a 'project' ripe for cultivation, while others regarded such efforts as patronising.

The man in the street, like the highbrow, was treated as a species to be classified and analysed. So who was he and why did cultural commentators concern themselves so much with him? Sometimes the term was used to describe the working-class man, but more often it denoted the relatively unrefined middle-class man.[55] In 1922 Francesco Berger defined the man in the street as 'the up-to-date phrase for the average man', a person who was neither learned nor ignorant and who took his opinions ready formed from his daily newspaper, becoming himself 'the mouthpiece of contem-porary opinion'.[56] In other words, the man in the street was effectively the middle-class middlebrow, although the latter term was not yet widely being used. And there were an awful lot of 'men in the street': this was a period in which a sense of growing panic was emerging among cultural elites about the growth of a sprawling suburbia and the rise of the middle-class func-tionary. The figure was of little interest at the individual level, Berger argued,

52. Percy A. Scholes, *Everybody's Guide to Broadcast Music* (London: OUP/Hodder and Stoughton, 1925), pp. 107, 108, 114.

53. Ibid., p. 176.

54. Scholes defied the reader to suggest a single man who used to enjoy Bach and now listens to nothing but jazz. Ibid., p. 227.

55. 'A. G.', 'Art and the Man in the Street', *MM*, 2/4 (April 1922), 106.

56. Francesco Berger, 'The Man in the Street', *MO*, 45/534 (March 1922), 515.

'yet the aggregate forms an enormous power, which the minority may not respect but cannot ignore'.[57] The explicit gendering of the term obviously deserves comment. Female tastes, insofar as they might have differed from male tastes, were rarely discussed explicitly in the mainstream or musical press. Male nouns and pronouns were invariably used, but we should not assume that the tastes discussed were necessarily exclusive to men: there were undoubtedly also 'women in the street'.

Sometimes slightly different versions of the term were employed. Critics occasionally used the term 'the Plain Man', which was something slightly more specific: unlike the man in the street he could be said to have a definite interest in the arts, but his busy working life prevented him from devoting much attention to them.[58] And the journalist (and later bestselling novelist) J. B. Priestley coined the term 'broad brow' rather than middlebrow in an essay first published in *The Saturday Review* in 1926. In Priestley's view, highbrows and lowbrows were equally problematic because of their tendency to be 'sheeplike'. 'Low' was 'the fat sheep with the cigar from City or Surbiton' and 'High' 'the thin sheep with the spectacles and the squeak from Oxford or Bloomsbury', but both were incapable of independent thought and uncritical. For example, the highs 'move in one well-drilled mass from one artistic fashion to the next, all making the same gestures of contempt and admiration'.[59] The broadbrow, on the other hand—with whom Priestley himself identified—had eclectic tastes ranging from Russian dramas to variety shows, grand opera to boxing booths, and was able to exert independent thought.[60]

The British 'man in the street' was not the same beast as the cultivated peasant one could supposedly find in other nations: a figure much idealised in contemporary reports by commentators hoping to shame their compatriots. Henry Russell estimated that 80 per cent of the English-speaking races (thus, audiences not only in Britain but in nations such as America, Canada and Australia) were more or less indifferent to opera whereas 'On the continent, and particularly in Italy, the man in the street, the peasant who can neither write nor read, is interested in singers and in operatic

57. Ibid., 515.

58. Walpole, Preface to Francis Toye, *The Well-Tempered Musician: A Musical Point of View* (London: Methuen and Co., 1925), p. vii.

59. J. B. Priestley, 'High, Low, Broad', in *Open House. A Book of Essays* (London: William Heinemann Ltd., 1927), pp. 162–7, p. 164. Priestley's essays were originally published in *The Saturday Review*. The highbrows would doubtless have been equally critical of Priestley, a writer who was overlooked because of his Grub Street journalism in the 1920s and his later popular commercial fiction, and rejection of Modernism. For further reading, see John Baxendale, *Priestley's England: J. B. Priestley and English Culture* (Manchester: Manchester University Press, 2007).

60. Priestley, 'High, Low, Broad', pp. 166–7.

Figure 3.1 The Old Vic Theatre, Lambeth (b/w photo), English photographer (twentieth century) Private Collection. © Look and Learn/Bridgeman Images.

singers in particular'.[61] Similarly, Agnes Savill argued that the audience in Paris was 'drawn from every class of the people', and that opera in all the major cities of Italy and Germany was priced at levels similar to the Old Vic (Figure 3.1), meaning that 'opera is indeed the recreation of the people'.[62]

Yet although the level of knowledge possessed by the British man in the street of popular caricature was inferior to that of his continental counterpart, he was not so much a person who knew nothing about music as

61. Russell, *The Passing Show*, pp. 286–7.
62. Agnes Savill, 'Opera and the People', *The English Review* (September 1928), 327–31, 329.

someone who knew something and could perhaps be enticed to learn more.[63] His tastes were in some respects limited but by no means entirely uninformed. The Deputy Director of the BBC wrote in *Opera* magazine in 1923 that 'We English are notoriously unmusical, not one man in a hundred enjoys Wagner, not one in a thousand can listen to Beethoven.'[64] This was, however, something of an overstatement: Rose argues that 'there was a substantial working-class audience for Beethoven', thanks to their wide participation in choirs and orchestras, particularly in northern industrial cities.[65] A group of Sheffield manual workers who were surveyed in 1918 about their cultural interests were asked to state whether they had heard of various key historical figures. Of the 22 members of the 'intellectual' group, eight knew Beethoven's name, as many as had heard of Arthur Sullivan.[66]

There was a widespread perception that 'plain men' preferred 'plain tunes' and popular ballads certainly remained favourites, especially 'Home Sweet Home', which was characterised as 'the perfect expression of one of their deepest sentiments'.[67] On the other hand, a reasonable amount of 'serious' music appeared on the man in the street's radar: he attended an annual performance of *Messiah*, had seen a few operas such as *Carmen*, and could whistle 'Là ci darem la mano', Weber's 'Huntsman's Chorus', and the soldiers' chorus from *Faust*.[68] Francis Toye, music critic of *The Morning Post* from 1925 and later an important biographer of Verdi, argued that 'the modern democracy, amazingly ignorant, incredibly ill-educated though it may be, is beginning to grope after the pleasures of real music'.[69] It had picked up this taste from hearing snippets of serious music in cinemas and tea shops and on gramophone records and was now eager to find out more about the music of Verdi and (more surprisingly, on the face of it) Wagner.

The general public beyond those who regularly attended operatic performances was evidently knowledgeable enough about the basics of popular opera for operatic plots to be referenced regularly in popular fiction. But it was likely to be suspicious of the 'trappings' of opera in its most glamorous manifestations and of its rituals, about which it was widely presumed one

63. At a talk given at the Incorporated Society of Musicians, Hugh Allen divided musical people into three categories: 1) people who really know; 2) those who think they do; and 3) those who think they do not, but do (the man in the street)'. Anon., 'The "Man in the Street" Again', *MM*, 4/2 (February 1924), 29.

64. The Deputy Director of the British Broadcasting Company, 'Broadcasting: Its Possibilities and Its Future', *Opera*, 1/5 (May 1923), 20–1, 20.

65. Rose, *The Intellectual Life of the British Working Classes*, p. 206. He also cites interviewees who recalled hearing Beethoven in early cowboy films (p. 202).

66. Ibid., p. 194.

67. Coulter, 'An open letter to Dame Clara Butt', 229.

68. Berger, 'The Man in the Street', 515.

69. Toye, *The Well-Tempered Musician*, p. 69.

had to be 'in the know', an assumption that still persists today. This view is reflected in comments from Richard Capell (then music critic for *The Daily Mail* and editor of *The Monthly Musical Record*) who wrote in 1930 that 'Those great continental opera-houses which suggest such possibilities of musical pleasure may also strike us as rather alarmingly official in look, and uncomfortably like temples, where faith is congealed in formularies'.[70]

Unsurprisingly, *Opera* magazine made a strong case for 'opera for the people', and overtly declared its commitment to the engagement of 'the man in the street', announcing its manifesto to be that 'Opera in England, must be made the pastime of democracy'.[71] Numerous personalised anecdotal accounts reinforced the point that the BNOC's performances were for ordinary people rather than any sort of social elite. For example, *Opera* published a story in which a 16-year-old barber's apprentice from Bradford saved a shilling a week from his pocket money to buy tickets for the opera. Heart-warmingly, the orchestra paid for three seats for him during the last few days of the season, at which point he had run out of money.[72]

The BNOC made much of its efforts to take opera to working-class men who occupied a rung lower on the social ladder than the middle-class man in the street. Perceval Graves, the BNOC's Publicity Manager, wrote of touring round factories in northern cities, giving talks about opera in cheerless canteens during the workers' lunch breaks. Graves would tell the plots of operas, with music examples performed by a singer colleague, and explain that the 'grand' in 'grand opera' did not mean highbrow: the knock on effect was a demonstrable increase in ticket sales.[73] He argued that music's social and health-giving benefits should inspire benefactors to follow Beecham's lead in funding it, since 'The sedative effect of the right music on neurotics, and the tonic properties of community singing in the factory, should fire their imagination and loosen their purse strings'.[74]

Opera clearly did have a large audience among 'ordinary people', but some publications called into question whether it was really appreciated by the much-discussed man in the street; indeed as one journalist wrote 'There have been more words and "hot air" expended lately on the subject of popularising opera than on any other controversial musical matter'.[75] A crude caricature by *The Musical Standard* revealed that the man in the

---

70. Richard Capell, *Opera* (London: Ernest Benn, Ltd., 1930), p. 9.

71. The Editor, 'Hands Off Opera!', *Opera*, 1/7 (July 1923), 6–7, 7.

72. A Man in the Queue, 'Stray Notes: National Opera News', *Opera*, 2/4 (April 1924), 24.

73. Graves wrote: 'That these operatic samples created a demand for opera in bulk was later shown by the box office. Hundreds of pounds worth of tickets can be credited to this source alone'. Perceval Graves, 'Opera in Town and on Tour', *The Sackbut*, 8 (June 1927), 332–4, 333.

74. Ibid., 334.

75. Anon., 'Opera for the Plain Man', *MM*, 4/10 (October 1924), 187.

street was capable of enjoying opera, whereas orchestral music was considered to be the real 'highbrow' music: '"I love to hear good singers, if they don't jabber in some foreign language. But an orchestral concert is above me"'.[76]

As well as revealing a suspicion of non-texted classical music, this quotation demonstrates the perceived necessity of translating opera into English in order to appeal to British audiences. This was of course the policy of the touring companies and the Old Vic. Covent Garden, meanwhile, returned to performing operas in the original languages during the second half of the 1920s.[77] (The latter had been the policy instated by Augustus Harris at Covent Garden in the 1890s. Prior to that, the policy had been to translate all operas, whatever their nationality, into Italian.) Some critics suggested that opera might have a greater dramatic effect in the original language, but such suggestions tended to attract outraged accusations of snobbery from those aspiring to democratise opera.[78] *Opera* magazine exalted the democratic virtues of opera in English, the editor making the case for opera in a language 'which is intelligible to "the classes and the masses" alike'.[79] In the same periodical, Samuel Langford, a determined adversary of musical snobbery who usually wrote for *The Manchester Guardian*, attacked 'the outrageous man of culture' whom he characterised as wanting to keep opera in its original languages explicitly so as to keep it out of reach of 'the mass of the people'.[80] He argued that the translation of opera into English was absolutely essential, since 'nothing is more detrimental or indeed fatal to the general love of music in any vocal form than the common use of alien tongues'. Such debates about whether or not to translate opera rumble on vehemently today: the practice has arguably become redundant since the introduction of surtitles, yet English National Opera continues to present singing in English as central to its distinctive identity and its business model.

As we have seen, the man in the street was almost certainly familiar with operatic 'bleeding chunks'.[81] This form of listening attracted snobbish comment from critics of various dispositions. A. H. Fox-Strangways, chief

76. J. Raymond Tobin, 'Music and the man-in-the-street', MS, 24/446 (18 October 1924), 132.

77. Rodmell, *Opera in the British Isles*, p. 54.

78. Toye was unusual in critiquing the general policy on operatic translation (whilst admitting that it was unlikely to change), arguing 'Wotan, rendered into English, is not quite Wotan, and Tosca, screaming anglicised imprecations against Scarpia, can never wholly preserve the full flavour of her native latinity'. Francis Toye, *The Well-Tempered Musician: A Musical Point of View* (London: Methuen and Co., 1925), p. 204.

79. Editorial, No title, *Opera and the Ballet*, 2/5 (May 1924), 5.

80. Samuel Langford, 'What of Opera?', *Opera*, 2/3 (March 1924), 14–15.

81. In Berger's words, 'it is only these few stray bits or similar ones that have "caught on" with the "man in the street"'. Berger, 'The Man in the Street', 515.

music critic for *The Observer* and founder of the academic journal *Music & Letters*, condemned fragmented listening in *The London Mercury*, writing that 'An opera is, in fact, not primarily a mine of quotations. Those who regard and value it as that will never understand opera'.[82] Although the *Mercury* was a cultural magazine that spanned the highbrow-middlebrow divide, Fox-Strangways was clearly presenting an unashamedly highbrow agenda here, since middlebrows were less concerned about the purity of cultural texts, as we shall see presently. It is noteworthy to see a similar attitude being adopted even by Edward J. Dent (an advocate for 'popular opera' in his strong support of the Old Vic), who posited the person who came to opera by hearing isolated fragments in celebrity concerts as 'dangerous'. Although this type of listener was theoretically capable of enjoying good music if it was presented to them in the right way, Dent conceded, he or she was 'undiscriminating', unable to analyse whether their enjoyment of a piece of music was the result of the music, the words, or some external factor such as the singer's clothes.[83] Such comments exhibit a purist attitude towards opera, a reverence for the musical 'work concept'—however problematic that might be with regard to opera—and a dismissive attitude to the intelligence of the average listener.

In contrast, there was respect in some quarters for the way in which the man in the street listened to music, which was posited, paradoxically, as 'purer' than that of the musical expert, who was 'normally a mass of prejudice without knowing it'.[84] *The Musical Mirror* was a publication that actively spoke for the man in the street and, despite its coverage of some serious music, was resolutely sceptical about highbrow attitudes. Insofar as this periodical was concerned, listening to opera for pleasure was not a problem; indeed entertainment was the beginning and the end of the matter. The magazine proposed that the popular audience did not go to concerts to be educated but with the 'laudable' aim of being moved or amused, concluding that 'None but artistic or social snobs (or critics) go to concerts for any reason superior to that of deriving pleasure'.[85] Listening for pleasure

---

82. A. H. Fox-Strangways, 'Chronicles. Music: National Opera', *LM*, 12/67 (May 1925), 92–4, 93.

83. Edward J. Dent, 'The World of Music', *ILN*, 30 December 1922, 1084–5.

84. 'Devana', 'The "Popular" Audience', *MM*, 2/6 (June 1922), 170. There is a striking similarity here with music journalism in Italy at the turn of the century and beyond, where music periodicals regularly undermined the authority of their own critics by holding up ordinary listeners as the ideal critics for responding to music emotionally rather than intellectually. For further reading, see Alexandra Wilson, 'Defining Italianness: The Opera that made Puccini', *The Opera Quarterly*, 24/1–2 (2008), 82–92 and Alexandra Wilson, 'Music, Letters and National Identity: Reading the 1890s Italian Music Press', *19th-Century Music Review*, 7/2 (2010), 99–116.

85. Devana, 'The "Popular" Audience', 170.

was, furthermore, sometimes presented as an innately British tendency, if not exactly as a national virtue. Denis Laird of *The Musical News and Herald* played on the stereotype of the nation of shopkeepers and argued that the hard-working British, exhausted after the shutters had gone down at the end of the day, wanted entertainment that did not require study: intellectual laziness was therefore a fair gibe, but intellectual incapacity was not.[86]

Occasionally some periodicals published articles by journalists using names such as 'a man in the street' or, as in the case of the BNOC's *Opera* magazine, 'A man in the queue'. So lauded was the man in the street then, that some journalists apparently wanted to emulate him. Or was this a strategy for engaging readers by making them feel as though the critics were not lofty intellectuals but ordinary people just like themselves? In fact, *Opera* was prepared to admit the plain truth of the matter: that it was commonplace for periodicals to employ some writers who were not experts and pseudonyms were merely a cover for ignorance. A correspondent going by the name 'Our Unsophisticated Critic' reported that the first thing that had to be done when a new magazine was launched was for the editor to divide the writers into two classes: those who knew something about the subject could use their own names, while those who did not would hide behind a *nom-de-plume*.[87]

Other commentators, however, baulked at the idea that the 'man in the street' should be accorded the authority to pass comment upon high culture, something that was more commonly the case with music than other forms of art. L. Castle wrote in *The Musical Standard* in 1923 that 'the ordinary person in the street thinks that he has quite the same right to criticise a piece of music as a musical critic', whereas he would look at you dumbfounded if asked to criticise a sculpture.[88] Similarly, Harvey Grace argued for respect to be paid to those who were actually qualified to write about music, contrasting the disrespect shown towards them with the respect accorded, at least outwardly, to expert architects, painters, or writers.[89] Such outspokenness about music, compared with a lack of willingness to comment upon the other arts, seems rather perverse given the specialist technical vocabulary involved in discussing music, but would appear to suggest that music was regarded as something that operated merely at the emotional level.

86. Denis Laird, 'Wanted—A Mussolini', *MNH*, 65/1651 (17 November 1923), 426.
87. Anon., 'London Xmas Season. By Our Unsophisticated Critic', *Opera*, 1/2 (February 1923), 24.
88. L. Castle, 'The Attitude of the General Public Towards Music', *MS*, 21/409 (19 May 1923), 161.
89. Harvey Grace, 'Music and Musicians', *Yorkshire Post and Leeds Intelligencer*, 8 December 1924, 7.

This lack of reverence for music, compared to that which might be found in other European nations, can perhaps be attributed to a widespread lack of knowledge about it, which spanned the class spectrum. Even very cultured British people often knew little about opera. Dorothy Short, writing in the art journal *Apollo* in 1925, remarked upon the fact that while the average cultivated person knew a reasonable amount about canonical writers and poets and about contemporary art, music was a particular blind-spot: indeed, such a person 'seems to be almost proud of his incompetence' in this area.[90] A knowledge of music in general—let alone opera specifically—was quite simply not a part of the educated British man or woman's general education.[91] This created a suspicion about it that merely fuelled the contemporary confusion about where to situate opera within the new cultural categories.

RAISING TASTES

There were lively discussions during the 1920s about whether the musical establishment ought to try to educate the man in the street. On the whole, those members of the musical establishment who cared deeply about opera believed that raising the taste of British audiences was crucial, even if there were concerns that such efforts might seem condescending. (As the middlebrow *Musical Mirror* contended, 'How to raise the taste of the masses without being offensively patronising, is a problem that we have always with us'.[92]) A large number of general books about opera, aimed at beginners, were published during the decade, and often went through several editions.[93] More broadly, a veritable industry of music appreciation classes and talks sprang up during the 1920s. Such endeavours attempted to overturn the negative stereotypes that were sometimes associated with opera. First, it was deemed necessary to get past the idea that opera was boring. For example, *The Gloucester Journal* reported that a Mr F. A. Wilshire of

90. Dorothy Short, 'Music and Culture', R. Sydney Glover (Ed.), *Apollo: A Journal of the Arts, Vol 2 July to December 1925* (Nendeln, Liechtenstein: Kraus Reprint, 1976), pp. 53–4, p. 53.

91. 'It cannot I think be gainsaid that a knowledge of the great things of music is a part of an educated man's ordinary general culture'. Percy A. Scholes, *The Second Book of the Gramophone Record* (London: Oxford University Press, 1925).

92. Anon., 'Music Today: Music for the Masses', *MM*, 8/10 (October 1928), 253.

93. See, for example, Northcott's *Covent Garden and the Royal Opera*, whose first edition of 1921 sold extremely well, with a second edition published in 1924. Other popular books on opera included: Leo Melitz, *The Opera-Goers' Complete Guide: Comprising 268 Complete Opera Plots, with Musical Numbers and Casts* (London and Toronto: Dent, 1925); Anon., *Opera at Home* (London: The Gramophone Company, 1921); Paul England, *50 Favourite Operas: A Popular Account Intended as an Aid to Dramatic and Musical Appreciation* (London: Harrap, 1925).

Bristol had given a talk to the local Rotary Club, in which he 'said there was a general idea that grand opera was a dry, dreary, miserable sort of business—something analogous to Einstein's Theory of Relativity, and that it was only highbrow people who understood it'.[94] Second, it was deemed necessary to demonstrate that opera was not intimidating. Perceval Graves, on a 1924 publicity tour for the BNOC, gave several mid-day addresses in Leeds in which he stressed that opera was supposed to be popular enter-tainment and that 'the epithet "grand" was needlessly alarming'.[95]

The BNOC was particularly active in opera education, both for children and for adults. Its house magazine took its educational remit seriously, not only by publishing articles about opera intended to broaden its readers' knowledge but by promoting supplementary educational products: a series of BNOC books known as the National Opera Handbooks was advertised with the slogan 'Read them before hearing the opera and treble your en-joyment'.[96] *Opera* magazine regularly contained supplements outlining the plots of operas in the BNOC repertory and Figaro also found it noteworthy that the BNOC published plot summaries in their programmes, indicating that this was a rarity at the time.[97] In 1923 the magazine adopted as the header for its editorial the quotation 'opera is the supreme instrument for the aesthetic and emotional education of the whole nation', words bor-rowed from Peter Green, Canon of Manchester and Chaplain to H. M. The King, uttered in the context of hearing an opera for the first time at the age of fifty.[98]

Furthermore, *Opera* magazine devoted a good amount of space to the question of how people might be 'converted' by opera on the radio, once again serving its own interests.[99] The BNOC Covent Garden production of *The Magic Flute* on 8 January 1923 was the first ever opera broadcast on radio, and the first studio broadcast, on 8 October of the same year (Gounod's *Roméo et Juliette*) also featured a cast primarily drawn from members of the same company.[100] The magazine even published articles

---

94. Anon., 'Grand Opera. Address to Gloucester Rotary Club', *Gloucester Journal*, 29 October 1927, 1.

95. Anon., 'Opera in Leeds', *Yorkshire Post and Leeds Intelligencer*, 10 December 1924, 8.

96. Inside cover, *Opera*, 1/2 (February 1923). The series editor was Mr A. Corbett-Smith and the operas covered were *Parsifal, The Mastersingers, Tristan and Isolda* [sic], *The Ring, The Magic Flute,* and *The Marriage of Figaro.*

97. Figaro, 'The Operatic World', *MO*, 47/555 (December 1923), 253–4, 253.

98. Peter Green, 'What it Feels Like to Hear Opera for the First Time at the Age of Fifty', *Opera*, 1/7 (July 1923), 12–14, 12.

99. The company's artistic director, Percy Pitt, was appointed music adviser to the BBC in 1923. Meirion Hughes and Robert Stradling, *The English Musical Renaissance, 1840– 1940: Constructing a National Music*, 2nd edn (Manchester: Manchester University Press, 2001), p. 102.

100. J. C. W. Reith, 'Broadcasting Opera', *Opera and the Ballet*, 2/6 (June 1924), 13–14.

by leading BBC directors, including J. C. W. Reith himself. Reith praised the BNOC for its enthusiasm for broadcasting, something that had assisted the BBC in fulfilling its own aims: 'It must be remembered that theatre opera transmissions would not have been possible had it not been for the broadminded attitude and foresight of the BNOC. This organisation was amongst the first to see a potential aid in broadcasting, and to support the BBC's endeavour to give radio audiences the benefit of the highest forms of musical art. We have since broadcast every London season of the BNOC'.[101]

Reith's article demonstrated the way in which the BBC, like the BNOC, was attempting to reach out to an audience not yet necessarily familiar with opera. The question of how to convey the plot of an opera was something that was much debated in the BBC's infancy: for this reason, opera was considered to be more difficult to broadcast than other forms of music. In the early days of opera broadcasting, the announcer not only read out the plot in advance but talked over the music, in order to explain to the audience at home what was going on onstage.[102] This policy prompted complaints from listeners, but the BBC defended it.[103] After quipping that a listener had threatened to turn up at Covent Garden and shoot anybody who dared to talk over the production of *Siegfried*, Reith explained to the readers of *Opera* that although the interpolated remarks seemed sacrilegious to some, they had helped many.[104]

Nevertheless, it is clear that some listeners perceived opera, as encountered for the first time on the radio, to be highbrow. The BBC received numerous letters of protest about its 'heavy' programming—despite the fact that only a small proportion of the repertoire broadcast in these early years was classical—from correspondents who said they wanted to relax when they got home from work.[105] There was an immediate outcry when

---

101. Ibid., 13.

102. 'We had no means of telling whether our listeners, many of whom had probably never seen an opera performed, would be able to follow the dramatic situation. To assist matters therefore, the plot of the opera was read prior to the transmission, thereby establishing a precedent from which we have never since departed. In addition to this, with the aid of another microphone, the invisible audience were kept informed of the progress of events on the stage. These interpolations were superimposed over the opera transmission, the interpolator—or interpreter, one should say—being ensconced on the stage itself, in the prompt-box'. J. C. W. Reith, 'Broadcasting Opera', *Opera and the Ballet*, 2/6 (June 1924), 13–14, 13.

103. A letter of 31 January 1929 from B. V. Darbishire to Percy Pitt complained that in a performance of *Samson and Delilah* the music was interrupted 18 times. The correspondent asked whether this was an experiment and if so whether it could be abandoned. BBC WAC R27/326/1 Music Gen—Opera—General Memos 1929–34.

104. Reith, 'Broadcasting Opera', 14.

105. Doctor has calculated that in 1925, classical music represented 12.02 per cent of the total hours of transmission and 18.05 per cent of the hours devoted explicitly to music, rising to 15.79 per cent/25.07 per cent by 1927 and 19.32 per cent/32.15 per cent by 1929. Popular/light music still made up a larger percentage of the total music broadcast, although serious music

the corporation began to increase its number of opera broadcasts. And it is interesting to note that in this context many correspondents lumped opera in with forms of music that were generally considered more highbrow. For example, *The Nottingham Evening Post* reported in 1925 that 'the vast majority of listeners are exasperated beyond measure and wearied to death of grand opera, symphony, Elizabethan atrocities, and the like'. This newspaper attempted to whip up populist, anti-intellectual feeling by calling in almost jingoistic terms for the organisation of 'a great national protest against the musical crank with a passion for the unmelodious and inexplicable', and 'virile propaganda for really good, tuneful, expressive, and cheerful music of the kind that stirs the blood and rouses the emotions and brings back to us memories of happy days'.[106]

Opera magazine, by contrast, made much of the fact that ordinary people were being converted to opera through broadcasting.[107] It published a first-person article by an unnamed office boy, who told a story about an evening when he and the office typist, Peggy, stayed at work late into the evening—even forgetting to have dinner—so captivated were they by something 'very wonderful' on the wireless.[108] They discovered by looking in a newspaper that it was a BNOC broadcast of *The Mastersingers*. This was of course still an era when 'self improvement' was fashionable: clerks from the London suburbs were striving for self-education, reading literature in cheap editions, visiting museums and galleries, and attending concerts.[109] The office boy—whom we might see as the even more humble younger cousin of E. M. Forster's Leonard Bast—visited Covent Garden the next day and found that he could afford a couple of gallery tickets for himself and Peggy. The story was, of course, a piece of overt propaganda for the BNOC's own collaboration with the BBC, but its general premise

and serious discussion programmes tended to be broadcast at peak times. Jennifer Doctor, *The BBC and Ultra-Modern Music, 1922–1936: Shaping a Nation's Tastes* (Cambridge: Cambridge University Press, 1999), pp. 40, 49. Hann reported in *The Spectator*: 'when the Broadcasting Company increased the number of opera performances in its programmes, there immediately came an outcry, whether representative or not there is no telling, against "Too Much Opera". If that was a true ballot from those millions of listeners, then here is an end to all our schemes'. Hann, 'Opera—If You Will', 8.

106. Anon., 'BBC's Fare. Continued Protests against Unpopular Programmes. Do Listeners want Musical Tastes Developing?', *The Nottingham Evening Post*, 26 October 1925, 7.

107. Such reports contradict McKibbin's claim that the interwar BBC's policy of giving the general public a taste for serious music was unsuccessful. He writes: 'There is ... no evidence that this happened, any more than the apparent enthusiasm during the war for "good" literature denoted any significant change in what people wished to read'. McKibbin, *Classes and Cultures*, pp. 386–7.

108. An Office Boy, 'My First Opera', *Opera*, 2/4 (April 1924), 8.

109. Carey, *The Intellectuals and the Masses*, pp. 59–61. On the clerks and other office boys, see Rose, *The Intellectual Life of the British Working Classes*, pp. 401–21.

is backed up by the praise Rose cites for the early BBC opera broadcasts, from working-class audience members who evidently found the listening experience transformative.[110]

Opera companies also worked in partnership with recording companies to expand the audience for opera, which would of course have benefits for both parties.[111] Numerous talks about music were given up and down the country, illustrated by examples on gramophone record, while gramophone societies held public 'recitals'.[112] *Opera* magazine was full of stories of everyman characters listening to opera on record. There was, for instance, the account of 'Smith', previously a lover of band music. Smith's initial classical choices were deemed 'bad' because 'he selected names, international names, rather than music'—recordings by celebrity singers, in other words—but with repeated listening came to tire of them and to appreciate a more serious repertoire.[113] Eventually he was inspired to seek out a BNOC performance of *La bohème*, where, thanks to the gramophone, 'he felt that the opera in some undefined way belonged to him', and even started to enjoy orchestral music, a repertoire he had previously considered too highbrow.

It is interesting to find Nellie Melba—in spite of her precious attitude towards changing audiences at Covent Garden—celebrating the fact that broadcasting and the gramophone were 'the two most eloquent missionaries to the musical heathen in our midst'.[114] The religious overtones to this comment should not go unnoticed. There was undoubtedly a missionary zeal to some of the attempts to broaden the audience for opera. In a particularly clear example, a south-London based clergyman named Father R. H. Green ran an 'opera club' at his church in a deprived area of Battersea in the early 1920s. Green invited his younger parishioners to join him after evensong each Sunday to talk through the music and plot of an opera, aided by gramophone examples. After eighteen months, Father Green's club had grown to number thirty members and his parishioners, who had previously regarded Wagner's music as mere 'noise', now 'know *The Ring* by heart'.[115]

110. Rose, *The Intellectual Life of the British Working Classes*, p. 204.

111. H. V. Higgins, Chairman of the Grand Opera Syndicate, Covent Garden, wrote in the preface to a small book published by the Gramophone Company: 'The publication of *Opera at Home* should . . . lead to a material increase in the numbers and enthusiasm of operatic audiences—a result in hoping for which I am not entirely disinterested'. Anon., *Opera at Home* (London: The Gramophone Company, 1921), p. 8. Higgins called the Gramophone Company 'an admirable missionary in the good cause' in familiarising the public with the art of great singers (p. 9).

112. For further reading on the gramophone societies, see the numerous reports of their activities in *Gramophone* magazine.

113. A. Clement Jones, 'The Wonderful Gramophone', *Opera*, 2/4 (April 1924), 32.

114. Nellie Melba 'A Musical Renascence', *MT*, 67/997 (1 March 1926), 259.

115. See Green's letter, 'Father Green's Opera Club', *Gramophone*, 2/12 (May 1925), 501.

Furthermore, so enthused about opera were these poor parishioners that eighteen of them misguidedly signed up for Isidore De Lara's ill-fated 'National Opera Scheme' when he came to visit the club, handing over their hard-earned pound on the spot.[116]

What, then, do all these stories tell us about opera's place in the battle of the brows? Like those in the previous chapter, they tell us that the people in the 1920s audience for opera—whether critics or ordinary members of the public—were extremely difficult to categorise. Some Britons were evidently fearful of opera; some, knowing very little about it, presumed it *must* be highbrow. And yet many so-called men (or women) in the street, once introduced to a little opera, evidently felt able to embrace it without prejudice as just another form of entertainment. What is strikingly clear from the analysis above is that no group seems to have wanted to adopt opera as the private preserve of a limited social group or something for which one required special knowledge or social cachet in order to appreciate. Indeed, precisely the opposite was the case: the most lofty highbrows of the era were keen to distance themselves from opera as something that was rather beneath them, too frivolous to merit proper artistic respect. In short, these were not 'opera snobs': rather, they were snobbish *about* opera. Meanwhile, other critics took opera very seriously but were advocates of serious opera for all. Thus, it starts to become abundantly clear that when thinking about operatic attitudes of this period, a simplistic highbrow-lowbrow dichotomy is a most unhelpful frame of reference. The truth of the matter was far more complicated, and far more interesting: opera occupied a messy and complicated space in the middle. Might we go so far as to call opera middlebrow?

116. As reported in: Leonard Spalding, 'The Forum: Grand Opera a Necessity?', MNH, 69/1756 (21 November 1925), 464.

CHAPTER 4

✧

Boundaries

For all the efforts to separate out the high from the low in the 1920s, encounters between the two could be found wherever one chose to look. The archetypal interwar collision between different cultural spheres is epitomised in a brief account by Ursula Greville (editor of *The Sackbut*) of a trip to a London cinema in 1929. Greville was watching a private screening at the Wardour Street Film House of *The Street Girl*, a film about an impoverished New York jazz band. The curtain rose upon Tito Schipa singing what Greville called 'that lovely song from *L'elisir d'amore*, which, when I am a millionaire, I shall get C. B. Cochran to do with a Compton Mackenzie translation'.[1] Here film meets jazz, meets opera, meets revue, meets popular fiction. Attitudes towards such culture clashes varied. Highbrow commentators, whether their field was literature, fine art, or music, were concerned with formal purity and united by a suspicion of the blurring of formal boundaries. Middlebrow commentators, on the other hand, actively encouraged boundary crossing. They also enthusiastically embraced new media technologies and were untroubled by the recycling and re-adaptation of culture, whether manifested in adaptations of best-selling novels for the theatrical stage or the new suburban mock-Tudor houses that caused purists so much angst.[2]

In this chapter I consider how opera's refusal to adhere to rules about cultural purity acted as a barrier to its acceptance into the highbrow bracket, and propose that opera sat somewhere closer to the middlebrow. As we have already seen, opera was capable of taking a place alongside

---

1. Ursula Greville, 'Excursions', *The Sackbut*, 10/2 (September 1929), 29–31, 31.
2. Trewin, *The Gay Twenties*, p. 29; Napper, *British Cinema and Middlebrow Culture*, p. 10.

an eclectic range of other types of music in the broad, mixed tastes of the average man in the street, in a way that string quartets, for example, were not. Furthermore, opera acted within the marketplace in ways that seemed to blur the dividing line between high and low. Some arguments that took place in the 1920s about opera's cultural 'impurity' were old: debates about the perceived problem of blending music with drama dated back centuries, but were still being discussed vehemently during this period. However, some of the arguments about opera and cultural purity that raged in the 1920s were prompted by new encounters between opera and other forms of entertainment, and by the blurring of boundaries between them.

Historically, opera had long rubbed shoulders with many forms of popular entertainment: operatic highlights had made their way into music halls—both as fodder for mockery and, conversely, a way of demonstrating the halls' respectability and ambition—and brass band arrangements.[3] Equally, popular ballads such as 'Home, Sweet Home' were sometimes interpolated into operas (regularly, for example, into the letter-writing scene in The Barber of Seville) and found themselves nestling cheek-by-jowl alongside operatic arias in the pick-and-mix concerts that were given by operatic stars. These practices continued in the 1920s: witness, for example, the way in which operatic excerpts were performed by Mr Fred Roper's Piccadilly Follies as part of an end-of-pier cabaret show in Portsmouth in 1927.[4]

The dividing lines between opera and more populist forms of entertainment were therefore permeable, and becoming more so. This tendency offended the highbrows' obsession with formal purity and complicated opera's cultural pigeonholing. Significantly, however, highbrow critics were not usually—with a few exceptions—attempting to defend opera's 'purity' or expressing concern about the quality of opera being demeaned when they baulked at cultural mixing. Rather, they were damning opera precisely because it lent itself so well to commercial commodification and to collaborations with film, popular music, fictional potboilers, and much more besides. At the very moment when there seemed to be a compelling need to assign labels, opera's historically vexed cultural status was becoming more problematic than ever before.

3. Opera singers and ballerinas were brought into the music halls from the 1890s, at a point where impresarios wanted to attract a more middle-class audience (Weber, The Great Transformation of Musical Taste, p. 291; see also Burrows, Legitimate Cinema, p. 98). The Victorian music hall and brass band repertoires are discussed in depth in Russell, Popular Music in England.

4. Anon., 'South Parade Pier Cabaret', The Portsmouth Evening News, 19 July 1927, 3.

OPERA'S 'UNLAWFULNESS'

Before turning to opera's encounters with new media, let us examine the question of its perceived inherent impurity—its identity as, in J. B. Priestley's words, 'the mongrel art'.[5] Romantic aesthetic principles asserting the superiority of absolute music had cast a long shadow, and opera's status as an amalgam of several different art forms became doubly problematic at a time when commentators felt obliged to slot cultural products into distinct categories. These historical concerns were international ones, yet Samuel Langford, music critic for *The Manchester Guardian*, complained in 1924 that:

> England is more troubled even than other countries with the sort of ascetic philosopher
> who sees in music but the discipline of pure form, and looks upon every poetic associ-
> ation with music, whether in opera, programme music, or even song, with suspicion.[6]

Music critics exhibited widespread snobbery about opera being a 'bastardised' art form—in the sense of the music being adulterated or contaminated by its combination with other art forms—and the word, whose connotations were stronger than they would be today, was used explicitly. Columnists for *The Musical Times* were predictably quick to make this observation, calling opera 'a bastard art that has achieved respectability by the sheer tenacity of its existence' and 'a composite product whose lawfulness we need not deny, but whose artistic rank we must class as secondary'.[7] Yet opera's 'lawfulness' was indeed something that had to be ascertained and confirmed, with some critics questioning whether it had the right to call itself an art form at all. For instance, the young lecturer, biographer, novelist, and broadcaster Basil Maine called opera 'a form so incongruous that it refuses to fit in with our preconceived theories of art, however anxious we may be to accommodate its presence'.[8] The perceived problem with opera

---

5. J. B. Priestley, 'On Overlooking Covent Garden', in *Open House: A Book of Essays* (London: William Heinemann Ltd., 1927), pp. 49–54, p. 50.

6. Samuel Langford, 'What of Opera?', *Opera*, 1/3 (March 1924), 14–15, 14. Langford also attacked highbrow critics for their insistence that opera be performed in the original language: the 'outrageous [men] of culture who would . . . keep most first rate opera from the mass of the people' (p. 15).

7. Frank Howes, 'Some Varieties of Operatic Experience', *MT*, 66/990 (1 August 1925), 713–14, 713; Arthur L. Salmon, 'The Artistic Values in Opera', *MT*, 61/930 (1 August 1920), 519–20, 520.

8. Basil Maine, 'Acting in Opera', in R. Sydney Glover (Ed.), *Apollo: A Journal of the Arts, Vol 6 July to December 1927* (Nendeln, Liechtenstein: Kraus Reprint, 1976), pp. 16–18, p. 16; Basil Maine, 'Is Opera Absurd?', in Glover (Ed.), *Apollo: A Journal of the Arts, Vol 6 July to December 1927*, pp. 147–9, p. 147. Scaife dismisses Maine as an 'amateur' writer about music. Scaife, 'British Music Criticism in a New Era', p. 37.

as an amalgamation of several art forms was that the worth of its constituent components was watered down.

In the numerous books on opera that were published during the 1920s, whether beginners' guides or detailed analyses aimed at the more informed reader, authors—even if well disposed to opera—almost invariably dealt with the question of opera's 'confused' status before moving on to other matters. A prime example is a book of 1929 entitled *Eurydice, or the Nature of Opera* by the poet and journalist Dyneley Hussey, who was at the time of writing a music critic for *The Times*.[9] *Eurydice* was part of a large series of introductory books (the 'Today and Tomorrow' series), each named after an appropriate figure from mythology, ancient history, or the Old Testament. While the majority of the other titles included the phrase 'the future of' (*Heraclitus, or the Future of Films; Cassandra, or the Future of the British Empire*, for example), the expression 'the nature of' was chosen for the book about opera.[10] This variation from the series norm is both intriguing and telling, indicating that opera was so puzzling as to need its very nature pinning down, while perhaps also suggesting that the art form's future existence was not perceived to be guaranteed. Although Hussey took a positive attitude towards opera himself, he felt obliged to deal with a key operatic problem, namely that 'The charge brought against opera, as a form, is that it is a hybrid, a mixture of oil and vinegar, a spoiling of two good things'.[11]

Many of those involved in writing and performing operas themselves gave short shrift to the widespread criticism of opera's composite nature. For example, Rutland Boughton—one of the few really successful British opera composers of the era thanks to his hit *The Immortal Hour*—argued that such anxieties were expressed only by 'theorists' and were an irrelevance to the people who composed, performed, and enjoyed opera.[12] Thomas Beecham spun the point more optimistically, positing opera's hybrid nature as a selling point, precisely the 'hook' that would attract listeners who didn't know much about it. He stated in a speech at the Leeds Luncheon Club that 'Opera properly done is the most appropriate medium of conveying not only music but other arts to the unsophisticated mind of the average person. Opera is an amalgam, a combination of all the arts'.[13]

9. Dyneley Hussey, *Eurydice, or the Nature of Opera* (London and New York: Kegan Paul, Trench, Trubner and Co. Ltd./E. P. Dutton & Co., 1929).

10. As Overy notes, these popular pocket books aspired to resurrect the traditional literary format of 'the pamphlet' and formed part of a wider literature on the future of civilisation. Overy, *The Morbid Age*, p. 18.

11. Hussey, *Eurydice, or the Nature of Opera*, p. 9.

12. Rutland Boughton, 'The Future of Opera in Great Britain', *MNH*, 64/1630 (23 June 1923), 610–11, 610.

13. 'Music in England: Sir Thomas Beecham's Criticism', *The Times*, 2 October 1928, 11.

And yet on the other hand it is striking to note that opera promoted aesthetic discomfort—in some cases even loathing—from within the musical community itself.[14]

OPERA'S ABSURDITY

Related to discussions about opera as a hybrid or bastardised art form was a long-standing cliché attributable originally to Samuel Johnson about opera being an 'irrational art'. This too was still alive and well during the 1920s, and journalistic articles abounded with titles such as 'Is Opera a Luxury, a Habit, or Just Absurd?', as Basil Maine put it in *The Musical News and Herald*.[15] Opera was far more prone to being ridiculed by critics than other forms of art, even if these too had their absurdities.[16] And while literary parody was good-natured, the mockery of opera was sharper edged. Again, criticism of opera often came from within the specialist music press.[17] That highbrow critics should have dismissed opera as ridiculous is unsurprising. More interesting is the fact that those involved in promoting opera should have felt the need to discuss and in some cases attempt to justify its supposed strangeness.[18] Percy Scholes, for instance, began his book *A Miniature History of Opera* (first published in *The Radio Times*) with the declaration that 'Opera is a "rum thing" and as such takes some explaining'.[19]

Opera had long been parodied in British popular culture—sometimes affectionately, sometimes less so—for its convoluted plots, for the way in which characters sing different things simultaneously, and for the way in which trains of private thought are expressed in extravagant public fashion. A prime example of this ridiculing—which reveals a long-standing British suspicion of the art form as a faintly preposterous cultural import—was the genre of the Victorian burlesque, which combined humorous texts

14. See, for instance, Francesco Berger, 'Opera in England: The Native Form', *The Times*, 6 October 1928, p. 10. Berger was a pianist, composer, and tutor at the Royal Academy and the Guildhall School of Music.

15. Basil Maine, 'Is Opera a Luxury, a Habit, or Just Absurd?', *MNH*, 73/1833 (1 November 1928), 280.

16. 'More heavy sarcasm is poured out over opera in one season than painting and literature receive in half a century'. Philip Page, 'Realism in Opera', *LM*, 18/105 (July 1928), 290–7, 290.

17. An anonymous writer for *The Musical Standard*, for instance, wrote in 1920 that 'quite a lot of opera is frankly ridiculous; the operatic "chestnut" is pretty hard to swallow, when it is badly sung, vilely acted and odiously staged'. Anon., 'Notes and Comments. An Opera Tax', *MS*, 16/342 (23 October 1920), 139.

18. For one article among many that grappled with opera's lack of 'logic', see Horace Shipp, 'On Being Entertained', *The English Review* (June 1927), 756–8.

19. Percy A. Scholes, *A Miniature History of Opera: For the General Reader and the Student* (London: Oxford University Press, Humphrey Milton, 1931), p. 11.

with well-known operatic arias.[20] During the 1920s the tradition continued within the context of the revue, in which performers wore comical wigs and body padding and put on warbling, out-of-tune operatic voices.[21] Sometimes the tributes were affectionate and received in good spirit. In 1929, for example, *The Daily Mirror* reported that Luisa Tetrazzini had enjoyed watching the young Gracie Fields burlesque her performance of an aria from Ambroise Thomas' *Mignon* in a variety show by Archie Pitt called *The Show's The Thing* at the Lyceum.[22]

Philip Page, writing in *The London Mercury*, went so far as to claim that opera's unintentionally comic and absurd aspects were significant factors in its appeal to audiences. He noted that a large portion of the audience attended the opera 'with an expectant semi-grin, half in the hope that something untoward will happen and half with the unshakable conviction that the whole thing is rather amusing anyhow'.[23] There were two factors that made opera inherently, albeit unintentionally, comical. The first was the chance of something going wrong with the staging (as we have seen, this was a common occurrence). The second was the fact that although opera in English was the norm—and considered necessary—it did have its humorous side, exposing the banalities of a text that might have seemed more profound in the original language. The instruction to shut a door, for example, was more amusing when sung in English than in Italian.[24]

For some highbrows, it was the visual aspect of opera that was the problem. Opera was acceptable only if this element was removed, whereby a semblance of cultural purity was restored. Page observed that many self-styled 'superior listeners' would flock to the Queen's Hall on Monday nights to hear the all-Wagner programmes but could not be induced to listen to the same music at Covent Garden.[25] In similar vein, some did attend Covent Garden but spent the entire performance refusing to open their eyes, instead 'plunging their faces into their hands the moment the curtain is about to rise'.[26] In these circumstances a restricted-view seat was a veritable boon.

20. See Roberta Montemorra Marvin, 'Verdian Opera Burlesqued: A Glimpse into Mid-Victorian Theatrical Culture', *Cambridge Opera Journal*, 15/1 (2003) and Joanne Cormac, 'From Satirical Piece to Commercial Product: The Mid-Victorian Opera Burlesque and its Bourgeois Audience', *Journal of the Royal Musical Association*, 142/1 (2017), 69–108.

21. Philip Page, 'Realism in Opera', *LM*, 18/105 (July 1928), 290–7, 290.

22. Anon., 'Mme Tetrazzini Burlesqued', *The Daily Mirror*, 24 October 1929, 2. See also http://graciefields.org/wordpress/the-shows-the-thing/.

23. 'The more spectacular the opera the more pleasurable is the anticipation of minor catastrophes'. Page, 'Realism in Opera', 290.

24. Ibid., 292.

25. Ibid., 291.

26. Ibid., 291.

Intriguingly then, although there were debates during the 1920s about whether opera on the radio was pointless (because one could not see the stage action), some commentators saw it as having distinct advantages precisely *because* it allowed the listener to escape the absurdity of the stage action. Sometimes a radio broadcast could prompt a reviewer to consider a composer's oeuvre afresh: removing fatuous stage business could even redeem a 'bad' opera. In a review of a radio broadcast of *Rigoletto* in 1926, for instance, *The Musical News and Herald* reported that 'however stagey and melodramatic [Verdi's] operas may seem to be in the theatre, it would be difficult to find anything more completely and dramatically successful than the broadcast version of the last act of *Rigoletto*.'[27] Given the doubtless poor sound quality of these early broadcasts, to consider them preferable to watching a staged performance was certainly saying something.

During this period, one also finds critics expressing antipathy towards the visual and dramatic aspects of opera specifically because they underlined the similarities with the new medium of film. For Harvey Grace, writing as 'Feste', opera was inherently ridiculous because, unlike oratorio, it left nothing to the imagination. Allying the opera audience with the 'mindless' audience for film, he argued that if people wanted to see stories acted out they should go to the cinema, 'where that particular kind of mental deficiency is provided for.'[28] Opera's supposed realism was, Grace argued, crude and childish, its stories ridiculous and its texts stilted. Such comments are revealing. One might assume that the arrival of cinema would have led those engaged in cultural categorisation to differentiate opera from it by labelling it as highbrow. Yet this was not necessarily the case: rather, the emergence of cinema merely underlined opera's middlebrow or even potentially lowbrow characteristics.

OPERA AND FILM

Many discussions—both approving and disapproving—took place about the ways in which opera was merging with film during the 1920s. There were 3,300 cinemas in Britain by the end of the decade, and the threat that cinema posed to opera in terms of taking away audience members—and even tempting away performers because of a lack of operatic opportunities

---

27. Anon, 'Salesmanship at the BBC', *MNH*, 71/1794 (28 August 1926), 161.

28. 'Feste', 'Ad Libitum', *MT*, 66/990 (1 August 1925), 698–701, 701. A mixture of snobbery and moral panic may be found in Colson's remark that 'At present the cinema is evil for the young and is, I am convinced, responsible for not a little of the great interest in juvenile crime' (Colson, *Those Uneasy Years*, p. 121).

for British singers—was much debated.[29] At the end of 1929, *The Musical Mirror* published a cartoon in which a film producer asks an auditioning opera singer 'Are you accustomed to singing without an audience?', to which the singer replies sadly, 'I am! That's what brought me here'.[30]

Film was often held up as the art form of the masses, and parties who were sceptical about or opposed to operatic subsidy and operatic funding schemes repeatedly held up the example of cinema (like sport) as a genuinely populist form of entertainment that had no need for financial assistance.[31] Commentators expressed considerable concern about audience members abandoning opera for the cinema, and in particular feared this would signal the death knell for regular visits by touring opera companies to small provincial towns.[32] This remains a concern today, although the current threat is perceived to be an opera-on-opera one, the fear being that cinema screenings of live operas from the Met and the Royal Opera House will not so much build new audiences but take an existing audience away from local opera performances.[33] On the other hand, there remained an optimism in the 1920s that opera would never be completely supplanted—as has proved to be the case over the long term—because ultimately nothing could match the performer's live, physical presence.[34]

Despite anxieties about the threat posed by cinema, many commentators viewed it as something that could be used in order to complement and indeed generate interest in opera. Opera and film regularly entered one another's domains, unsurprisingly so, given the aesthetic debts that the newer medium owed to the older. There were also of course many early silent films of operas, or sections from them, with live accompaniment provided by the cinema musicians.[35] These were an important way of disseminating operatic stories to a wide public; lift operators and street boys would undoubtedly have watched such films as Cecil B. DeMille's *Carmen* starring Geraldine Farrar.[36] Early cinemas were often constructed not just for the

29. Gale, *West End Women*, p. 69.

30. *MM*, 9/12 (December 1929), v.

31. See, for instance, Anon, 'Half a Million for Opera!', *MNH*, 69/1755 (14 November 1925), 437–8.

32. Figaro, 'The Operatic World', *MO*, 52/614 (November 1928), 125–6.

33. Such suspicions appeared to be borne out by a 2013 research study undertaken by the Guildhall School of Music and Drama and English Touring Opera. http://www.gsmd.ac.uk/about_the_school/news/view/article/new_research_suggests_work_to_be_done_before_cinema_broadcasts_bring_in_new_audiences_for_opera/ (accessed 8 November 2017).

34. Figaro, 'The Operatic World', *MO*, 52/613 (October 1928), 23–4.

35. Opera's influence on early film scores—postdating our period—has been well documented. See, for example, Matthew Bribitzer-Stull, *Understanding the Leitmotif: From Wagner to Hollywood Film Music* (Cambridge: Cambridge University Press, 2015) and Jeongwon Joe and Sander L. Gilman (Eds.), *Wagner and Cinema* (Bloomington: Indiana University Press, 2010).

36. Rose, *The Intellectual Life of the British Working Classes*, p. 203.

projection of films but as multi-functional variety theatres and there was often a stage in front of the screen for live performance: singers were employed to sing at cinemas, before and during the projection of films.[37] Silent film screenings were often preceded by prologues closely or loosely related to the subject matter of the film, comprising a variety of different forms of entertainments that might include selections of operatic arias and/or operatic overtures.[38]

Covent Garden itself, furthermore, was sometimes used as a picture house, attracting both a new audience and opera regulars.[39] If we take the films screened there in 1922 as a case study, we can see the appeal they would have had to Covent Garden's usual opera audience. The plot of the Franco-Belgian film *Atlantide* (directed by Jacques Feyder) recalled numerous operatic *femmes fatales*, while the Italian film *Theodora* (Leopoldo Carlucci) was based upon a play by Victorien Sardou, whose *La Tosca* had inspired Puccini's opera. J. Stuart Blackton's *The Glorious Adventure*, meanwhile, starred a glamorous Society figure doubtless known personally to many in the Covent Garden stalls—Lady Diana Manners.[40] Religious epics that featured quasi-operatic spectacle were also shown at Covent Garden, including the Cecil B. DeMille film *The King of Kings* (1927), which was much discussed in Society magazines. There was even an operatic feel to the films' paratexts: film-goers were presented with theatre-style programmes containing cast lists and detailed synopses, which often contained twice as many pages as those distributed at operatic performances.

There were, furthermore, attempts to bring opera and film together more directly. There had, of course, been a decade's worth of silent films of operas by the 1920s and there was much anticipation of the possibility, once technology was at a more advanced stage, of projecting a performance of an opera at the cinema with both visuals and sound. The idea of recording the voices and orchestra and juxtaposing them with an original film starring different performers was also welcomed, on the grounds that one could then have characters who both looked and sounded the part.[41] On

37. Rebecca D'Monté, *British Theatre and Performance, 1900–1950* (London: Bloomsbury, 2015), p. 97.

38. For further reading, see Julie Brown, 'Framing the Atmospheric Film Prologue in Britain, 1919–1926', in Julie Brown and Annette Davison (Eds.), *The Sounds of the Silents in Britain* (New York: Oxford University Press, 2013), pp. 200–21.

39. The *ILN* stated in 1922 that Covent Garden was 'now becoming a recognised home of large-scale film plays'. Anon., 'Films on the Grand Scale: *L'Atlantide*', *ILN*, 18 February 1922, 229.

40. Programme booklet, *Atlantide*, Royal Opera House, Covent Garden [V&A Theatre and Performance Collections, production box: Covent Garden Theatre, 1922].

41. 'The advantage of having slender Isoldes and Brunhildas [*sic*] to look at as well as heavenly voices to listen to would be enormous'. Iris Barry, 'It Talks and Moves', *The Spectator*, 5006 (7 June 1924), 915–16, 915.

the other hand, some critics were sceptical about the future of filmed opera. W. J. Turner, in a disparaging review of a film of *Der Rosenkavalier* (1926), argued that film and opera were completely different art forms. In film, 'the eye is in a state of restless expectation', and so an opera such as *Tristan and Isolde*, with its long passages of dramatic inactivity, would have to be heavily revised for any film adaptation.[42] Turner foresaw a future for film operas but believed that they would have to be composed especially: it is interesting to note that his objections were practical rather than ideological.

It was widely anticipated that film technology might in future be routinely used as a scenic device in the theatrical staging of opera, images being projected on to the back of the set.[43] (By 1929, Bohuslav Martinů would actually set a jazz-influenced opera—*Les trois Souhaits*—on a film set, although the opera was not performed in Britain at this time.) There were also discussions about ways of using cinematic technology to create surtitles *avant la lettre*. Prompted by the theory that many people were not attending the opera because they were fearful of not being able to understand the words (even when in English), a reader of the BNOC house magazine *Opera* wrote in with the suggestion that the text of an opera be projected on to a screen, cinema-fashion, during performances. This would not only assist the audience but a judicious arrangement of mirrors would also enable the singers to see them, helping with their cues.[44] It is remarkable to find this being discussed so early in the twentieth century: surtitles were not actually introduced in Britain until the 1980s.

Opera's language barrier was regularly debated during the 1920s, as we have already seen, in order to make the case for opera in English. The idea of displaying the text in the matter of cinematic inter-titles was picked up with curiosity in the music press, if not much enthusiasm. Figaro responded to the proposal as 'extraordinary', labelling it 'the most cutting criticism of operatic music and of British singers' diction that I have yet read'.[45] (Similar arguments continue to be made today, as the letters page of the contemporary *Opera* magazine often reveals, particularly in response to English National Opera's policy for using surtitles even for operas performed in English

---

42. W. J. Turner, 'The World of Music: Film Opera', *ILN*, 16 October 1926, 738.

43. Figaro reported that 'A novelty dubbed "cinema-aided opera" is to be launched early in the New Year at the New Polytechnic. It is to take the form of grand opera aided by the kinema, a combination of synchronised moving pictures depicting scenes from opera, with vocal items interpolated'. Figaro, 'Whispers from the Wings', *MO*, 50/592 (January 1927), 362.

44. Anon, 'Diction in Opera', *MNH*, 64/1629 (16 June 1923), 585.

45. Figaro, 'The Operatic World', *MO*, 47/555 (December 1923), 253–4, 253. The *MNH* saw both sides of the coin, writing 'The idea is so brilliant that it will surely be taken up eagerly, here or elsewhere', although added, 'But wouldn't it be simpler to get artists whose diction is good?' Anon., 'Diction in Opera', *MNH*, 64/1629 (16 June 1923), 585.

translation.) There was, moreover, another school of thought that proposed that it was not in fact essential for audiences to understand the text of an opera. Despite his scorn elsewhere for academic purists who privileged absolute music, Turner observed in *The Illustrated London News* that although many people failed to understand the story of *The Magic Flute* they had not been at a disadvantage because 'The finest music requires no words to assist it; words are, in fact, totally irrelevant even in opera'.[46]

Commentators of the day expressed contrasting perspectives on operatic accessibility and the boundaries with other forms. For ultra-highbrow commentators such as Grace, the fact that opera was engaging with such a facile form of entertainment as cinema was proof positive of its lack of artistic credentials. Figaro, in contrast, was not in the anti-operatic highbrow camp, treating opera respectfully and intelligently in his column in *Musical Opinion*, yet exhibiting certain hallmarks of the highbrow in his concern for formal purity. He was concerned about the threat posed to opera by its integration with other forms, and he baulked in 1923 at the idea of 'film opera', calling it a 'horror'.[47] Yet a few years later, even this critic acknowledged that opera would be forced to adapt cinema's technologies in order to beat it at its own game, reporting ways in which foreign opera houses were using technology in order to launch a 'war on the film boom'. The State Opera in Berlin, he noted, was employing moving scenery and the Charlottenburg opera house was using microphones to amplify the voices of 500 choristers who couldn't fit on to the stage. He speculated that in the future operas would use microphones, gramophones, and projected images.[48]

Commentators writing for broadly 'middlebrow' publications were predictably untroubled by the interactions between cinema and opera. *The Musical Mirror* was a periodical not particularly well disposed to opera and inclined to regard it as an aloof form. Thus, for this publication, the mingling of opera with cinema was an opportunity rather than a threat: a way of making opera more accessible. Its correspondents viewed the idea of the quasi-surtitles as a welcome democratising initiative that would encourage more people to go to the opera.[49] And most positive of all was Philip Page in *The London Mercury*, who observed that cinema had fostered a new love of spectacle from which opera might take inspiration. He argued that emulating cinema's realistic spectacle and paying attention to the eye as well as

46. W. J. Turner, 'The World of Music', *ILN*, 3 June 1922, 822.

47. Figaro, 'The Operatic World', *MO*, 47/555 (December 1923), 253–4, 254.

48. Figaro, 'The Operatic World', *MO*, 52/620 (May 1929), 719–20, 720.

49. 'A cinematograph guide to the plot as the opera proceeded would be of inestimable value to the uninitiated opera-goer, and very possibly lead to larger audiences'. Symphonicus, 'Heard in the Interval', *MM*, 3/6 (June 1923), 165.

the ear offered opera a chance to counter its aforementioned rather laugh-able image and attract a large new audience, writing 'This is grand opera's fresh chance and it may mean the removal of all difficulties if it is prop-erly taken'.[50] Opera would also do well to learn from the cinema in terms of promotional techniques. Thus, if those involved in putting opera on were willing to be open-minded, the future could be bright.[51]

High-profile singers of the day were routinely asked in interviews about their attitudes towards film and the possibility of appearing in it. Some dis-played a nuanced awareness of the vexed cultural politics of the time, the fact that opera and cinema had not yet settled down into an easy relation-ship with one another. In her autobiography Maria Jeritza wrote of going to the cinema for relaxation, although appeared slightly reluctant to admit it, asking 'will I be accused of being a "lowbrow", as you call it . . .?'[52] She was cagey about the possibility of appearing in films herself: less enthusiastic about the prospect of appearing in films 'mute', but obviously tempted by the publicity opportunities offered by performing to an audience of mil-lions.[53] She evidently already considered herself to have a similar status to the film stars like Mary Pickford, Douglas Fairbanks, and Charlie Chaplin whom she enjoyed watching on screen, writing that in the interests of not being stared at she often took the precaution of wearing her hat low down over her face in order to avoid being recognised.[54] There is, furthermore, some evidence that film was having an influence upon her operatic prac-tice: she became renowned for a particular type of melodramatic posturing on stage that led Ernest Newman to liken her to a 'bad film actress'.[55]

Others were more overt about their ambitions to appear on the silver screen and untroubled by any anxiety about opera's boundary crossing. In 1923 Luisa Tetrazzini, three months away from her fifty-second birthday and matronly of physique, confided to an interviewer that her greatest ambition was to be a film actress and that she was 'just mad on' William S. Hart and his cowboy stunts. A cartoon on the cover of *The Musical Mirror* depicted her dressed as a cowboy and shooting a gun, headed 'The girl of the golden West'.[56] And by the end of the decade, singers such as Frieda Hempel were being given contracts to appear in the talkies.[57] Such

50. Page, 'Realism in Opera', 297.
51. See, for example, James M. Glover, 'The Music Box', *The Stage*, 2459 (17 May 1928), 15.
52. Maria Jeritza, *Sunshine and Song: A Singer's Life* (New York and London: D. Appleton, 1924), p. 178.
53. Ibid., p. 260.
54. Ibid., p. 179.
55. Ernest Newman, 'English Opera', *MT* (1 May 1926).
56. Cover, *MM*, 3/3 (March 1923).
57. Piacevole, 'Heard in the interval', *MM*, 9/8 (August 1929), 199.

boundary-crossing by star singers certainly complicated opera's status as high art, something I shall discuss further in Chapter 6.

OPERA AND JAZZ

The permeable boundaries between opera and film were, then, fostering new creative opportunities at the same time as contributing to the difficulties in categorising opera. Much the same applied to opera and other forms of music. Opera and jazz were often held up as occupying different ends of a musical spectrum during the 1920s, but in fact the situation was not quite as clear cut as some liked to claim. Derek Scott has demonstrated that what he calls a popular music 'revolution' first came about during the nineteenth century, when popular music began to assert distinctive stylistic forms, techniques, and characteristics.[58] A fissure emerged between the concepts of high art and mass culture, at least in the major cities of Western Europe, with the consequence that musicians increasingly specialised in one area or the other, and from the 1880s onwards popular music started to be considered as 'lesser'.[59] However, it is clear that the divide would become wider still after the First World War, with the emergence of jazz appearing to usher in a decisive split between opera and popular song.[60] This was a consequence both of a widening stylistic divide between the two and of the growing impulse to categorise different forms of musical activity. A high-profile opera singer might still perform Victorian popular ballads in the concert hall, but would be unlikely to cross over into singing jazz.

Even though scholars may retrospectively have pinpointed the siphoning off of 'classical music' from 'music' more generally as having taken place in the nineteenth century, the 1920s critics clearly discerned this to be a process that was still ongoing. It is telling that R. W. S. Mendl wrote in 1926 that 'We hear so much nowadays about a distinction between classical and popular music', suggesting that the division between the two had been far less clear-cut before the War.[61] Insofar as Mendl was concerned, the growing use of the term 'classical music'—directly related to growing attempts to codify different types of music—was off-putting to listeners and had done a great deal to harm the music appreciation movement. Mendl reinforced

---

58. Scott, *Sounds of the Metropolis*, p. 3.

59. Ibid., pp. 4, 10.

60. Scott, *The Record of Singing* 2, p. 103. James Nott observes that between 1918 and 1939 the audience for pop music grew to an unprecedented extent and the provision of it became far more commercialised. James J. Nott, *Music for the People: Popular Music and Dance in Interwar Britain* (Oxford and New York: Oxford University Press, 2002), p. 2.

61. Mendl, *From a Music Lover's Armchair*, p. 2.

the point that jazz and classical music were 'set in antithesis to one another as though one were bad and the other good' and pointed to 'violent
and slashing attacks' that the musical establishment were in the habit of
launching upon jazz.[62] However, he argued that the roots of syncopated
dance were to be found in Western art music as well as in African music.

Educationalists also discussed the schism between different types
of music as a matter of current concern. In a 1925 study of music in
schools, Thomas Wood argued that music was divided nowadays into two
'classes': serious and popular. The latter scored heavily over the former because it was heard at dances, cafés, and music halls and widely advertised,
even if 'The musician pure and simple will hold that popular music is outside the pale'.[63] Wood argued that 'serious' music was written by 'masters
of their art' who were not motivated by financial gain and did not follow
fashions; it was not always easy to understand and could sometimes only be
appreciated after repeated hearing. Popular music, on the other hand, had
its place as a form of recreation but appealed to one's 'lower instincts': it was
light, catchy, tuneful, commercial, and topical, but it never aspired to make
you think.[64]

Some commentators observed that the divide that had been placed between 'classical music' and 'popular music' was not only an artificial one but
one that was wider in England and the United States than anywhere in continental Europe. Francis Toye, critic for *The Daily Express* and *The Morning
Post*, proposed that if one were to ask a Frenchman who the most popular
national composer was, he would say Gounod or Massenet; ask an Italian
and he would say Puccini. If one asked an Englishman, however, he would
say 'Mr Smith Robinson', a well known, commercially successful composer
of ballads.[65] Thus, in Europe, it was still possible for an opera composer to
be considered a composer of 'popular music', whereas at home the term had
different connotations: opera was coming to be considered too rarefied by
certain sectors of the general public to merit the label.

Yet despite the fact that jazz and opera were often posited as polar opposites, numerous discussions took place during the 1920s about the ways in
which they were coming together in unexpected ways. There was speculation among music journalists about whether composers might start to mix

62. R. W. S. Mendl, *The Appeal of Jazz* (London: Philip Allan and Co., 1927), p. 25.

63. Thomas Wood, *Music and Boyhood: Some Suggestions on the Possibilities of Music in Public,
Preparatory and other Schools* (Oxford/London: Oxford University Press/Humphrey Milton,
1925), p. 51.

64. Ibid., pp. 53–4.

65. Francis Toye, *The Well-Tempered Musician: A Musical Point of View* (London: Methuen
and Co., 1925), pp. 53–4. On Toye's journalism, see Scaife, 'British Music Criticism in a New
Era', p. 36.

the two styles of music by writing jazz operas. Reports of early performances of Krenek's *Jonny spielt auf* in Germany and Austria attracted interest
from the British press, as did American experiments with the genre.[66] In
1922, for example, Otto H. Kahn, Chairman of the Metropolitan Opera
Company, invited Irving Berlin, Jerome Kern, and George Gershwin to
write a jazz opera for the company, although the project ultimately failed
to come to fruition.[67]

The Musical Standard took a particular interest in this topic, asking in
1925 why, since jazz could be heard everywhere else—in theatres, ball-
rooms, concert halls, and restaurants—it shouldn't also be heard at the
opera house.[68] For the unsigned author of this article, merging opera and
jazz would be a democratic move, because 'then the opera house could no
longer be feared as the gilded resort of the highbrow and the *awfully* musical, but could come into line in popular esteem with the plutocratic night
club and the "house full" revue'.[69] The comments about the opera house
being the preserve of the 'awfully musical' stand in sharp contrast to the
view held by most serious critics that the audience for opera was more lowbrow than the genuinely 'musical' audience that favoured orchestral concerts and chamber music.

Bits and pieces of jazz were already finding their way into the 'gilded'
opera house, albeit during the periods when opera was off the menu. A cartoon published in *Opera* magazine in 1923 showed, via a series of frames, a
music critic at Covent Garden becoming increasingly disconcerted to find
himself present not at an opera but a 'George Robey Jazzaganza'.[70] Robey's
show was an American-style revue called *You'd Be Surprised*, billed as being
in 'two acts and fourteen surprises', presented under the management of
theatre and film studio owner Oswald Stoll and performed ten times a
week (every evening plus three matinées). Robey, a music hall comedian
and pantomime dame turned variety star, was given top billing on the programme, with other high-profile acts including the ballet dancers Lydia
Lopokova and Leonide Massine, the Savoy Havana Band, and the 'Jolly
Jazzaganza Girls'. The programme also featured Arabian acrobatics and a
corps de ballet, demonstrating the eclectic range of performers involved

66. See, for instance, Anon., 'A Jazz Opera that Caused Riots in Vienna', *ILN*, 18 February
1928, 253.

67. Anon., 'Jazz Opera?', *Time*, 4/22 (1 December 1924), 18. That same year, however,
Gershwin would write a short jazz opera called *Blue Monday*, which was performed on
Broadway but pulled immediately.

68. Anon., 'That Jazz Opera', *MS*, 25/453 (24 January 1925), 23–4, 23.

69. Ibid., 24.

70. Anon., 'You'd Be Surprised!', *Opera*, February 1923, 19.

and the way in which the show cut across highbrow-lowbrow categories.[71] Many press reviews were negative about the piece (which would ultimately have only a short-lived run), portraying it as a piece of brash Americana— expensively staged but loud, shrill, and not particularly funny.[72] Angry comments were made about Robey's 'presumption' in appearing at Covent Garden, but Robey was well aware of the incongruity of performing there and played up to the fact, both with quips during the show and a variety of teasing advertisements poking fun at opera.[73] His many fans were as as- tonished as the imaginary highbrow critic to find him performing in such a venue.

If middlebrow commentators regarded jazz as an antidote to opera's sup- posed 'aloofness', some of those committed to formal purity objected to the fact that opera and jazz were being mixed, if not on the stage then in other formats. In 1927 Figaro complained that 'Something ought to be done ... to stop the filching of themes from great operas by jazz bands', pointing to reports of melodies being lifted from *Tosca*, *Faust*, and *Tannhäuser*, and writing that he had recently received a piece called 'The *Meistersinger* Rag'.[74] Similarly, there were reports in 1923 of Puccini seeking damages for pla- giarism after learning that melodies from *Tosca* and *Madama Butterfly* were being reworked as foxtrots and sold throughout the United States.[75] Such blendings of jazz and classical music were all the rage during this period, as witnessed by the fact that Mendl devotes a chapter to 'ragging and jazzing the classics'. Whether or not you regarded this as a problem defined your position on the highbrow–middlebrow spectrum.

BESTSELLERS

Opera also interacted during this period with popular fiction—just as it had during the nineteenth century—most obviously through the way in which operatic characters appeared regularly in middlebrow novels or stories serialised in popular magazines. Singers and impresarios, widely perceived to have colourful lifestyles, were seized upon by authors as juicy

71. Programme, 'You'd Be Surprised', Royal Opera House, Covent Garden, 5 February 1923 [V&A Theatre and Performance Collections, production box: Covent Garden, 1923].

72. See the unattributed press clippings in V&A Theatre and Performance Collections, pro- duction box: Covent Garden, 1923: Anon., 'Covent Garden Theatre. "You'd Be Surprised"' and H. J. H. 'Jazzaganza at Opera House'.

73. Trewin, *The Gay Twenties*, pp. 48–9; James Harding, *George Robey and the Music-Hall* (London: Hodder and Stoughton, 1990), p. 111.

74. Figaro, 'Whispers from the Wings', *MO*, 50/595 (April 1927), 678.

75. Anon., 'Turning Opera into Fox-trots', *MM*, 3/11 (November 1923), 329.

protagonists. Most notably, the female Italian opera singer was used as an enticing emblem of sexual licence in a variety of types of fiction. Susan J. Leonardi and Rebecca A. Pope observe that a shift took place in the early twentieth century in the way in which the prima donna was represented in fiction. Having previously been posited as corrupted by her profession yet still sympathetic, she suddenly (in response to the threat of the New Woman and burgeoning feminism) took on a much more vicious guise, 'deliberately luring victims, usually men, to her sensual lair—her body—and systematically picking their bones'.[76] This model of the dangerous diva is found in Vera Brittain's novel *The Dark Tide* (1923). Daphne Lethbridge, the novel's nondescript heroine, marries her tutor at Oxford, the caddish Mr Sylvester, who proposes to her on impulse immediately after being rejected by her more studious tutorial partner, Virginia Dennison. Daphne's new husband treats her cruelly and allows himself to be lured away by an Italian opera singer who bears a physical resemblance to Virginia. Virginia herself does not become an adulteress, but the thinly sketched opera singer acts as an obvious conduit.

1923 also saw the publication of F. Britten Austin's 'The Spell of Calypso: A Romance of Love in Italy' in *Nash's and Pall Mall Magazine*, a story that makes the 'singer as siren' trope central. A ship's captain recounts a sojourn in Naples during which he had become transfixed by a young, slim Italian soprano—'the antithesis of the fleshly operatic prima donna'— making her unexpected and triumphant debut in a performance of *La bohème*.[77] From the moment of their first passionate embrace, it is clear that 'Mimì' has a powerful grip upon him that he cannot resist: she becomes the archetypal *femme fatale*, the Calypso to his Ulysses. And where obsession leads, disaster must follow: fêted by every opera house in the land, she refuses to sign a prestigious contract unless he remains with her. Since the captain cannot imagine reducing her to the suburban life of a naval wife, he attempts to flee, only for there to be a tragic accident as she pursues his ship doggedly in a motor boat. The story itself takes on the qualities of an opera, complete with an oily impresario and old hag of a prospective mother-in-law as stock villains.

Other correlations were drawn between opera as an art form and popular novels. In 1924, *The Musical Standard* likened the contemporary arguments surrounding opera to the stuff of cheap fiction, arguing that 'the vicissitudes of opera in England', so full of acrimonious disputes, 'would afford material

76. Susan J. Leonardi and Rebecca A. Pope, *The Diva's Mouth: Body, Voice, Prima Donna Politics* (New Brunswick, NJ: Rutgers University Press, 1996), p. 50.

77. F. Britten Austin, 'The Spell of Calypso: A Romance of Love in Italy', *Nash's and Pall Mall Magazine*, 70/357 (January 1923), 382–92, 385.

for a volume of romances of extraordinary interest'.[78] Sometimes critics likened opera to popular fiction in order to reinforce its middlebrow status, its failure to correspond to highbrow norms. Occasionally, however, the strategy was reversed: damning correlations were drawn between opera and 'difficult' literary fiction precisely in order to construct it as highbrow. Complaining about 'novels you have to work hard to enjoy', *The Bookman* remarked that:

> There is a world of affectation about this. Vain, simple people mouth nothings of spurious appreciation and superficialities over the fashion of the hour. Opera is the most cursed at the moment. You are not 'au fait' unless you can exchange the meaningless jargon of the stalls and dress circle and drawing-room.[79]

More positively, opera was sometimes contrasted favourably with poor quality novels, *The Musical Standard* arguing that performing, listening to, or reading about opera was a better way to spend one's time than reading silly novels or attending vapid revues. Furthermore, attending the opera was just as accessible as such activities: 'Opera, like other things, is merely a habit'.[80]

There were even endeavours to create new operas that would have similar audience appeal to short stories. On the justification that 'These are the days of brevity—the days of the shorter novel, the smaller picture, the shorter articles in newspapers, the shorter play',[81] Hugh Allen, Principal of the Royal College of Music, commissioned in 1922 a series of operas lasting in the region of fifteen to twenty minutes from British composers, which were referred to in the press as 'tabloid operas'.[82] Allen's initiative was simultaneously a way of stimulating the cause of English opera—they demanded only small resources and could therefore be staged in any town or village, including by amateur opera companies—and an explicit strategy to use the forms employed by other areas of culture in order to expand the audience for opera. He proposed that they could also be performed 'as adjuncts to other entertainments in theatres, variety houses, or even cinemas', presumably with the intention of enticing an audience for opera that usually

78. Lyricus, 'Wanted—A Permanent National Opera House', *MS*, 23/434 (3 May 1924), 144.

79. Bookman, 'Take a Week-End Off!', *The Yorkshire Evening Post*, 19 May 1923, 6.

80. Anon., 'Opera Evenings', *MS*, 21/409 (19 May 1923), 156.

81. Anon., '15-Minute Operas', *MM*, 2/6 (June 1922), 168.

82. The expression 'tabloid' to denote 'short' in the operatic context was used on both sides of the Atlantic. In 1925, *Time* reported an experiment at the Hippodrome, Manhattan, where *Aida* was reduced from 180 minutes to 80 and presented in 'tabloid form' and noted that 'it was seen that US citizens who read tabloid newspapers, chew tabloid gum, can appreciate grand opera when its glories are compressed'. Anon., 'Tabloid Opera', *Time*, 5/10 (9 March 1925), 15.

preferred to see a play or a film. This comment is interesting for being an admission that opera was increasingly having to cling to the coat tails of other forms of entertainment for survival. On the more positive side, we see an acceptance that opera and various forms of popular culture could happily exist side by side. The scheme to promote these short operas—which included Vaughan Williams' *The Shepherd of the Delectable Mountains* and Charles Wood's *Pickwick*—was welcomed, even if some commentators expressed surprise that the initiative should have sprung from such an august institution as the RCM.[83]

The worlds of opera and popular fiction coincided in another way in the 1920s: gramophone recordings of opera were frequently likened— sometimes approvingly, sometimes contemptuously—to popular novels. Records and novels were both referred to as 'best-sellers', an expression recently imported from America that carried ambiguous connotations in an age when concepts of highbrow, middlebrow, and lowbrow were being repositioned.[84] Parallel debates about the commercialisation of reading and the commercialisation of listening took place during the 1920s: both were concerned not only with discussions about the commodification of art but with deciding who had the right to consume culture. Arguments took place about whether mass literacy prompted progress or, conversely, heralded the decline of civilisation; one can point to similar debates about whether recordings were a tool to raise taste or whether their effect was to lower it. The difference was that whereas the debates about literature were centuries old, albeit reaching a fever pitch, those surrounding recordings were new.

Longstanding concerns about the growth of the reading public, about what this public should read and how it should read, took on a new intensity during this period, due to the massive expansion in the production of and market for popular genre fiction, regarded by many as the most pernicious form of reading matter, and the decisive split between it and modernist literature.[85] In interwar Britain, popular novels were reaching ever-growing

83. As the *Musical Mirror* observed: 'It is something to write home about when the austere Royal College of Music descends from its lofty pedestal and shows such signs of a progressive spirit and an intelligent interest in musical matters that concern the public at large. Opera concerns the public at large—or should do'. Anon, 'Tabloid Operas', *MM*, 2/6 (June 1922), 172.

84. The term 'best-seller' was first used in Britain in the 1920s, having been current in America from the 1890s and used interchangeably with the expression 'big seller'. Billie Melman, *Women and the Popular Imagination in the Twenties: Flappers and Nymphs* (Basingstoke: Macmillan, 1988), p. 41. In 1920s usage the expression was either hyphenated or written as two separate words.

85. The cultural pessimism expressed by the Leavises merely put a new twist on an age-old anxiety about the expansion of the reading public and the immorality of popular literature. See Ian Haywood, *The Revolution in Popular Literature: Print, Politics and the People, 1790– 1860* (Cambridge: Cambridge University Press, 2004) and Patrick Brantlinger, *The Reading*

numbers of readers and the worrying implications of reading such material were much discussed by highbrow commentators. British intellectuals during this period were profoundly concerned about the growth of mass culture and its effects upon both high art and social hierarchies. This debate reached its high watermark at the turn of the 1930s in F. R. Leavis's *Mass Civilisation and Minority Culture*, whose contention was that the profusion of reading matter was making it difficult for people to acquire discrimination.[86] His wife Q. D. Leavis argued in *Fiction and the Reading Public* (1932) that too many people were reading, and reading the wrong things.[87] There were simply too many books.

To guide the new reading public through the vast array of choice available to them, a growing body of literature attempted to steer the 'new reading public' away from the bad and towards the good. A 1926 book by W. E. Simnett entitled *Books and Reading* contained advice on 'methods of reading', 'libraries and their use', and 'how to form a private library', as well as listing recommended titles in areas ranging from ancient classics to contemporary fiction.[88] The book began by defining its target audience, presenting it as a work not for the cognoscenti but for the 'great new *potential* reading public' that had emerged since the War and was turning in larger numbers to serious literature. Simnett explained that he was particularly keen to reach a younger readership that was likely to be confused by the profusion both of reading materials and other distractions.[89]

Similar attempts were made during the 1920s to police the new audience's listening habits. And just as there were considered to be too many novels available to the general public, we can find many complaints during the interwar period that there was too much music around in ordinary life. Thanks to the new possibilities technology offered for transporting music, it was never possible to escape from it. Bright Young Things were blasting loud jazz from portable gramophones as they drove in convertible cars or punted down the Cam or the Cherwell, and Percy Scholes even speculated that explorers probably took gramophones with them on Arctic expeditions.[90] At the opposite end of the social spectrum, the citizens of a Durham mining town would sit outside their houses, their gramophones

Lesson: The Threat of Mass Literacy in Nineteenth-Century British Fiction (Bloomington and Indianapolis: Indiana University Press, 1998).

86. F. R. Leavis, *Mass Civilisation and Minority Culture* (Cambridge: The Minority Press, 1930), p. 18.

87. Q. D. Leavis, *Fiction and the Reading Public* (London: Chatto and Windus, 1932), p. 19.

88. W. E. Simnett, *Books and Reading* (London: George Allen and Unwin, 1926).

89. Ibid., p. 5.

90. Percy A. Scholes, *The First Book of the Gramophone Record* (London: Oxford University Press, 1924), p. vii.

blasting out everything from Chaliapin to 'Yes! We Have no Bananas'.[91] The eclectic listening that the gramophone encouraged was part of its supposed problem. So too was the fact that record companies could be equally undiscriminating in the sorts of music they promoted. As *The Yorkshire Post* observed in 1929 about Columbia's recording catalogue, 'High-brows and low-brows alike can make their choice and be content'. Bach, Brahms, Italian opera, popular ballads, Yankee songs, variety acts, and organ solos all featured: 'it is all one to Columbia'.[92]

The advent of modern recording technology was an important factor in driving the mass culture industry and as such prompted a sense of anxiety about a decline in artistic authenticity—many British comments from this period anticipate by a decade Walter Benjamin's argument about mechanical reproduction leading to the loss of an art work's aura.[93] Related discussions took place about the impact of technology upon taste formation. Lionel R. McColvin, the author of the volume on art in the 'Today and Tomorrow' series, argued: 'The mechanical factor, by making the fourth-rate accessible, *generated a desire for the fourth-rate*'.[94] McColvin went so far as to talk about the 'degeneration' of taste, and argued that many people were conservative, governed by ignorant prejudices and 'intellectually and spiritually incapable of appreciating good art'.[95] The rhetoric of his commentary may come across as aloof, but he also demonstrated a desire to make the best art more accessible than it was currently, even if he acknowledged simultaneously that there was no absolute scale of good taste and many people would be averse to having their tastes improved.[96]

Just as Simnett's book attempted to guide new readers in how to read, numerous books were published in this period instructing a new mass audience on how to listen, and the desire for instruction was considered to be growing as more people gained access to serious music via the gramophone. Scholes was particularly active in this regard, publishing numerous books, including *The First Book of the Gramophone Record* (which quickly spawned a sequel) in which he recommended fifty good records, including arias by Purcell, Handel, and Mozart, and guided readers through the works' main musical themes.[97] He even provided a guide to the other guides, devoting a whole chapter of *Everybody's Guide to Broadcast Music* to

91. Rose, *The Intellectual Life of the British Working Classes*, p. 203.

92. Anon., 'Catholicity of Taste', *Yorkshire Post and Leeds Intelligencer*, 21 March 1929, 4.

93. Walter Benjamin, 'The Work of Art in the Age of Mechanical Reproduction', in Hannah Arendt (Ed.), *Illuminations* (London: Pimlico, 1999), 211–44.

94. McColvin, *Euterpe, or the Future of Art*, p. 15.

95. Ibid., pp. 26, 35, 37.

96. Ibid., pp. 28, 38–9.

97. Scholes, *The First Book of the Gramophone Record*, p. viii.

'helpful publications for opera lovers', which would furnish them with plots before attending a performance.[98] There were, furthermore, books and a large number of magazine articles dedicated to advising readers on the best works of music to be found on record.[99]

Although those parties who were making the case to expand the audience for opera considered the dissemination of opera via recordings to be a useful democratising strategy, it prompted further anxiety among the highbrows. During the 1910s the gramophone had prompted snobbery among musicians and not been taken seriously, as a commentator looking back from 1920 observed:

> Highbrows, we may be sure, frowned upon it. To possess a gramophone argued a vulgarity of taste on the part of the owner; to enjoy it put him outside the pale of those circles which discuss esoteric mysteries over the teacups.[100]

Across the course of the 1920s, gramophones would come to occupy a more important place in domestic life, whatever one's position on the highbrow-lowbrow spectrum, leading the *ILN* to report in 1922: 'It can now be said that the gramophone has come into its own as a serious member of the family of musical instruments'.[101] Singers, initially sceptical about recording, increasingly embraced its possibilities (Figure 4.1 depicts Nellie Melba making a gramophone recording in 1920). Yet highbrow snobbery about the commodification of music on record remained. Short operatic arias, detached from their original context, were particularly susceptible to such treatment. Ironically, as other scholars have discussed in detail, the early recording industry favoured opera above other musical repertoires as a way of conferring respectability and high social prestige upon its products.[102]

As recordings became more widely available to the public, debates began to take place among self-styled cultural guardians about the expansion and changing character of the listening public and about what these new listeners ought or ought not to hear. Even after becoming respectable, the gramophone continued to be regarded by serious music specialists as

98. Scholes, *Everybody's Guide to Broadcast Music*, pp. 100–26. Books that he recommended included Kobbé, *The Complete Opera Book* (G. P. Putnam's Sons); Krehbiel, *A Book of Operas, their Histories, their Plots, and their Music* (Macmillan); McSpadden, *Opera Synopses* (Harrap).

99. See, for instance, the reviews in *Gramophone* and the columns by 'Stylus' in the *ILN*; *Opera at Home* (The Gramophone Company); and Percy Scholes, *The First Book of the Gramophone Record* and *The Second Book of the Gramophone Record*.

100. D. C. Parker, 'The Gramophone and Education', *MS*, 9 October 1920 (16/341) 130–1, 130.

101. Stylus, 'The Talking Machine', *ILN*, 13 May 1922, 724.

102. See, for instance, Michael Chanan, *Repeated Takes: A Short History of Recording and its Effects on Music* (London and New York: Verso, 1995).

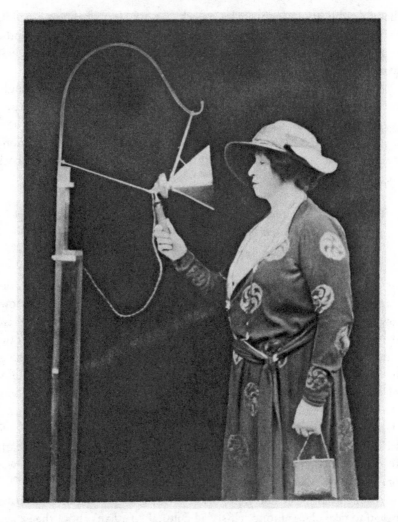

Figure 4.1   Nellie Melba recording at Chelmsford in 1920. Unattributed photograph. © Mary Evans Picture Library.

a potentially dangerous force, opening up the floodgates for undiscerning people to enjoy and own music.[103] And composers were even perceived to be starting to write explicitly in such a way as to exploit the new commercial possibilities offered by recording technology. Commenting upon the British premiere of *Il trittico*, for instance, Edward Dent argued that most of the arias in *Il tabarro* were 'very obviously designed for the purpose of gramophone records, as they can all be taken out and performed by

103. See, for example, Figaro, 'The Operatic World', *MO*, 48/569 (February 1925), 478–9.

themselves'.[104] He was more positive about *Gianni Schicchi* but noted that 'Needless to say, there is in this opera too a chance for the gramophone', pointing in particular to the tenor's aria 'Firenze è come un'albero fiorito', whose presence in the opera seemed to him to have no particular dramatic justification. (A Puccini scholar might, of course, beg to differ.)

Opera recordings were advertised in much the same way as new novels and it is significant that one of the people who played a particularly important role in promoting recordings was himself a novelist: Compton Mackenzie, founding editor of *Gramophone* magazine. Mackenzie understood intimately the world of the bestseller and, in typical middlebrow fashion, was at ease with the idea of cultural products being adapted into other formats. His second novel, *Carnival* (1912), had sold in colossal numbers and been reworked as films, stage plays, broadcast plays, and the libretto for a broadcast opera.[105] Others in the *Gramophone* circle were also popular novelists, including Mackenzie's brother-in-law, the writer Christopher Stone, and Archibald Marshall, whose books about English country house life sold extremely well in the United States for a period of about a decade.[106] Marshall and Mackenzie wrote a book called *Gramophone Nights* in 1923, in the introduction to which Mackenzie drew an explicit connection between gramophone records and novels, expressing a desire to see the establishment in the future of libraries of music similar to the great libraries of literature of the present day.[107] Already, scores and books about music were being regularly borrowed from the widely used public libraries: *The Musical Mirror* quoted the Chief Librarian of Wigan, a Mr A. J. Hawkes, as saying, 'After fiction, the second most popular section in the Wigan library is the music section'.[108]

Mackenzie was particularly keen to attract intelligent, middle-class readers and listeners, arguing the importance of promoting the message that the gramophone was not just a toy for 'tired, rich business men' on the one hand or 'nitwits who like humming' on the other.[109] In the first issue of *Gramophone* he explained that the magazine would endeavour to work with the recording industry to promote records that were 'distinguished by musical merit'.[110] In order to attract the intelligent listening public and to expand the readership for his magazine, Mackenzie drew explicitly upon his

104. Edward J. Dent, 'Puccini's *Triptych*', *The Athenaeum*, 4704 (25 June 1920), 837–8, 838.

105. Compton Mackenzie, *My Record of Music* (London: Hutchinson, 1955), p. 43.

106. Ibid., pp. 73, 68.

107. Ibid., p. 68.

108. 'Dominant', 'Round the Provinces', *MM*, 3/3 (March 1923), 87. On library usage in the era, see Pugh, '*We Danced All Night*', p. 328.

109. Mackenzie, *My Record of Music*, p. 82.

110. Anon., 'A School of Salesmanship', *The Gramophone*, 1/1 (April 1923), 2.

knowledge of the publishing industry. He advised record companies to note that 'no great publishing business has ever been built up by publishing rubbish'—a questionable claim indeed on current evidence—and stressed the importance of the steady-selling backlist over the ephemeral bestseller.[111] Interestingly, Mackenzie shared the view that the literary market was oversaturated, arguing that overproduction threatened the future of literature by 'stifling it with mediocrity'.[112]

Mackenzie therefore distanced himself from the most populist fiction of the day and allied himself explicitly with what would later come to be called the middlebrow, both in terms of literature and arguably in terms of music. For this, however, and for his lack of formal musical training he was sometimes mocked in highbrow musical circles. 'Schaunard' of Musical Opinion (A. J. Sheldon, also music critic for The Birmingham Post), for instance, was contemptuous about the contradiction between Mackenzie's 'defective musical education' and the fact that he was presenting himself as an authority on music.[113]

Mackenzie attributed the fact that the second issue of Gramophone had sold out to its inclusion of a feature on all of the available recordings by the soprano Amelita Galli-Curci.[114] Galli-Curci was the first singer to achieve worldwide fame through recording rather than live performances and undoubtedly the best-selling recording artist in early to mid-1920s England. Initially discovered in Chicago, she was given a recording contract in 1917 after taking New York by storm, and became particularly famous for her rendition of 'the Shadow Song' from Meyerbeer's Dinorah. Her British reception further illustrates some of the parallels that were drawn between popular records and popular novels during the 1920s. Her success was akin to that of contemporary popular novelists both in terms of earning power and visibility within the media and, like them, she prompted considerable anxiety among those who sought to act as guardians of the nation's culture.[115]

Galli-Curci's records were explicitly compared to popular novels and posited as the latest must-have commodities. For example, in Opera and

111. Mackenzie, My Record of Music, pp. 68, 82.
112. Ibid., p. 120.
113. Schaunard, 'Stray Musings', MO, 49/580 (January 1926), 357–9, 357.
114. Mackenzie, My Record of Music, p. 79.
115. Galli-Curci's fee for her 25 concert tour of the British Isles in 1924 was reportedly £25,000. Cited in Anon, 'Galli-Curci-Itis', MT, Vol.65/No.981, 1 November 1924, 1000–1, 1000. On high-earning authors of the early twentieth century and their celebrity status, see Stefan Collini, Common Reading: Critics, Historians, Publics (New York: Oxford University Press, 2008), p. 237 and Clive Bloom, Bestsellers: Popular Fiction since 1900 (Basingstoke: Palgrave Macmillan, 2002), p. 1.

its Stars, a 1924 book profiling the most famous singers of the day, the author, Mabel Wagnalls, wrote that '[Galli-Curci's] records began to be talked of like the latest best-seller in books. Not to have heard her "Caro Nome" made you as *déclassé* as not to have read *Main Street* or *This Freedom*.'[116] The American Wagnalls knew her popular fiction: she was, herself, the author of historical novels with titles like *The Palace of Danger: A Story of La Pompadour* and *Miserere*, which was about an opera-singing nun. *Opera and its Stars*, published simultaneously in New York and London, interspersed plot synopses with interviews with Maria Jeritza, Mary Garden, Frieda Hempel, Geraldine Farrar, Nellie Melba, Emma Eames, Emma Calvé, Lillian Nordica, Lilli Lehmann, and Marcella Sembrich, and was dedicated 'to those who love music but have no opportunity to familiarize themselves with grand opera'.[117] The very fact that opera was being written about by an author of cheap women's fiction epitomises the 'problematic' position it was capable of occupying in the middlebrow. With its sycophantic interviews conducted in prima donnas' hotel suites and its breathless descriptions of trunks overflowing with evening dresses, it was ostensibly little more than a piece of puff, a mouthpiece for whatever propaganda the singers in question and their agents wanted to promote.[118] Nevertheless, Wagnalls' seemingly throw-away remark exposes why popular recording artists such as Galli-Curci were treated with suspicion by members of the intelligentsia.

To the highbrows, likening Galli-Curci's recordings to the new phenomenon of the literary bestseller was no compliment, since the latter genre was seen as being more commercial than artistic. Furthermore, the bestseller is almost by definition ephemeral, its specific appeal to the contemporary zeitgeist often guaranteeing a short shelf life. One of the novels cited by Wagnalls, *This Freedom*, by Arthur Stuart-Menteth Hutchinson (a former editor of *The Daily Graphic*), was a polemical, anti-feminist morality tale about an emancipated career woman who is ultimately punished for her independence when her family is beset by a series of catastrophes. It had been the smash hit of 1922, and was in its sixth edition by 1924, but its

---

116. Mabel Wagnalls, *Opera and its Stars: A Description of the Music and Stories of the Enduring Operas and a Series of Interviews with the World's Famous Sopranos* (New York and London: Funk and Wagnalls, 1924), p. 2.

117. Ibid., p. v.

118. Whilst interviews with literary celebrities typically took place in the home (as discussed in Richard Salmon, 'Signs of Intimacy: The Literary Celebrity in the "Age of Interviewing", *Victorian Literature and Culture*, 25/1 (1997), 159–77, 166–7), those with celebrated opera stars—often visiting London or New York from overseas—were usually conducted in hotel rooms, which kept both interviewer and reader at a more distant remove from the subject's 'real life'.

appeal would fail to last.[119] Ironically, Galli-Curci's success was ultimately to be similarly short-lived: only eight years after her sensational discovery, her voice was already on the decline by the time of her UK tour in 1924.

Singers were seemingly aware that their records were objects that people coveted and consumed in much the same way as novels. In order to counter an association with transient forms of culture, they sometimes consciously distanced themselves from the best-seller market by speaking publicly about their own literary interests. Galli-Curci was quoted by a British regional newspaper as having said 'I do not think anyone could call me a "highbrow" in music or anything else'.[120] However, one of the supposedly self-penned articles about her that appeared in the immediate run-up to her British visit constructed her as an avid reader with eclectic tastes, including serious classics. She spoke of her enthusiasm for the works of Kipling, Conrad, Stevenson, and the American short story writers Bret Harte and O. Henry, but also of a perhaps implausible childhood love of Goethe, Schiller, Lessing, Uhland, Heine, Cervantes, Voltaire, and Zola—all read in the original languages, she claimed—and expressed a particular fondness for the works of Balzac, Shakespeare, and Dante.[121]

The vocabulary of moral and physical danger used to discuss lowbrow novels also crept into discussions of Galli-Curci's visit. A particularly scathing anonymous article (possibly by Harvey Grace) that appeared in *The Musical Times* the month after her appearances in London was entitled 'Galli-Curci-itis', constructing the current enthusiasm for the soprano and her records as an infectious disease.[122] This headline tapped into the lingering Victorian practice of characterising fashionable trends such as football and cycling as 'epidemics'.[123] It also recalled the specific correlations that were drawn between reading and illness during the nineteenth century, with commentators depicting reading as an enfeebling and fatiguing practice. Voracious reading was often referred to in the nineteenth century as a 'habit' or 'vice' and likened to the consumption of alcohol, tobacco, or opium.[124] Such analogies to intoxicating substances were still current in the

119. For a more extended discussion, see Billie Melman, *Women and the Popular Imagination in the Twenties: Flappers and Nymphs* (Basingstoke: Macmillan, 1988), p. 62. For further reading on 1920s bestsellers, see Clive Bloom, *Bestsellers: Popular Fiction Since 1900* (Basingstoke: Palgrave Macmillan, 2002).

120. Amelita Galli-Curci, 'The Doom of Jazz. Songs a Famous Singer Likes to Have by Her', *The Hull Daily Mail*, 7 October 1924, 4.

121. Amelita Galli-Curci, 'Galli-Curci's Ever Green Pastures', *The Sketch*, 8 October 1924, 88–9.

122. Anon, 'Galli-Curci-Itis', *MT*, 65/981 (1 November 1924), 1000–1.

123. Jennifer R. Sheppard, 'Sound of Body: Music, Sports and Health in Victorian Britain', *Journal of the Royal Musical Association*, 140/2 (2015), 343–69, 362.

124. Kelly J. Mays, 'The Disease of Reading and Victorian Periodicals', in John O. Jordan and Robert L. Patten (Eds.), *Literature in the Marketplace: Nineteenth-Century British Publishing and*

interwar period, as seen in the likening of reading light novels to 'a sort of mental dram-drinking' (Simnett) and 'a drug habit' (Q. D. Leavis).[125]

Sectors of the musical establishment suggested that recordings and the surrounding celebrity culture were as deleterious as the worst popular novels and represented a regressive step for the nation's musical taste. In the view of the unsigned author from *The Musical Times*, Galli-Curci's concerts had not so much elevated taste as set it back.[126] On another occasion Harvey Grace (writing again as 'Feste') reported that there had recently been a lot of public discussion about the extent to which popular tastes ought to be pandered to. Particularly troubling, in his view, was the fact that 'As usual there has been insistence on the old cry that the fact of a novel or a piece of music having an enormous sale is proof of some kind of merit'.[127] For Grace the success of popular songs and presumably also of popular opera singers, was 'In the fashionable jargon of today, [...] a particularly virulent case of mass psychology and herd instinct'.[128] (He cites the specific example of the recent hit 'Yes! We Have no Bananas', a novelty song from the 1922 Broadway Revue *Make It Snappy*, recorded by American Broadway performer Eddie Cantor, which was often held up as the epitome of a musical bestseller, the opposite of refined taste.[129])

Within the musical context, then, the term 'bestseller' was far from being a compliment in the eyes of serious musicians: popularity and commercial success worked in direct opposition to cultural worth. An advertisement for piano music published in *Musical Opinion* in 1923 deliberately drew attention to the critics' hostility towards anything that might be called a 'bestseller', writing:

> There has arisen among a certain class of superior critics a pose of speaking in a contemptuous tone of 'bestsellers' as if to suggest that a composer who is so unfortunate, or lucky, as to write a very popular piece ought to be thoroughly ashamed of himself.[130]

Reading Practices (Cambridge: Cambridge University Press, 1995), pp. 165–94, pp. 171, 173. See also Karin Littau, *Theories of Reading: Books, Bodies and Bibliomania* (Cambridge: Polity Press, 2006).

125. W. E. Simnett, *Books and Reading* (London: George Allen and Unwin, 1926), p. 11; Leavis, *Fiction and the Reading Public*, p. 19.

126. 'During the past few weeks the Galli-Curci craze has shown that the public is, after all, pretty much where it was twenty-five years ago'. Anon., 'Galli-Curci-itis', 1000.

127. 'Feste', 'Ad Libitum', *MT*, 65/974 (1 April 1924), 314–16, 314.

128. Ibid., 316. As David Ayers states, 'References to crowds, herds, masses, or the "man in the street" are commonplace in pessimistic cultural commentary of the 1920s'. David Ayers, *English Literature of the 1920s* (Edinburgh: Edinburgh University Press, 2004), p. 99.

129. Cantor was a member of the Ziegfeld Follies revue and recorded many popular phonograph recordings. The huge marketing campaign given to the song (including bananas being given away free by bandleaders to audience members) is discussed in Nott, *Music for the People*, p. 218.

130. Anon., 'Best Sellers' (ad in front of) *MO*, 46/547 (April 1923), 632.

The term was more likely to be used for operas than for other types of music: Figaro wrote in 1922 that 'Opera on the whole . . . has so far hardly emerged from the "best seller" stage'.[131] This critic, as we have seen, was enthusiastic both about opera and about building audiences for it but he uses the term 'bestseller' disparagingly here, lamenting the limited nature of the repertory, the endless churning out of the same few popular hits, and the fact that the bestseller had to cater to what he called 'the lowest common multiple'.

In terms of its association with other cultural genres, then, it would appear clear-cut that opera occupied that hazy ground known as the middle-brow during the 1920s, once again nullifying the idea of any simplistic 'Great Divide'. It is plain to see that opera was, as Figaro put it, 'coquetting' with cinema.[132] It was also, for that matter, flirting with jazz and dallying with popular fiction. Opera was gregarious, sociable, and flighty, and it refused to be confined to its box. Opera's interactions with new and ostensibly more popular media appalled the most purist of self-styled musical highbrows, but many opera goers simply didn't care. If we were to step back in time and take a tour around 1920s London, we would find opera rubbing shoulders in vibrant and exciting ways with other forms of entertainment and creating new opportunities both creative and social. For all the fearfulness about opera's decline during this period, this was surely a sign of an operatic culture in good health, testimony to the fact that opera was categorically a part of 'everyday life'.

131. Figaro, 'The Operatic World' *MO*, 45/540 (September 1922), 1034.
132. Figaro, 'The Operatic World', *MO*, 51/601 (October 1927), 27–8, 28.

CHAPTER 5

✧

Repertories

The debate about how to classify opera was further vexed by the fact that there were perceived to be hierarchies within the art form itself. Some highbrow commentators were prepared to tolerate certain types of opera: early opera was acceptable, as were some more cutting-edge recent works, but much of the nineteenth-century repertoire was an unfashionable blind-spot. The works from one end of this period (the *bel canto* repertoire) placed too much emphasis upon visual spectacle and vocal excess to pass muster with the high-brows, while those from the other (the works of Puccini and his contemporaries) were too overtly emotional. The degree of disdain high-minded critics expressed towards opera depended, too, upon the opera's nationality: German operas were generally regarded, with certain exceptions, as more tolerable than the Italian repertory. Such attitudes had a long intellectual history and were not limited to the British context or the 1920s, but during this period they become intertwined with the bigger debate about the categorisation of art forms. Furthermore, they would shape attitudes towards opera in the decades to follow.

Middlebrow commentators did not share any of the aforementioned prejudices about national schools of opera, but sometimes expressed different ones of their own. Some of their number voiced strong opinions about works that were or weren't acceptable to British tastes or suitable to be performed by British singers. Those promoting opera, meanwhile, tried hard to assert the concept of music as a universal language, with the editor of *Opera* magazine arguing that 'it is unfortunate that in surveying the works which compose the modern repertoire of music-drama, many people lay unnecessary stress upon the nationality of the composers . . . What does it matter who may write the music, as long as it is good music?'[1] Before analysing these issues in detail, it is necessary first to provide a contextual overview of the sorts of operas being performed in Britain during the 1920s. This was a key historical moment when the British operatic repertory was being shaped.

THE 1920S REPERTORY

During the early 1910s, Thomas Beecham had made concerted efforts to enrich British operatic culture, particularly by expanding the repertoire through the introduction of such recent works as *Salome* and *Elektra*. After the War, however, this spirit of adventure had to a large extent ebbed away. Among the 1920s music establishment there was a keenly felt sense that Britain was becoming a backwater in terms of the sorts of operas being staged. The performing repertory was dominated by German and Italian operas, with a healthy number of popular French operas but very few Russian or central European works. There was also a tendency to cling to the tried and tested. Although Puccini's *Il trittico* and *Turandot* arrived at Covent Garden relatively swiftly, they were exceptions to a general rule: new operas were, for the most part, no longer crossing the Channel with the speed that they had a decade or two earlier, if at all.[2] In Germany, by comparison, 418 performances of *Jonny spielt auf* had been staged in 1927–8 alone and there had been a noticeable growth of interest in the works of Janáček.[3] The latter visited London briefly in 1926, and some of his chamber works were performed at the Wigmore Hall, but there was no prospect for the time being of any of his operas being staged in Britain.[4] 'Where are the new post-war works?', cried Figaro in 1926, 'Anywhere but in London, where blood transfusion has long been needed to save the ailing patient'.[5]

The sense that the operatic repertory was becoming a 'museum culture' was clearly beginning to dawn upon critics during the 1920s. At the start of the decade, Leigh Henry referred explicitly to the season at Covent Garden as 'a museum catalogue' and noted that whereas fashions in dress were

---

1. Anon., 'Editorial', *Opera*, 1/1 (January 1923), 5.

2. The 1910s saw the premieres of new operas by Humperdinck, Wolf-Ferrari, Zandonai, Méhul, Montemezzi, and even such obscure names as Waltershausen and Camussi. Rodmell, *Opera in the British Isles*, p. 83.

3. Wilhelm Altmann, 'The German Operatic Repertory', trans. Whyte Monk, *The Sackbut*, 9 (December 1928), 168–70, 168, 170.

4. Rosa Newmarch, 'A Czechoslovak Composer: Janáček in England', *The Times* (1 May 1926), 12.

5. Figaro, 'The Operatic World', *MO*, 49/584 (May 1926), 805–6, 806.

changing rapidly and radically, tastes in opera seemed to be ossifying: 'The most unsophisticated flapper, the most credulous dowager would object to having a bustle palmed off on to them as the latest Paris mode; but our musical old women accept any antediluvian monstrosity as representative of contemporary foreign taste and originality.'[6] Even when newer works arrived in Britain they rarely entered the performing canon; indeed, rather than growing, the repertory was actually starting to shrink.[7]

A small number of operas had become 'safe draws' and critics were disparaging of the regularity with which they came around. (One often hears similar complaints from today's opera aficionados about the long runs of bankable *Traviatas* and *Bohèmes* at Covent Garden.) Figaro was positive about the way in which some more recent popular works such as *Madama Butterfly* were drawing in new audiences, but dismissive of the old warhorses ('one would not lament too much if *Trovatore* went back on the shelf to gather more cobwebs').[8] He believed that it would only take one decent performance of a good opera to lure the 'half-musical' (whom he defined as 'the musically half-educated and hyper-sentimental among the middle-classes in the suburbs and provinces') away from their usual fare of 'musical soufflés': *Faust, Rigoletto*, and *Cav* and *Pag*.[9] The latter double bill was performed with such regularity that Richard Capell, in yet another culinary metaphor, referred to it as 'the ham and eggs of opera'—a comment that reinforces the fact that opera, or at least certain types of opera, could be comfortably categorised as unpretentious everyday entertainment during this period.

Notwithstanding critical concerns about a limited repertory, many audience members were evidently lapping up the predictable fare that was on offer. Joseph O'Mara, a singer-turned-impresario, claimed that his touring company was thriving in early 1920s Britain precisely because it played safe in the works it put on. He told *The Musical Mirror* in 1923 that provincial support for opera was more reliable than in central London, and that regional audiences still enjoyed works that would be regarded as old-fashioned in the capital, principally the 'English Ring' (also known as the

6. Leigh Henry, 'Opera and Ballet', *MS*, 15/331 (22 May 1920), 173.

7. 'The repertoire does not grow; on the contrary, it tends to shrink. One would be inclined to say that, so far as modern inspiration goes, a phase of opera is definitely passing'. Anon, 'Can Opera Survive the Dole?', *MNH*, 71/1807 (27 November 1926), 465–6, 465.

8. '*Butterfly* has advertised opera like no other work before or since'. Figaro, 'The Operatic World', *MO*, 50/598 (July 1927), 967–9, 968; Figaro, 'Giacomo Puccini: 1858–1924', *MO*, 48/568 (January 1925), 381–3, 383.

9. Figaro, 'The Operatic World', *MO*, 52/616 (January 1929), 331–2, 331. On the growing critical impatience with *Faust* in particular, see Figaro, 'The Operatic World', *MO*, 44/529 (January 1921), 312.

'Irish Ring'): Michael William Balfe's *The Bohemian Girl*, William Vincent Wallace's *Maritana*, and Julius Benedict's *The Lily of Killarney*.[10] O'Mara claimed, moreover, that some regional theatres would not book the company unless they performed *The Bohemian Girl* on Saturday nights and that, by comparison, some Wagner operas such as *Tristan and Isolde* did not attract enough audience members to cover the costs of paying the orchestra.

And yet, the repertory of other touring companies testifies to a surprisingly adventurous appetite on the part of some regional audiences. The BNOC, notably, performed a surprising array of different types of opera and sometimes eschewed predictable favourites. Its repertory was vast: it produced 26 operas during its first 33-week season. Although the company's repertory included popular works such as *Carmen* and *Tosca*, it also featured such novelties as Debussy's *Prodigal Son* and Offenbach's *The Goldsmith of Toledo*.[11] (Its avoidance, at least initially, of Verdi operas other than *Aida* was a matter worthy of note.[12]) And for its regular residency at Covent Garden, the company adopted a conscious policy of trialling more unusual works with a single performance, such as *The Abduction from the Seraglio* in 1923.[13] Unfortunately, the company's laudable ambition surpassed what was realistically possible: an embarrassment of riches sometimes ran the risk of becoming simply an embarrassment. Performing more than twenty operas and rehearsing continually in up to four theatres at a time meant that performance standards inevitably suffered; many critics advised the company to halve its repertory and concentrate on quality rather than quantity.[14]

However misguided, the BNOC's efforts nevertheless demonstrate a laudable intention to challenge the narrowness of the current British operatic repertory, and there is evidence that their policy of taking serious opera to all was warmly received, at least in certain locations.[15] The company

10. Symphonicus, 'Heard in the Interval', *MM*, 3/9 (September 1923), 261.

11. The operas were as follows (and as billed here): *Rhinegold, Valkyrie, Siegfried, Dusk of the Gods, Tristan, Mastersingers, Parsifal, Tannhäuser, Figaro, Seraglio, Magic Flute, La bohème, Madam Butterfly, Tosca, Louise, Aida, Il trovatore, Samson and Delilah, Cavalleria rusticana, Pagliacci, Carmen, Faust, The Prodigal Son*, a staged version of Bach's *Phoebus and Pan, The Goldsmith of Toledo* (Offenbach), and *Hansel & Gretel*. Paget Bowman, 'A Year of Opera', *Opera*, 1/3 (March 1923), 15–16, 16.

12. John W. Klein, 'Early Verdi', *MO*, 47/554 (November 1923), 159–60, 159.

13. Herman Klein, 'British National Opera Company: The Revival of Mozart's *Seraglio*', *MNH*, 64/1607 (13 January 1923), 27–8, 27.

14. Dent argued that 'An opera does not necessarily get better played the more you play it. On the contrary, it often gets worse and worse. It is quite impossible for the BNOC to go on in this fashion and retain the respect of serious musicians'. Edward J. Dent, 'The World of Music. Opera—Comic and Grand', *ILN*, 1 March 1924, 376.

15. A growing sense of frustration with the narrow British repertory can be traced across the lifetime of *Opera* magazine. See, for instance, Aylmer Buesst, 'Those Other Operas I should Like to Hear', *Opera and the Ballet*, 2/8 (autumn 1924), 22–3.

demonstrated great perceptiveness in tailoring its repertory to the tastes of audiences at individual theatres: local BNOC committees advised on what would be most appropriate. In industrial Bradford, a city of textile mills, the works performed were of a more 'popular character', since it was agreed that Bradford people were, as yet, not sufficiently advanced in their tastes to give adequate support to 'highbrow' opera.[16] But the definition of what was a 'popular' opera and what was (or wasn't) a 'highbrow' one was sometimes surprising: the works in question put on in Bradford were hardly frivolous fare, including as they did *The Valkyrie* and *Otello*.

On the whole, however, little more than ten miles down the road in Leeds, the BNOC could be bolder in its choices. Leeds was a thriving regional cultural centre, partly through being a university city and partly thanks to the rich tradition of concerts and music festivals at Leeds Town Hall that had developed since the mid-nineteenth century.[17] By 1926, a report on the BNOC's autumn visit to Leeds emphasised that the most 'popular' works had been omitted because of public interest in more advanced fare.[18] Leeds audiences were reputedly mistrustful of British operas: Vaughan Williams' *Hugh the Drover* and Holst's *The Perfect Fool* did badly there in 1924.[19] On the other hand, they lapped up the works of Wagner: when polled on their favourite BNOC productions, *The Ring*, *Mastersingers*, *Aida*, and *Tristan* came out top. The Leeds audience was also noted for its understanding of operatic etiquette, with reports that at the BNOC's Leeds performances of *Parsifal* in 1926 the large audience was 'correspondingly well-behaved, and there was none of the hooliganism which is generally present in British opera audiences, the music being in no case interrupted by untimely applause'.[20]

Even beyond Leeds, however, putting on Wagner led to extremely good box-office takings for the company, and by 1929 the company was able to report that *The Mastersingers* was drawing larger audiences than *Faust*.[21] There was a certain novelty to rediscovering Wagner, whose works had been removed from the British repertory during the War.[22] But the composer's popularity would grow and grow across the course of the decade: in 1927

16. Anon., 'Bradford and Opera', *Yorkshire Post and Leeds Intelligencer*, 18 December 1926, 11.

17. For further reading, see Rachel Milestone, '"A New Impetus to the Love of Music": The Role of the Town Hall in Nineteenth-Century English Musical Culture', unpublished doctoral thesis, University of Leeds, 2009.

18. I. E., 'Leeds. British National Opera Co.', *MS*, 28/500 (20 November 1926), 167.

19. Anon., 'Opera in Leeds', *Yorkshire Post and Leeds Intelligencer*, 10 December 1924, 8.

20. H. T., 'The Opera Season in Leeds. *Parsifal*', *Yorkshire Post and Leeds Intelligencer*, 6 November 1926, 12.

21. Anon., 'Music Today: the BNOC Report', *MM*, 9/2 (February 1929), 29.

22. Tunbridge, 'Singing Translations', 55.

The Musical News and Herald went so far as to report that 'Wagner now reigns supreme in the provincial towns that at one time asked for the so-called popular works'.[23] Wagner's music dramas were also popular at the Old Vic, where they sat happily alongside popular French and Italian favourites (albeit no Puccini operas until 1926 because the royalties were too expensive).[24] Regional audiences that lacked the apparent sophistication of those at Covent Garden were evidently capable of enjoying the most demanding of operatic works and would buy tickets for them without fear or prejudice.

The repertoire at Covent Garden itself was somewhat unadventurous in the early 1920s but began to diversify as the decade progressed, in tandem with rising performance standards. Critics expressed pleasure at the announcement of the 1926 season, deemed to be comprised of 'intelligent' works: *Falstaff* and *Otello* as well as 'the inevitable *Rigoletto*'; *Gianni Schicchi* 'instead of the hackneyed *Madama Butterfly* and *La* [sic] *Tosca*'.[25] Curiosities such as *Mefistofele, I gioielli della Madonna, L'heure espagnole* and *Manon* also appeared. But some critics remained frustrated: W. J. Turner longed to hear some works by Méhul, Weber, or even Rossini, Donizetti, or Bellini, and argued that 'it would be in the best interests of Puccini's music if his operas were given a rest for a few seasons'.[26] New continental operas, meanwhile, remained conspicuous by their absence, as indeed did British works. Holst's *The Perfect Fool* was performed at Covent Garden by the BNOC in 1923, but the majority of British operas were put on by the Old Vic (where Baylis promoted the works of her friend Ethel Smyth), the Carl Rosa Company, the BNOC in the regions, or the conservatoires, or received their first performances abroad.[27]

23. G. C., 'The Work of the B.N.O.C.', *MNH*, 72/1823 (15 December 1927), 456.

24. Gilbert, *Opera for Everybody*, p. 36. When the first Puccini opera arrived, *Madama Butterfly*, it proved 'instantly and almost embarrassingly popular' with audience members; hundreds of people were turned away from the first performance. The Old Vic Theatre, Annual Report 1926–7, p. 7 [V&A Theatre and Performance Collections, production box: Old Vic Theatre, 1927].

25. Percy Colson, 'The Covent Garden Opera Season', *Apollo*, 3/15 (March 1926), 171–2, 171.

26. W. J. Turner, 'The World of Music: Operatic Revivals', *ILN*, 22 June 1929, 1110. Turner pointed to the absence of works such as *Guillaume Tell, La sonnambula, La favorite, Don Pasquale, Ernani, Un ballo in maschera, La forza del destino*, or *Macbeth*.

27. The Carl Rosa premiered a large number of British works including Joseph Holbrooke's *Bronwen* (1929). The BNOC premiered Ethel Smyth's *Fête Galante* in Birmingham in 1923 and Holst's *At the Boar's Head* in Manchester in 1925. The RCM, meanwhile, put on works such as Vaughan Williams' *Hugh the Drover* (1924) and *Sir John in Love* (1929) and Ethel Smyth's *Entente Cordiale*. For a list of works, see White, *A Register of First Performances of English Operas*, pp. 94–8.

EARLY OPERA VERSUS 'GRAND OPERA'

If the performing repertory was to some extent failing to modernise, there were other glimmers of diversification, even if they had comparatively little impact upon the mainstream opera-going public. The 1920s saw a rising interest, at least in small circles, in Classical and pre-Classical opera. Works that we would consider to be firmly in the repertory nowadays were still regarded as novelties. Mozart's works became a speciality at the Old Vic, where they were performed in new translations by Edward Dent. However, they were by no means staples of the repertory elsewhere: the opportunity to hear *Don Giovanni* at Covent Garden in 1926, for instance, was widely reported as an event of considerable note.[28] (The work had long been included on a list of works 'to be selected from' at Covent Garden, in order to pique interest, but seemingly without a genuine intention to stage it.[29])

If Mozart was a comparative rarity, then earlier opera was a largely mysterious entity insofar as the opera-going public was concerned. Purcell's *Dido and Aeneas* was an exception, having been widely performed in the 1900s and 1910s,[30] but Handel's operas were almost entirely unknown in Britain.[31] By the latter half of the decade, pockets of more unusual repertory were starting to appear, but only with a limited circulation. Most notably, the Universities of Oxford and Cambridge spearheaded an operatic early music revival. Dent, Fellow of Music and Professor at Cambridge from 1926, was a powerful advocate for the cause of early opera, making the case for it in his book *Foundations of English Opera*.[32] The fact that Dent straddled the worlds of academia and journalism (writing for *The Athenaeum* and *The Illustrated London News*) meant that he was also able to promote early opera, as well as to report upon new operas he had heard in Europe, to a wider readership and potential audience.[33]

28. 'Not every day is *Don Giovanni* to be heard'. D. C. Parker, ' "Don Giovanni" at CG', *MS*, 27/492 (31 July 1926), 22. The opera had been performed regularly at Covent Garden in the 1870s, but had later fallen from favour. Rodmell, *Opera in the British Isles*, p. 10.

29. Dyneley Hussey, 'The Coming Opera Season', *The Saturday Review*, 139/3629 (16 May 1925), 522–3, 523.

30. Boughton, *The Glastonbury Festival Movement*, p. 7.

31. 'The present generation is really intimate with only three or four of Handel's choral works and practically ignorant of his operas, of which he wrote forty'. Anon., 'Handel's Operas', *MS*, 27/487 (22 May 1926), 159.

32. Edward J. Dent, *Foundations of English Opera: A Study of Musical Drama in England During the Seventeenth Century* (London: Cambridge University Press, 1928).

33. For biographical context on Dent, see Annegret Fauser, 'The Scholar Behind the Medal: Edward J. Dent (1876–1957) and the Politics of Music History', *Journal of the Royal Musical Association*, 139/2 (2014), 235–60.

Over in Oxford, meanwhile, members of the University performed Monteverdi's *Orfeo* (edited by Jack Westrup, then a student at Balliol, and translated into English by Robert L. Stuart, a graduate of Corpus Christi) in December 1925 at the Oxford Playhouse: this was the first complete staged performance of the work in modern times.[34] *The Musical Times*, which ran a series of articles on the opera to coincide with its revival, noted that the audience in Oxford was appreciative of the work's 'astonishing vitality and beauty'.[35] But this audience was, according to A. H. Fox-Strangways, a rather special one, sufficiently sophisticated to appreciate the work's historical significance.[36] Yet Fox-Strangways seems to have underestimated the wider interest in the endeavour. It is striking that *The Daily Mail* should not only have reported on the Oxford experiment but have done so in very positive terms, praising the work for sounding fresh and vivid and arguing 'The Oxford enthusiasts deserve high credit for rediscovering [Monteverdi's] surprising genius'.[37]

The Oxford University Opera Club was officially established in 1926, and put on Gluck's *Alceste* in the December of that year, conducted by Dr W. H. Harris of New College.[38] Subsequent repertory included *L'incoronazione di Poppea* (1927), *Der Freischütz* (1928), and *The Bartered Bride* (1929, now at Oxford's New Theatre).[39] In 1929 the Club's founder Robert Stuart attempted to take its repertory to wider audiences by setting up the Oxford Festival Opera Club, an outfit planning to give short seasons of opera in English in London, hopefully in a West End Theatre, and then tour to the provinces.[40] At the Scala Theatre near Tottenham Court Road,

34. Anon., 'Oxford University Opera Club 50th Anniversary Appeal', slip contained within programme for *Orfeo*, The Oxford University Opera Club 50th Anniversary Production, 1975 [Oxford University Opera Club Programmes, Bodleian Library shelfmark 17405 d. 27 (box 1)].

35. F. S. H., 'Monteverdi's *Orfeo* at Oxford', *MT*, 67/995 (1 January 1926), 61.

36. 'It was necessary, of course, that the audience should know that Monteverde [*sic*] "mattered", and that was more likely to be the case at a University; elsewhere, people would just have said "all recitative," and have absented themselves'. A. H. Fox-Strangways, 'Music and Musicians. Some Problems of Opera', *The Observer* (13 December 1925), 10.

37. The Music Critic, 'An Antique Opera. Monteverde's *Orfeo* at Oxford', *The Daily Mail*, 9 December 1925, 14.

38. Gluck's *Alceste*: programme for the Oxford University Opera Club production, 6–11 December 1926 [Oxford University Opera Club Programmes, Bodleian Library shelfmark 17405 d. 27 (box 1)]. The early travails of the OUOC are discussed in Robert Ponsonby and Richard Kent, *The Oxford University Opera Club: A Short History 1925–1950* (Oxford: The Potter Press, 1950).

39. Monteverdi's *L'incoronazione di Poppea*: programme for the Oxford University Opera Club production, 6–10 December 1927 [Oxford University Opera Club Programmes, Bodleian Library shelfmark 17405 d. 27 (box 1)]. Weber's *Der Freischütz*: programme for the Oxford University Opera Club production, 27 November–1 December 1928; Smetana, *The Bartered Bride*: programme for the OUOC production, 26–30 November 1929.

40. Anon., 'The Oxford Festival Opera Company', *MO*, 52/619 (April 1929), 628.

the troupe performed works including *Dido and Aeneas, Giulio Cesare, La finta giardiniera, Alcestis*, and *Der Freischütz* in the winter of 1929–30.[41] This was a radical step, but the season was poorly promoted and proved to be a disappointment both in terms of artistry and ticket sales.[42]

Despite the weaknesses of the Oxford troupe, many critics welcomed their efforts. Some advocated that this sort of repertory could be the saving grace of British operatic culture: the opera of Mozart's time and earlier—and particularly 'light opera' (by which they meant *opera buffa*)—was constructed as better suited to British tastes than everything that had followed since. For Leigh Henry, a preponderance of 'grand opera' (a synonym for tragic nineteenth-century opera in general), which he likened to a 'grotesque and ponderous monster', was responsible for making opera 'a thing apart'.[43] Henry noted that in other areas of music there had, in recent years, been a backlash against popular showmanship and the extravagant 'Barnum-and-Bailey'-style performance aesthetic of the Victorian era. (A prime example was the so-called 'monster concert' typically put on at Wembley—in Henry's words, 'the musical equivalent of The Fattest Woman on Earth'—which was now passing out of favour.) In the sphere of opera, however, the grandiose had lived on as a white elephant but was, according to Henry, doing nothing to develop a taste for opera in the country as a whole.

Similarly, Edwin Evans—a champion of new music—wrote in the high-brow art journal *Apollo* that grand opera 'is not the classic opera, but its Byzantine offspring'.[44] He considered this repertory to have originated in an 'obese period', which also created concerts on a huge scale at the Albert Hall and the Handel Festival: 'institutions which we cannot conceive as being born in a world of *svelte* figures'. It is noteworthy that both Henry and Evans should have made their case against so-called grand opera by reference to overweight bodies. Such comments reflect a 1920s distaste for what were seen as the flabby, bloated, and out of control artistic forms of the nineteenth century—a reaction against Victorian values—as well as perhaps making a veiled reference to the large operatic ladies of the popular imagination, who seemed to sit at odds with the fashionable 1920s streamlined silhouette.

41. Advert for the London Opera Festival in Smetana, *The Bartered Bride*: programme for the Oxford University Opera Club production, 26–30 November 1929 [Oxford University Opera Club Programmes, Bodleian Library shelfmark 17405 d. 27 (box 1)].

42. Figaro, 'The Operatic World', *MO*, 53/629 (February 1930), 413–14.

43. Leigh Henry, 'Should Opera Be Opulent?', *MO*, 49/587 (August 1926), 1095–6, 1095.

44. Edwin Evans, 'Lyric Drama of Tomorrow', in R. Sydney Glover (Ed.), *Apollo: A Journal of the Arts, Vol 1 January to June 1925* (Nendeln, Liechtenstein: Kraus Reprint, 1976), pp. 93–5, p. 94.

Despite being a critic who embraced commercial culture, had eclectic musical tastes that went well beyond the Austro-German canon (with particular interests in modern French, Russian, and British music), and wrote enthusiastically about film music during the 1920s, Evans seemingly could not reconcile himself to 'grand' opera, and proposed a radical solution.[45] It would involve eliminating all elements that were merely pretentious (in other words the star system) or merely spectacular, and reducing the expense. He conceded that 'This would probably involve the "scrapping" of many— though not all— established favourites of the nineteenth century.'[46] I shall now examine the reception of these established favourites and the way in which different national schools of opera were more difficult than others to categorise.

ITALIAN OPERA

Italian opera had reigned supreme at Covent Garden in the Edwardian era but lost its pre-eminence after the War, and some commentators felt that it had little chance of ever recouping it.[47] (That said, Italian works had hardly disappeared altogether from the stage, particularly given the preponderance of Puccini performances.) The German seasons at Covent Garden in the mid- to late 1920s were considered by serious critics to have been far more successful artistically than the Italian seasons and notwithstanding the performances of a few outstanding artists—Rosetta Pampanini, Aureliano Pertile, and Mariano Stabile—there had been many weak productions of Italian works. Change would come in 1929 with the arrival of Rosa Ponselle, who had successes with *Norma* and *La Gioconda*, and Beniamino Gigli would sing in London in the early 1930s.

As had long had been the case in Britain, Italian opera was considered the most irrational and flippant of all branches of opera and it was the nineteenth-century Italian repertoire that the highbrows of the 1920s found the least tolerable. (Maria Jeritza is depicted in Figure 5.1 in the particularly maligned *Fedora* by Umberto Giordano.) For instance, Filson Young—a self-taught music writer and adviser on music programming at the BBC—wrote in *Apollo* that 'Italian music . . . ends for me with Lulli

45. Scaife, 'British Music Criticism in a New Era', pp. 35, 174–6.

46. Evans, 'Lyric Drama of Tomorrow', p. 94.

47. W. J. Turner, 'The World of Music: The Coming Opera Season', *ILN*, 9 April 1927, 656. On the reign of Italian opera at Covent Garden in the 1900s, see Rodmell, *Opera in the British Isles*, p. 81.

Figure 5.1 Maria Jeritza as the title role in Umberto Giordano's *Fedora*, 1922. © Mary Evans Picture Library/Imagno.

[*sic*] and does not begin again'.[48] Those critics who were well disposed to Italian opera reported snobbery from their fellow contemporaries; indeed, admitting a liking for the repertoire had almost become a source of embarrassment within elite musical circles, and anyone who took Italian opera seriously was likely to be dismissed as a 'country lout'.[49]

---

48. Filson Young, 'Music in a Life VII—Opera in England', in R. Sydney Glover (Ed.), *Apollo: A Journal of the Arts, Vol 3 January to June 1926* (Nendeln, Liechtenstein: Kraus Reprint, 1976), pp. 70–3, p. 70.

49. Schaunard, 'Stray Musings', *MO*, 52/622 (July 1929), 903–5, 904.

Underpinning such prejudices were long-standing anxieties about Italian opera's modularity, its collaborative model of production, its failure to conform to Romantic notions of the lone artistic genius, and its historic associations with an unthinking sector of 'Society'.[50] By all of these criteria, Italian opera failed to qualify as highbrow, at least so far as the highbrows themselves were concerned. And if this repertoire was criticised 'from above' as ridiculous and culturally impure, it was also mocked 'from below' by some middlebrow critics who were inclined to label it as pretentious and un-British. Then there was the supposed 'problem' that Italian opera was very popular, and thus accessible to the less intellectual sections of the opera audience, wherever they might sit on the class spectrum. Popularity is not, of course, necessarily a good thing; indeed, as Derek Scott has observed, since the rise of the modern entertainment industry in the later nineteenth century, commercial success has often been equated with inferior quality and unrefined taste.[51] On the other hand, Richard Capell of *The Daily Mail* suggested (without sarcasm) that certain types of Italian opera had the potential to become genuine popular entertainment. Notably, he pointed out that 'Those who like opera, but disclaim highbrowery should make a point of seeing *Gioconda*'.[52]

Even within the Italian repertory there were hierarchies, or rather different degrees of perceived awfulness. The *bel canto* repertoire was disdained by most opera companies in Britain at this time, although there were some signs of a re-emergence of interest.[53] Many highbrow critics regarded the works of Rossini, Bellini, and Donizetti as supremely old-fashioned and cliché-ridden, even if (or perhaps precisely because) middlebrow listeners enjoyed arias from such works when they heard them in celebrity concerts. For all this, critics were evidently surprised by how much there was to admire or at least enjoy in *Norma* when it was performed at Covent Garden in 1929, for the first time in some thirty years, as a vehicle for Rosa Ponselle.[54] Dent deemed it a great opera, in spite of its absurdities, and asked why it had fallen out of the repertory of even the most old-fashioned opera

50. For a detailed discussion of this problem within opera historiography more broadly, see Fabrizio Della Seta, 'Some Difficulties in the Historiography of Italian Opera', *Cambridge Opera Journal*, 10/1 (March 1998), 3–13.

51. Scott, *Sounds of the Metropolis*, p. 37.

52. RC, 'Mme Ponselle in *Gioconda*', *The Daily Mail*, 5 June 1929, 12.

53. Rodmell notes that *bel canto* was becoming unfashionable as early as the 1880s. For further reading on its British reception see Michelle Fillion, *Difficult Rhythm: Music and the Word in E. M. Forster* (Urbana, Chicago, and Springfield: University of Illinois Press, 2010), pp. 25–6.

54. The title role had last been sung at Covent Garden by Lilli Lehmann. Anon., 'Rosa Ponselle's Debut', *The Telegraph*, 29 May 1929 [V&A Theatre and Performance Collections, production box: Covent Garden Theatre, 1929].

companies.[55] Part of his agenda, however, was simply to demonstrate that native opera was even worse: *Norma*'s absence could not be attributed to its absurdity when British opera companies were still regularly performing works like *The Bohemian Girl*.[56]

Although a good deal of mid-period Verdi was performed, it too met with snobbery from the serious musical establishment, in part because of its very ubiquity. There was certainly relief that Verdi's early works had dropped out of the repertory, since these were considered to be 'poor stuff', characterised by 'mere virtuosity and sensationalism'.[57] Middle-period Verdi fared little better in the eyes of the highbrow critics. In one of the first significant English-language biographies of the composer, published in 1930, Francis Toye reported that critics were prone to dismissing *La traviata* and *Rigoletto* for their 'guitar-like orchestra', *Aida* for being 'flashy' and 'empty', and *Il trovatore* 'absurd'.[58] On the other hand, critics of the early 1920s expressed disappointment that the two Verdi operas acceptable to highbrow sensibilities, *Otello* and *Falstaff*, had not made it into the performing canon, being still regarded as too advanced for the general public.[59] By the latter part of the decade, *Falstaff* was being well received not only at Covent Garden but around the country, something that was held up as evidence of an improvement in provincial taste.[60] But Toye was open about the fact that Verdi's popularity beyond these works was a hindrance to his acceptance by serious critics, making the striking comment that 'There was no merit to be gained by professing admiration for a composer whose music could be enjoyed by anybody gifted with any musical receptivity whatever'.[61]

By this measure, other arguably even more accessible Italian operas prompted predictable squeamishness. *Verismo* works were criticised both by highbrow critics repulsed by their aesthetic weaknesses, and by middlebrow critics from across the spectrum concerned about the moral welfare of the audiences watching them. *Cavalleria rusticana* and *Pagliacci* were

55. Edward J. Dent, 'The Classic Art of Singing', *The Nation and the Athenaeum*, 29/19 (6 August 1921), 690/2, 692. See also E. B., 'Covent Garden Opera: *Norma*', *The Manchester Guardian*, 30 May 1929, 8.

56. Dent, 'The Classic Art of Singing', 692.

57. John W. Klein, 'Early Verdi', *MO*, 47/554 (November 1923), 159–60, 159.

58. Francis Toye, *Giuseppe Verdi: His Life and Works* (London: William Heinemann, 1930), xi. Toye's 495-page book was intended to introduce British readers to 'the music of a man about whom they knew less, perhaps, than about any other composer of equal standing' (xii). A second Verdi biography appeared near simultaneously: F. Bonavia, *Verdi* (London: Oxford University Press, 1930).

59. Toye, *Giuseppe Verdi*, p. 159.

60. For example, Anon., 'Music Today: the BNOC Report', *MM*, 9/2 (February 1929), 29.

61. Toye, *Giuseppe Verdi*, p. xii. For further reading on the German Verdi renaissance, see Gundula Kreuzer, *Verdi and the Germans: From Unification to the Third Reich* (Cambridge: Cambridge University Press, 2010).

performed by a wide variety of different types of company at the full spectrum of operatic establishments, from Covent Garden to the humblest of
provincial theatres. There was a perception, however, that these operas
were somehow crossing a highbrow-lowbrow divide when they were performed at Covent Garden. At a performance in 1928, it was reported that
the operas caused 'enthusiastic breaches of the decorum proper to that august house'.[62] The fact that a certain snobbery about the genre may be found
even in the assessment of a middlebrow commentator such as Capell—
who dismissed *Cav* and *Pag* as 'terse, bloody dramas of meridional peasant
life' in which 'the crudities are formidable'—would indicate that many
perceived them to be formulaic and unchallenging to the point of being
lowbrow.[63] They had, indeed, enjoyed a former parallel existence in the
world of popular theatre: in 1911, for instance, Leoncavallo had come to
the London Hippodrome to conduct a drastically condensed *Pagliacci* that
had been turned into a music-hall version that was performed twice daily,
billed by *The Times* as 'the sensation of the century'.[64] And yet paradoxically
even *Cav* and *Pag* were perceived as highbrow in certain contexts. W. H.
Kerridge, conductor of a local amateur operatic society, reported that, in
attempting to persuade his singers to explore a wider repertory than Gilbert
and Sullivan, he had programmed *Cavalleria* as 'bait', but found that the
work was 'too highbrow' for some.[65]

Critics often expressed surprise at the fact that home-grown performers
were able to interpret the roles convincingly in operas that were perceived
to be so profoundly at odds with the British character. In 1923, for example,
Figaro wondered at the fact that *Cav* and *Pag* 'always seem to get good and
vigorous interpretations by English companies, just as though their strident
clash of passions and prodigal wielding of the paint brush provide the stolid
Englishman with the opportunity to prove what a dog he can be when he
cares to let himself go'.[66] *Tosca*, on the other hand, was a step too far, in the

62. Anon., ' "Cavalleria" and "Pagliacci" ', Unattributed press clipping [V&A Theatre and
Performance Collections, production box: Covent Garden Theatre, 1928]. Capell noted that
'The Covent Garden gallery had an exciting evening, and at moments heads were lost and wild
noises (all well meant) entered at the wrong places'. Richard Capell, 'Singers in Sicilian Mood',
unattributed press clipping of 14 June 1928, presumed to be *The Daily Mail* [V&A Theatre and
Performance Collections, production box: Covent Garden Theatre, 1928].

63. Capell, *Opera*, pp. 74–5.

64. Matteo Sansone, 'The "Verismo" of Ruggero Leoncavallo: A Source Study of *Pagliacci*',
Music & Letters, 70/3 (August 1989), 342–62, 362.

65. W. H. Kerridge, 'Music and the People', *The Sackbut*, 9 (December 1928), 171–4, 173.
Kerridge's choir had 'no wish to be either uplifted or made to appreciate "highbrow" music'
(p. 174). Eventually he did introduce a mixed repertory but lost about thirty members. New
members joined but they were 'not all true workers; some of them wear black coats during
the day'.

66. Figaro, 'The Operatic World' *MO*, 46/545 (February 1923), 436–8, 436.

same critic's eyes, and not one in which British artists could possibly shine, since 'A drama of such hectic passion, fiendish torture and death . . . calls for qualities which do not get even a sporting chance of development in a land of fogs, gloom and early closing'.[67]

The sort of snobbery about Puccini's music that would linger on until the late twentieth century was already in wide evidence in this period.[68] British highbrow commentators of the 1920s tapped into the full panoply of Puccini stereotypes that were circulating internationally, including the one about him being a meretricious craftsman with commercial nous, able to manipulate listeners who in principle should have known better.[69] Yet it was difficult to ignore his expertise at creating theatrical effect. Constant Lambert argued that Puccini's was 'the only operatic music that is perfectly adapted to its medium', that he was 'an artist who thought operatically', in the same way that D. W. Griffiths or Pudovkin thought cinematically.[70]

Characterising Puccini as a proto-cinematic composer—whether as a compliment or an insult—certainly situated him somewhere in the middlebrow. So too did a broader range of tropes in Puccini reception: his appeal to women and the middle classes; the domestic settings of many of his operas; and the constant refrain that he was a composer who knew his own limitations and pandered to conventional tastes.[71] However, some British commentators placed him lower in the cultural pecking order. An unsigned critic for *The Saturday Review*, for example, called *Il tabarro* and *Suor Angelica* two 'tabloid stories of illicit love', using the sort of terminology that might usually be associated with the crudest forms of journalism or cheap potboiler novels.[72] Puccini was degrading the entire operatic art form, dragging it down into 'the gutter, into the brothels and to the gallows' by setting material that was all well and good in rags read by decadents and degenerates, but 'certainly no concern of art'.[73] There is little ambiguity in

---

67. Figaro, 'The Operatic World', *MO*, 47/558 (March 1924), 580–1, 580.

68. Cecil Gray wrote in his study of contemporary composers that 'No living composer is more despised and execrated by the leaders of musical opinion today in every country'. Cecil Gray, *A Survey of Contemporary Music*, 2nd edn (London: Oxford University Press/Humphrey Milford, 1927), p. 240. On Puccini's Italian reception, see Wilson, *The Puccini Problem*.

69. Gray, *A Survey of Contemporary Music*, p. 240.

70. Constant Lambert, 'Puccini, a Vindication', *MILO*, 1/3 (Christmas 1929), 9–11, 9.

71. Similarly, in literary terms, Rosa Maria Bracco defines the interwar middlebrow as writing that made no attempt to go beyond or deviate from comfortably familiar presentations, and that appealed strongly to women and the middle classes. Rosa Maria Bracco, *Merchants of Hope: British Middlebrow Writers and the First World War, 1919–1939* (Providence and Oxford: Berg, 1993), p. 10. On Puccini's broader reception in terms of class and gender, see Wilson, *The Puccini Problem*.

72. Anon., 'Puccini: Ineradicable Sentimentalism', *The Saturday Review*, 129/3374 (26 June 1920), 583–4, 583.

73. Ibid., 583–4.

this angry critique, which prefigures Joseph Kerman's notorious 1956 vilifi-
cation of *Tosca* as a 'shabby little shocker': Puccini's work was not so much
middlebrow as downright lowbrow in its tawdriness.[74]

WAGNER

German opera was, on the whole, considered in a more favourable light
than Italian by serious opera critics, who often commented upon the jolt
that they experienced on the move from the German to the Italian portion of the Covent Garden season, or vice versa. In the summer of 1925,
for example, Percy Colson complained that the Opera Syndicate should
have let audiences down more gently because the transition between *Die
Meistersinger* and *Lucia di Lammermoor* was 'too great a fall' (not to mention
the fact that they had then added insult to injury by programming *Fedora*,
which he called 'one of the world's worst operas and quite beneath criticism').[75] Similarly, Ernest Newman wrote to his wife in the same season
'after *Der Rosenkavalier* and *Meistersinger, Tristan* and *Walküre* I had the sensation of being locked up in a home for the feeble-minded, and of having to
listen all day to the childish lispings of the unfortunate inmates'.[76]

Wagner was an unusual composer in cutting across highbrow–middlebrow
boundaries in interesting ways and in pleasing both the highbrow critics and
ordinary opera-goers, although there were also grumblings, from both 'above'
and 'below', about the subject matter of his works being alien to British audiences.[77] If Wagner's works had originally been promoted in Britain by what
George Bernard Shaw called 'an inner ring of superior persons', they had gone
on to be very widely performed by the 1880s and 1890s.[78] Many Wagnerians
of the later nineteenth century were intellectuals or eccentrics who were considered to be proponents of a variety of radical new attitudes, such as socialism,
vegetarianism, universal suffrage, or free love.[79] By the 1920s, however, his

74. Joseph Kerman, *Opera as Drama*, new and revised edn (London: Faber and Faber, 1989),
p. 206.

75. Percy Colson, 'Music News and Notes', in R. Sydney Glover (Ed.), *Apollo: A Journal of the
Arts, Vol 2 July to December 1925* (Nendeln, Liechtenstein: Kraus Reprint, 1976), pp. 120–2,
p. 120.

76. Vera Newman, *Ernest Newman: A Memoir By His Wife* (London: Putnam, 1963), p. 56.

77. 'I suppose one must be German to take a real interest in the doings of Wotan and his
tiresome family, for nobody in the present day attaches the slightest importance to Wagner's fu-
tile philosophizing and his abnormal psychological opinions'. Percy Colson, 'Music, News and
Notes', in Glover (Ed.), *Apollo: A Journal of the Arts, Vol 2 July to December 1925*, pp. 59–60, p. 59.

78. Anne Dzamba Sessa, *Richard Wagner and the English* (London: Associated University
Presses, 1979), pp. 11, 143.

79. Ibid., p. 148.

appeal had broadened: he was regularly referred to as 'the most popular operatic composer of the day',[80] and his works were perceived as simultaneously popular and intellectual. Among opera recordings, HMV's excerpts from *The Ring* vied for the top spot in public popularity with *La bohème*.[81] And when the BNOC came to Bristol in 1921, *The Western Daily Press* reported that 'It is no longer the custom to scorn Wagner's music-dramas as "highbrow" and "caviare to the general"'.[82]

We have already seen that Wagner's works were highly profitable for the touring opera companies who performed to socially mixed audiences in the provinces. *The Manchester Guardian*, for instance, reported packed houses in Manchester for the BNOC's *The Mastersingers* in 1926, in what was otherwise a somewhat indifferently attended season.[83] Such was the appetite for this repertory that a critic was able to remark upon the fact that *Parsifal*'s absence from the Theatre Royal in Leeds for a period of three years had left audiences champing at the bit.[84] Wagner was also becoming more central to the repertory at Covent Garden: *The Ring*, previously performed only occasionally, would by the mid-1920s become the principal event of the international season (two complete cycles eventually being performed during the four-week German season, and selling out quickly), something that represented a marked change in public taste since the war.[85]

Almost everyone, it seemed, was mad about Wagner. By the late 1920s, members of high society increasingly frequented the German portion of the season as well as the Italian.[86] And there was a very definite sense that the audience for Wagner had begun to expand and to diversify since the War. Some new audience members had developed a taste for Wagner's music at Sir Henry Wood's Promenade Concerts; others had encountered his music via pianolas or gramophones, or by reading about it in books.[87] Da Capo of *The Musical News and Herald* disparaged the traditional Wagner enthusiasts at Covent Garden as a very specific, snobbish type: 'Your Covent Garden highbrow gives you to understand that he is there for a higher moral purpose

---

80. Figaro, 'The Operatic World', *MO*, 51/609 (June 1928), 881–2, 881.

81. G. M. Thomson, 'Britain's Favourite Gramophone Records', *The Strand Magazine*, 67 (January 1929), 70–77, 72.

82. F.M.L., 'The British National Opera Company. Programme of the Bristol Visit', *The Western Daily Press*, 5 September 1922, 7.

83. 'The Mastersingers, March 1926' in Neville Cardus (Ed.), *Samuel Langford: Musical Criticisms* (London: Oxford University Press, 1929), 36.

84. I. E.., 'Leeds. British National Opera Co.', *MS*, 28/500 (20 November 1926), 167.

85. W. J. Turner, 'The World of Music: The Grand Opera Season', *ILN*, 11 May 1929, n.p.

86. Anon., 'The Coming Season: A Forecast of 1929', *ILN*, 20 April 1929, 655.

87. Savill, *Music, Health and Character*, p. 135; The Editor, 'The "Ring", the Screen, and the High-brow', *MNH*, 62/1572 (13 May 1922), 591–2, 591.

than mere enjoyment: he (or she) is there to give intellectual support to a highly specialised esoteric cult'.[88] The new audience, however, was listening to Wagner in a new way, judging the works for themselves and attempting to break free from the quasi-religious veneration of leitmotifs.[89]

Where, then, did Wagner fit into debates about opera and the brows? It is clear that some people believed his music to be unequivocally highbrow. In a book entitled *Everybody's Guide to Broadcast Music*, Percy Scholes quoted the author of an angry letter to the BBC as having written:

> Your defence of the present undue infliction of highbrow music on a wireless audience is—in my opinion, backed by 90% of my friends—entirely fallacious, and mischievous. Your forcible feeding of the masses with heavy Wagnerian storm music is a huge mistake, and will drive the inarticulate "ninety-percenters" into aggressive *hostility* against ALL highbrow music—heavy or light.[90]

(The seemingly nonsensical expression 'light' highbrow music would suggest that this correspondent was using the term highbrow to denote all classical music.) However, the great box office success companies such as the BNOC had with Wagner productions would seem to contradict such assumptions. The company even published special Wagner supplements to its magazine, *Opera*, talking readers through the plot and music of his music dramas in an accessible manner.[91] It may seem striking that, at a time when opera was widely disparaged as foreign and incomprehensible, the most popular composer should have been the one who arguably made the highest demands upon the listener, the composer whose oeuvre was, in Huyssen's reading, 'the most ambitious high art of the nineteenth century'.[92]

Wagner was acceptable to the most anti-operatic of highbrows because they didn't really consider his music dramas to be opera: as Harvey Grace put it, 'Wagner was not so much an opera composer as a great symphonic writer who took the wrong turning'.[93] And yet several articles in *The Nation and Athenaeum* would suggest that some highbrows were beginning to tire of Wagner. Although many middlebrow periodicals called him the most popular composer of the

88. Da Capo, 'Operatic Types', *MNH*, 66/1680 (7 June 1924), 537.

89. The Editor, 'The "Ring", the Screen, and the High-brow', 591; Mendl, *From a Music Lover's Armchair*, p. 121.

90. Percy Scholes, *Everybody's Guide to Broadcast Music* (London: OUP/Hodder and Stoughton, 1925), p. 186.

91. See, for example, E. G. J., 'Ring of the Nibelung Supplement, No. 4: The Dusk of the Gods', *Opera*, 2/4 (April 1924), 25–8.

92. Huyssen, *After the Great Divide*, p. 35.

93. Harvey Grace, 'Music and Musicians', *Yorkshire Post and Leeds Intelligencer*, 8 December 1924, 7.

day, Edward Dent argued that 'Both as a composer and a philosopher, Wagner is at the present moment very much out of fashion; but it cannot be denied that he was by far the greatest musical personality of his century.'[94] In other words, being popular with the public meant that a composer was *ipso facto* out of favour with the highbrows.[95] The middlebrow novelist Hugh Walpole, meanwhile, sarcastically expressed his misgivings about going to Bayreuth for the grand re-launch of the festival in 1924 because 'Doesn't one know that Wagner is dead and that it is only the vulgar of heart and of purse who can care for him any longer!'[96] Walpole evidently didn't share this view—he went to Bayreuth and thoroughly enjoyed himself—but he had evidently been made to feel that Wagner was heartily old-fashioned.[97] Thus, we find an intriguing situation where Wagner was no longer seen as intellectual enough by the intelligentsia.

Some commentators of the 1920s went so far as to imply that Wagner's works were responsible for spawning various types of popular culture, making even this repertoire difficult to position within the new cultural categories. A correspondent wrote to *The Yorkshire Post* arguing that Wagner's later music had paved the way for two very different types of 'music without melody': Modernism and jazz.[98] Such attitudes were damning but the editor of *The Musical News and Herald* stated approvingly that Wagner was 'a craftsman of the theatre, and not a highbrow', crediting him with having 'invented the technique of the cinema.'[99] The author noted the resemblance between the leitmotif technique and filmic musical underscoring:

> You can point out that when any of the characters in the "Ring" is moved to action by some unuttered thought, and the orchestra reveals what is in his mind, that

94. Edward J. Dent, 'Music: The End of a Chapter', *The Nation and the Athenaeum*, 35/4 (26 April 1924), 113–14, 113.

95. A little while later, similarly, Dent wrote that London had been listening with delight to Wagner, but 'that only shows, as usual, how far London is behind the times'. In Germany, meanwhile, Wagner had been relegated to 'the classical shelf'. Edward J. Dent, 'Music: Towards a New Opera', *The Nation and the Athenaeum*, 35/14 (5 July 1924), 440.

96. Hugh Walpole, 'Bayreuth, 1924: An Impression', *The Nation and the Athenaeum*, 35/21 (23 August 1924), 640–1, 640.

97. The BNOC magazine reported Walpole's presence at the Festival and wondered whether it had regained its old position as 'all that is virile and progressive in music', having passed into oblivion during the past decade. Anon., 'The Problem of Bayreuth', *Opera and the Ballet*, 2/8 (autumn 1924), 42–4, 42. On Bayreuth's endorsement of the Nazi party and extreme nationalism during this period, see Levi, *Music in the Third Reich*, p. 6.

98. Verax, 'Low-brow Music', letter to *Yorkshire Post and Leeds Intelligencer*, 11 April 1928, 4.

99. The Editor, 'The "Ring", the Screen, and the High-brow', *MNH*, 62/1572 (13 May 1922), 591–2, 591. For further reading on the connections between Wagner's works and film, see Jeongwon Joe and Sander L. Gilman (Ed.), *Wagner and Cinema* (Bloomington: Indiana University Press, 2010).

is exactly what every competent cinema producer of today would do in the same circumstances.[100]

Wagner's sword motif, he argued, was the equivalent of the cinematic close-up, akin to a film maker zooming in on the gun of an Arizona cowboy. Although this particular author regarded it as a compliment to Wagner that he had fostered a new convention, above and beyond his other achievements, the highbrows, as we have seen, regarded any connection between the opera and the new world of cinema with suspicion: Wagner, by this measure, was no better than Puccini. Not even that most 'symphonic' of operatic composers could be considered to be adhering to cultural purity.

For those inclined to mock opera 'from below', meanwhile, the similarities between Wagner's operas and early films offered an excuse to poke fun. A correspondent for *The Musical Mirror* reported going to see a performance of *Tristan and Isolde* before returning home to read a Wild West novel called *Shotgun Magee* and discovering a surprising affinity between the two. Playing upon the long-running British strategy of mocking the pretensions of opera by creating an amusing clash between the supposedly highbrow and lowbrow, the author mused upon the possibilities for adapting the novel as an operatic libretto. He wrote:

> Its possibilities for musical dramatisation and idealism on Wagnerian lines are indeed rich . . . It is true that a Wild-West opera has been written in the form of Puccini's *Girl of the Golden West*, but this has never really captured the public's fancy. What is wanted is a full-blooded story that will capture the Wagner fans. We have ample material in *Shotgun Magee*, which could perhaps be made more attractive and clarified by being entitled, as a music drama, *Dave and Isabel*.[101]

VIOLENCE AND PASSION

What of Wagner's leading successor? Strauss's *Der Rosenkavalier* was undergoing a wave of particular popularity in 1920s Britain, with audiences rediscovering the work after the wartime ban on operas by living German composers.[102] The 1924 Covent Garden production with Lotte Lehmann, Delia Reinhardt, Elisabeth Schumann, and Richard Mayr, conducted by Bruno Walter, was marked down by many commentators as the stuff of

---

100. The Editor, 'The "Ring", the Screen, and the High-brow', 592.
101. John F. Porte, 'A Cowboy *Tristan and Isolde*', *MM*, 9/3 (March 1929), 70–75, 70.
102. On the wartime ban, see Rodmell, *Opera in the British Isles*, p. 123.

legend and the opera was revived at the theatre several times during the later 1920s.[103] This was a work that was capable of cutting across highbrow-lowbrow tastes: as one newspaper reported following a Covent Garden performance in 1925, 'the mezzo brows applauded as loudly as the high-brows, while the low-brows were enchanted with the lilt of the lovely waltzes and thought they must have been written by the other Strauss'.[104]

More recent operas by Strauss, however, prompted aesthetic criticism from the highbrows and distaste and incomprehension from the middle-brows, who were prone at times to assuming a stance of the moral high ground. By the 1920s, Strauss's career was being re-evaluated negatively by serious music critics, who perceived him to have gone off on an irreversibly downward trajectory since *Der Rosenkavalier*.[105] *Salome* and *Elektra* predated Strauss's supposed decline, but were nevertheless vigorously attacked by the highbrow critics during the 1920s. Even though Gray called *Salome* Strauss's 'masterpiece', he was still willing to acknowledge that the 'work as a whole is better than any of its constituent parts viewed separately'.[106] He likened Strauss's aesthetic to that of the author Emile Zola, in which the architectural power is 'remarkably impressive' but the details tasteless, vulgar, and 'a jumble of the most heterogeneous and dissimilar elements'.[107] Gray's comments here recall the early Italian reception of Puccini's operas, where references to decoration and detail were coded ways of saying that the works were too feminine, too frivolous, too bourgeois, and that they lacked Wagnerian organicism.[108] And, indeed, Gray even draws an explicit connection to the reviled Puccinian/*verismo* aesthetic, writing that in *Elektra*, 'when he has . . . to depict the tender womanliness of Chrysothemis or the love of Elektra for her brother, the result is very little different from what one would expect from Puccini or Mascagni'.[109]

Middlebrow commentators, meanwhile, applied metaphors of illness and physical pain to *Salome* and *Elektra*. To say that a piece of modern

103. *The Musical Mirror* reported that for the 1929 production, queues for *Der Rosenkavalier* began to gather at 7am and an 'old woman' of 60 said 'I'm going to wait twelve hours or so each day—for some weeks. And it's well worth it'; Piacevole, 'Heard in the Interval', *MM*, 9 (June 1929), 143.

104. Anon., 'Opera Filmed', *The Dundee Courier*, 16 December 1925, 8.

105. Cecil Gray argued in 1927 that 'From being a man of possibly unequal genius he has become a man of second-rate talent . . . No composer of such unquestioned eminence has ever suffered such a startling change of fortune, such a sudden and decisive reversal of a favourable verdict'. Gray, *A Survey of Contemporary Music*, pp. 50, 51. See also Eric Blom, 'A Late Strauss Opera' in Blom, *Stepchildren of Music* (London: G. T Foulis and Company, 1925), pp. 267–74.

106. Gray, *A Survey of Contemporary Music*, pp. 55, 56, 57.

107. Ibid., p. 56.

108. For further reading see Wilson, *The Puccini Problem*.

109. Gray, *A Survey of Contemporary Music*, p. 56.

music made the listener ill was much the same as dismissing it as mere noise: indeed, complaints of an 'ear-splitting cacophony' and an upset liver tended to go hand in hand.[110] Although a fan of *Der Rosenkavalier*, Capell's assessment of Strauss's oeuvre of the 1900s—which he characterises as decadent, wanton and downright unhealthy—drips with distaste: 'The Strauss of *Salomé* [*sic*] and *Elektra* is the barbaric invader making havoc in the scenes of old civilizations. This inheritor of Meyerbeer and Wagner spares no expense. He makes a tremendous music, all very loud, wasteful and intoxicated. We come out of it with bloodshot eyes and a headache.'[111] Strauss's music, then, was not only detrimental to the individual listener— in the sense of prompting a sensation akin to a hangover—but had more profound implications in defiling the whole operatic tradition.

W. J. Turner, in similar vein, characterised *Elektra* as something artificial: 'contrived, contrived, contrived', 'as lacking in imagination as a waxwork chamber of horrors', and with 'no real-life blood in it, only scarlet paint'.[112] The work left you feeling nervously exhausted, he argued, much as you would feel after witnessing a road accident. These comments suggest that the opera was perhaps too reminiscent, in the eyes of opera critics, of the sort of plays that were doing the rounds in the more commercial theatre. There was a considerable appetite in 1920s Britain for thrillers and horror dramas: audiences were, in the words of Hand and Wilson, 'eager for thrills and excitement—the artificial, high theatricality of on-stage horror, rather than the devastating reality of the horror that had so recently taken place on the battlefields'.[113] Critics were being particularly scandalised by the *Grand Guignol* plays being put on by José Levy at the Little Theatre, in which characters were drowned in acid baths or had their eyes stabbed out with knitting needles.[114] In similar vein, operas such as *Elektra* were too close to popular theatre for the highbrows and too violent for certain sectors of the morality-driven middlebrow.

If violence caused squeamishness on the part of middlebrow listeners, it was operatic love—the lifeblood of much popular Italian opera in particular—that made some highbrow critics squirm. The musicologist John W. Klein balked at opera's 'childish' tendency to repeat 'the same old story ... ad nauseam: a man either gets the woman he wants or he does not

---

110. Landon Ronald, for example, imagined a 'staunch conservative' uttering the words: 'When I go to a concert, Sir, I don't expect to have my intelligence insulted by listening to a lot of ear-splitting cacophony which gives me a headache and upsets my liver and causes me actual mental anguish'. Ronald, *Myself and Others*, p. 151.

111. Richard Capell, *Opera* (London: Ernest Benn, Ltd., 1930), p. 76.

112. W. J. Turner, 'The World of Music', *ILN*, 13 June 1925, 1174–8, 1178.

113. Hand and Wilson, *London's Grand Guignol*, p. 4.

114. Ibid., p. 3; Trewin, *The Gay Twenties*, p. 24.

get her'. Klein's objection was purportedly one of a lack of novelty—he argued that in other art forms people would rebel at the absence of variety—but it is also easy to discern a distaste for opera's (and particularly Italian opera's) emphasis upon high passions. He wrote

> I . . . believe that opera is held in contempt and derision by so many persons of musical taste simply because it is so full of passionate love let loose . . . I have often pitied those miserable artists who are compelled to indulge in long swooning ecstasies one night after the other. [115]

Figaro, responding with hostility to Klein, flagged up the latter's highbrow prejudices. Klein was characterising the love interest in opera as 'a sort of playing down to the mob', and if this were indeed the case, Figaro argued, opera should be extraordinarily successful rather than on its supposed deathbed, because 'It is . . . generally accepted, I think, that the war has been followed by a wave of eroticism'.[116] Long-running spats between contributors to a particular journal were a fairly common occurrence in this period, so it is unsurprising to find Klein then writing to the journal a second time to reassert his case. Sincere love was not a problem, he argued, but popular composers' habit of confounding lust with love was frankly unendurable: witness the contrast between the Mozartian noble conception of love and the Puccinian 'vulgar emotionalism and shrieking hysteria'.[117]

This was, of course, the era of Marie Stopes and debates about sexology, and as Maggie B. Gale has shown, 'questions of sexual and marital relationships became very much part of the popular discussion'.[118] The Lord Chamberlain kept a close eye upon seduction scenes in contemporary plays, with a ban on any scenes with two people in a bed.[119] It is unlikely that any opera productions of the day were particularly salacious; the problem was more one of a highbrow distaste for trivial matters of the heart. But highbrows may also have been painfully aware that operatic love stories

---

115. John W. Klein, 'Is Opera on its Death-Bed?' *MO*, 45/539 (August 1922), 960–1, 960. Klein wrote regularly for such periodicals as *The Musical Quarterly* and *Music & Letters*, and specialised in French opera of the Romantic period ('Obituary: John W. Klein', *MT*, 114/1568, October 1973, 1045). In 1922 he was happy to admit elsewhere to being a highbrow, writing: 'This indifference (or barbarism) on the part of the public is certainly extremely regrettable. It was not, however, my object to discuss the likes or dislikes of the mob, but the indifference—as far as opera is concerned—of people of musical tastes'. John W. Klein, 'Letters to the Editor: Is Opera on its Deathbed?', *MO*, 46/541 (October 1922), 40.

116. Figaro, 'The Operatic World', *MO*, 46/542 (November 1922), 129–30, 130.

117. Klein, 'Letters to the Editor: Is Opera on its Deathbed?', *MO*, 46/543 (December 1922), 242.

118. Gale, 'Errant Nymphs', p. 122.

119. Steve Nicholson, *The Censorship of British Drama 1900–1968. Volume 1: 1900–1932* (Exeter: University of Exeter Press, 2003), p. 225.

were not so different from the conventions of the literary romance, which was emerging as a distinctive genre in this period. Prior to the First World War, there had not been enough popular fiction for there to have been a real sense of 'genre fiction', but with the publishing deluge that followed the War, categorisation of different types of fiction was starting to be necessary by the mid-1920s.[120]

The widely exhibited fear of operatic lust was doubtless reflective of a particular type of Anglo-Saxon prudishness but also a barely disguised way of expressing a more general sense of revulsion for contemporary opera. For Klein, 'The more cultured section of the operatic community is undoubtedly acquiring a growing distaste for opera and all its absurdities and vulgarities'.[121] An anecdote he shared about a conversation overheard on the London Underground crystallises the way in which opera (or at least a certain type of popular contemporary opera) found itself in an awkwardly uncategorisable position: not highbrow enough for the highbrow critics but too highbrow for the man in the street. Klein professed to have heard a woman on the tube (whom he named 'Miss Brown') expressing a wish to hear *Madama Butterfly*. Her companion 'Mr Smith' retorted in an unrepeatable vernacular that he had 'not the least intention of witnessing any "such high-brow stuff"'. Klein's conclusion was that 'That is the mentality of the average citizen of His Majesty's realm. Fortunately opera has little to hope or to fear from him'.

AN UNOPERATIC NATION?

The subject matter of contemporary opera in particular, then, was often dismissed because it was too lustful, too violent, or disagreeable to British tastes in some other regard. (Puccini's *Suor Angelica*, for instance, was dropped from the Covent Garden run of *Il trittico* after only two performances because it was assumed that British audiences could not relate to its Catholic subject matter.[122]) Racial essentialism

---

120. Bloom, *Bestsellers*, pp. 108–9. For further reading on the cultural politics of the romance novel, see Alison Light, *Forever England: Femininity, Literature and Conservatism Between the Wars* (London and New York: Routledge, 1991).

121. Klein, 'Letters to the Editor', *MO*, 46/543 (December 1922), 242.

122. F. B., 'Puccini's *Trittico* at Covent Garden', *The Manchester Guardian* (19 June 1920), 12. Barrett noted in *The Musical Times* that 'in England . . . the convent is not well understood, and the listener is inclined to say "Why?" to the whole business, more especially when at the end Mme. Dalla-Rizza . . . appeared before the curtain with the child. Considered as music it is not unworthy, but the story lacks the necessary quality of attraction for this country'. Francis E. Barrett, 'Opera in London', *MT*, 1 August 1920, 547–8, 547.

was often pronounced in discussions about artistic taste and creativity. Filson Young argued that opera, whether Italian or Wagnerian, did not correspond to anything in British national life, which was 'sombre and austere' ('joy and real jollity are not part of its natural make-up').[123] Young's comments reflect a longer-standing suspicion of music per se, suggesting that the British were too respectable and hard working to have time or inclination for the performing arts and that British art tended to be sober in nature, with a preference for literature. And yet such arguments do not square with the British enthusiasm for music hall, musical theatre, and pantomime. Young also disputed the BNOC's oft-cited claim that Britain was 'rich in operatic talent', arguing that 'opera is essentially a product of the Latin temperament'. Similarly, Roger Quilter, who as a composer had something of a vested interest, argued the case for light opera, on the grounds that 'We are not a portentous people like the Germans, a dramatic people like the Italians or a people so steeped in classical tradition as the French; nor do we suffer overmuch from Slavonic moodiness'.[124] Time and again, then, so-called grand opera was presented as something alien to the national character and removed from the everyday.

Other commentators argued that operas were only capable of securing a genuine place in the hearts of British audiences if they dealt with themes that had a particular appeal to the British mentality, a nationalistic, protectionist view that flew in the face of the obvious, quantifiable appeal of popular foreign operas. Arguing against public subsidy for opera, Leigh Henry wrote in 1926 that:

> The only types of music which have ever sprung up or taken root in this country are such as have had immediate contact with our life in one form or another. Grand opera has never done this; we do not live melodramatically, however much our more romantic moments incline us to take melodrama as sensational fiction . . . Grand opera cannot ever be a British national institution because it is alien to the British nature. Are we then to provide an unearned increment to maintain this antipathetic alien in our midst?[125]

Meanwhile, the old arguments about Britain not being able to produce a vibrant operatic school of its own lingered on, and the rhetoric was often strikingly reductive, once again coming down to matters of national temperament. Although an opera composer herself, Smyth argued that British

---

123. Filson Young, 'Music in a Life VII—Opera in England', in R. Sydney Glover (Ed.), *Apollo: A Journal of the Arts, Vol 3 January to June 1926* (Nendeln, Liechtenstein: Kraus Reprint, 1976), pp. 70–3, p. 71.

124. Roger Quilter, 'Mainly about Light Opera', *Opera and the Ballet*, 2/6 (June 1924), 11–12, 11.

125. Leigh Henry, 'Should Opera be Opulent?', *MO*, 49/587 (August 1926), 1095–6, 1095.

people were unable to express passions and violent emotions easily in public, because they lacked 'incandescence' and were 'severely handicapped by [their] own most cherished ideals of behaviour'.[126] Smyth argued that British people were 'sluggish burners, and of that coal you cannot manufacture the terrific express-train heat that must be kindled between an artist and the art he is interpreting, if the heights and depths of passion are to be expressed'.[127] Smyth noted, however, that the 'slow tenacious' personality had its advantages. Echoing Cecil Forsyth's argument of 1911 that while the British might be unsuccessful at composing operas, they were very good at winning wars, she argued that the British character had broken Napoleon's power and allowed Britain to reassure the French and Italians in the last war that if the rest of the allies cried off, England would fight on alone.[128] The price to be paid for such heroic stoicism was that the British were not suited to the composition of great tragic opera: it was impossible to have it both ways. 'Light' opera was a different matter, and far better suited to the British character.[129]

Sometimes hypothetical operas that *would* appeal to the British people were suggested: the singer Robert Radford mused over the possibility of operas based on the lives of notable national figures such as Richard the Lionheart, Elizabeth I, Cardinal Wolsey, Sir Francis Drake, Mary Queen of Scots, Charles I, Oliver Cromwell, or Admiral Nelson.[130] A native British type of opera must 'grow out of the soil', Radford argued, in a comment evocative of the wider contemporary pastoral school of British music. Attempts to emulate the 'ponderous philosophy' of the Germans, the sugary style of the French school, or the passion of the Italians could only lead to failure.[131] The opera that came closest to achieving this distinctively 'English' quality was, of course, *The Immortal Hour*, a Celtic-themed opera peopled by fairies and druids. A critic for *The Telegraph* wrote in 1922:

> It is a British opera, not merely because it has been written by an Englishman, but because it possesses characteristics that are not found in German, Italian, or French opera. The text or story is as alien to the emotional plots of Puccini as to the Heroic Wagnerian stories or the phantastic medleys of some Straussian works.[132]

126. Smyth, 'An Iron Thesis on Opera',, 157.

127. Ibid., 158.

128. Forsyth, *Music and Nationalism: A Study of English Opera* (London: Macmillan, 1911), p. 2; Smyth, 'An Iron Thesis on Opera', 158.

129. 'There are historical reasons for thinking that the lighter forms of opera are those most suited to the English temperament in general'. Edward J. Dent, 'Music', *LM*, 1/3 (January 1920), 376–8, 377.

130. Robert Radford, 'The Future of Opera in England', *Opera*, 1/1 (January 1923), 6–8.

131. Ibid., 7.

132. Unattributed review in *The Telegraph*, 14 October 1922, cited in Hurd, *Rutland Boughton and the Glastonbury Festivals*, p. 150.

A cartoon of 1922 published in *The Musical Mirror*, meanwhile, took a more tongue-in-cheek attitude towards the question of what would make a good English opera. Headed 'A Fishy Opera', it depicts two portly singers: the man (presumably tenor) sings 'Hand me yon taters', hand imperiously outstretched, to which the soprano (clutching a bag of fish and chips in one hand and a salt shaker in the other) replies 'Never will I give up my 'taters'. A third principal—possibly intended to be a caricature of an operatic impresario—is marked out as the villain by his thin moustache, hooked nose, and clenched teeth, with more than a hint of anti-Semitic caricature.[133] In the background is a man smoking a pipe while frying fish and ballerinas dripping vinegar on to bags of chips. Boxes and signs in the background bear the slogans 'Pure malt vinegar' and 'Special tonight: cod steaks, halibut', while a box on the floor is marked 'Fishmonger, Grimsby'. Underneath the cartoon are the words: 'Richard Strauss has written a light opera with scenes in a pastry shop. What is to prevent some of our bright young British composers launching out on still more unconventional lines? A fried-fish shop, for example, would afford a striking and absolutely original setting for a really up-to-date opera'.[134]

The Strauss work in question was *Schlagobers*, not in fact a comic opera but a ballet, but it is easy to imagine that the latest hearsay about a work-in-progress that was not to be performed for another two years might well have become distorted en route from Vienna to London. The cartoon speaks volumes, both about the British reception of foreign works and about British cultural identities. The substitution of a fish and chip shop for a pastry shop is clearly intended to demonstrate the ridiculousness of Strauss's (supposed) light opera and other 'up-to-date works', and to bring opera down to earth along similar lines to the aforementioned imaginary cowboy opera. At the same time, there is an implication that anything foreign composers do, our composers can do better, and a certain pride is being taken in the fact that British tastes are so unpretentious.

This imaginary work is not just a generically British opera but one that is connected to a particularly down-to-earth type of Britishness: the words 'yon' and 'taters' suggest a Yorkshire setting, as does the box of fish from

---

133. The anti-Semitism that coloured contemporary perceptions of the impresario is transparent. See, for example, Henry Russell's description: 'The word "impresario" in London arouses visions of a gentleman with greasy black curls, a very large nose, huge diamond rings and dirty nails. These visions are not without some slight justification in the past'. Russell, *The Passing Show*, p. 287. Anti-Semitism was widespread in Britain during the 1920s and 1930s, particularly on the Left, intensifying in the aftermath of the War, the Russian Revolution, and the Balfour Agreement. See Fauser, 'The Scholar Behind the Medal', p. 252 and Julius, *Trials of the Diaspora*, p. 289.

134. 'A Fishy Opera' (signed J. Adams), *MM*, 2/1 (January 1922), 10.

nearby Grimsby. The clash between hyper-emotional opera that might be accused of taking itself rather too seriously and frank-speaking northernness was calculated to prompt humour. Indeed, the same strategy is still some-times affectionately deployed today. Witness, for example, the composition in 2017 of *The Arsonists*, a new short opera by Professor Alan Williams of Salford University and poet Ian Macmillan that was designed to be sung in flat northern vowels. This curiosity was reported in the tabloid news-paper *The Mirror* with the headline 'It's Nessun t'Dorma! First Yorkshire Opera to Challenge Posh Image of Art Form by Featuring Thick Northern Accents'.[135]

Of all conceivable 'culinary' operas, it would be hard to imagine one that could be more British than a fish-and-chip opera. This is posited as a subject matter to which the man in the street—much discussed in *The Musical Mirror* itself—could actually relate. Fish and chips were a staple of the working-class diet—although becoming more popular with the middle classes—particularly in the North.[136] Culinary metaphors were common in discussions of musical taste, whether good or bad. For instance, the BNOC's Perceval Graves used a reference to food in order to contextualise the particular popularity of Vaughan Williams' folksong-inspired *Hugh the Drover* in Sheffield: 'Yorkshiremen are still constant to their affection for wholesome British fare—roast beef, ale, and their famous pudding—and they simply swallowed the prize-fight in Act I'.[137] According to time-worn tropes, fancy foods were bad, hearty red meat dishes or good old plain fish dishes were good, and—more to the point—British.[138]

Opera's perceived pretensions, its villains and its high-flown lovers are resolutely brought down to earth in the fish-and-chip-shop opera cartoon; the way in which the art form, at times, aggrandises even the most banal subject matter is mocked by the dialogue about something as ordinary and boring as potatoes. As this and the other examples in this chapter have shown, music journalists of the 1920s and other commentators routinely stereotyped operatic works according to the perceived and often crude characteristics of their respective national schools. Assigning such labels

135. Jeremy Armstrong, 'It's Nessun t'Dorma! First Yorkshire Opera to Challenge Posh Image of Art Form by Featuring Thick Northern Accents', *The Mirror*, 20 October 2017, http://www.mirror.co.uk/news/uk-news/first-yorkshire-opera-challenge-posh-11379739 (accessed 10 October 2017).

136. There were 30–35,000 fish and chip shops in Britain by the late 1920s. Pugh, *'We Danced All Night'*, pp. 25, 95.

137. Perceval Graves, 'Opera in Town and on Tour', *The Sackbut*, 8 (June 1927), 332–4, 332.

138. In 1864, Henry Phillips had characterised the view from Italy and Germany of British music in the following terms: 'Has England got any national music? Roast beef and guineas, that is their national music'. Henry Phillips, *Musical and Personal Recollection During Half a Century*, Volume II (London: Charles J. Skeet, 1864), p. 277.

was, in effect, yet another way of pigeonholing artistic works and deciding where they sat on the highbrow-middlebrow-lowbrow spectrum. And despite the abundant evidence that opera was genuinely enjoyed by people of all classes, it still had to fight its corner against nationalistically driven prejudice and a peculiarly British type of anti-intellectualism which would, as the decades rolled on, increasingly posit opera as something stuffy, highbrow, and ultimately elitist.

CHAPTER 6

⌒

Stars

On the morning of Nellie Melba's farewell concert at Covent Garden in June 1926, the magazine *The Sphere* published a photograph of a group of cheerful-looking 'all nighters' on Floral Street raising celebratory cups of tea to the camera.[1] (A somewhat wearier-looking section of the queue is depicted in Figure 6.1.) Operatic stars of the old school were still sufficiently popular in the 1920s to attract Londoners to camp out in the hope of bagging a place in the cheap seats, a phenomenon usually prompted today only by a royal wedding or the release of the latest must-have and over-hyped technological gadget. Although new types of star would emerge during this period, threatening the pre-eminence of leading singers, the latter remained household names, appearing in tabloid newspapers and high-society magazines, and featuring prominently in the early recording catalogue. They had a strong appeal to those sorts of listeners who liked a bit of this and a bit of that—the emerging middlebrow—by virtue of their similarity to entertainers from the world of popular culture, their relaxed attitude to performing what we might term a 'crossover' repertory, and their endorsement of commercial products. For highbrow commentators, it was precisely the same factors that made the celebrity singer such a problematic figure.

There have, of course, been star singers ever since opera's earliest beginnings, together with an accompanying sense of moral panic that the cult of celebrity will automatically drive down artistic quality.[2] The status of such

1. 'An All-Night Queue for Madame Melba's Farewell Performance at Covent Garden', clipping from *The Sphere*, 12 June 1926 [V&A Theatre and Performance Collections, production box: Covent Garden Theatre, 1926].

2. On star singers of earlier eras, see, for instance: Suzanne Aspden, *Rival Sirens: Performance and Identity on Handel's Operatic Stage* (Cambridge: Cambridge University Press, 2013); Berta Joncus, 'A Star is Born: Kitty Clive and Female Representation in Eighteenth-Century English

Figure 6.1 The queue at Covent Garden for Nellie Melba's final performance, 1926. © Hulton-Deutsch Collection/CORBIS/Corbis via Getty Images.

singers, however, has changed over the centuries: Derek Scott argues that 'The modern type of star ... emerges with the entertainment industry and is differentiated by the way he or she is turned into a commodity'.[3] Scott identifies a significant moment of change within the music industry in the second half of the nineteenth century when singers started to employ agents who would negotiate to get them the highest fees. During this period, stars were essential to the operatic business model in London: a way of showing off the fact that Britain could source the best of anything from anywhere in the world.[4] Opera might have been thriving all over continental Europe, and in some respects with greater artistic integrity, but in terms of the star system—the worship of big names and a culture of high fees—London and New York were the two cities that reigned supreme. London's status in this regard, however, would come to be jeopardised after the First World War, as we shall see presently.

Musical Theatre', unpublished doctoral dissertation, University of Oxford, 2004; Beth Glixon, 'Private Lives of Public Women: Prima Donnas in Mid Seventeenth-Century Venice', *Music & Letters*, 76/4 (November 1995), 509–31; and J. Q. Davies, 'Veluti in Speculum: the Twilight of the Castrato', *Cambridge Opera Journal*, 17/3 (2005), 271–301.

3. Scott, *Sounds of the Metropolis*, p. 34.
4. Rodmell, *Opera in the British Isles*, pp. 9, 33.

While most critics had respect for jobbing opera singers, who were understood to be hard-working and dedicated to their craft, they expressed hostility to the particular brand of foreign singers who epitomised the star system, who were highly paid, over-exposed, and apparently shameless in their pursuit of celebrity status. The more middlebrow music publications that claimed to speak for the man in the street were less concerned by the star singers' blurring of formal boundaries but sometimes chastised them nevertheless, motivated by a desire to stand up for the interests of British singers. Certain sectors of the popular press, however, were more than happy to promote operatic celebrities—indeed to give them what many within the musical establishment regarded as excessive amounts of coverage—and there was evidently a public eager to listen to them and read about them.

Several different types of celebrity singer were problematic from the point of view of opera's cultural categorisation. First there were the pre-War stars now primarily doing the rounds in the concert halls: Melba, with her seemingly never-ending 'farewells', or Luisa Tetrazzini, who was ridiculed as an old-style prima donna, a throwback to the excesses of nineteenth-century diva worship who was at the same time adept at promoting both herself and various consumer goods.[5] But there were also younger opera stars who favoured the concert halls rather than the operatic stage (at least when in Britain), such as Amelita Galli-Curci, whose recordings were hyped to such an extent that she was able to sell out a concert at the Albert Hall eight months in advance without ever having set foot in Britain.[6] Finally, some of the younger generation of stars such as Maria Jeritza and Rosa Ponselle were acclaimed for their performances and treated as serious artists but simultaneously chastised for assuming so-called film star-like attitudes both on and off the stage.

It will not go unnoticed that all of the singers mentioned thus far are women. There were, of course, celebrated male singers during this era—notably Feodor Chaliapin, who returned to Covent Garden in 1926 for the first time since 1914 and was lauded as the most popular male recording artist of the era.[7] However, the popular press repeatedly lamented the lack

---

5. Melba's biographer wrote 'Melba, unfortunately, could not bring herself to retire, leaving us the memory of her exquisite voice in its full glory. We all tried to persuade her to give up singing in public. Alas, it was no use'. Colson, *Those Uneasy Years*, p. 33. Melba had reigned supreme at Covent Garden in the late Victorian years, singing in every season between 1897 and 1914. Tetrazzini starred there between 1907 and 1912. Rodmell, *Opera in the British Isles*, pp. 84–5.

6. Herman Klein, 'The Gramophone and the Singer', *The Gramophone*, 2/2 (July 1924), 40–43, 40.

7. On Chaliapin's popularity on record, see G. M. Thomson, 'Britain's Favourite Gramophone Records', *The Strand Magazine*, 67 (January 1929), 70–77, 72.

of a really engaging star tenor and there was a constant quest to find a 'new Caruso'.[8] Male singers were not perceived to be exploiting the new publicity mechanisms in the same manner; nor were they quite as appealing to the popular press or as loathed by the highbrow critics. Misogyny may be detected in discussions of the 1920s star singer: stereotypes of the fat, stupid prima donna abounded, often coupled with a hefty dollop of xenophobia. In this chapter I shall examine how the hostility expressed towards these women intersected with broader debates about cultural categorisation. As we shall see, the fact that these women deliberately adjusted their behaviour in order to compete with stars from other fields led to even greater condemnation from critics who regarded their promotional tactics as ever more egregious. Star singers had always attracted criticism but in the 1920s hostility to them hardened: for those of a 'superior' frame of mind, they were becoming not only figures of fun but objects of contempt, barely even worthy of the label 'musician'.[9]

Singer studies has become a thriving sub-discipline of opera studies in recent years.[10] However, where the present chapter goes further than other accounts is in analysing star singers of this period as quintessential figures of the middlebrow. An understanding of the strategies used by high-profile singers of the 1920s to negotiate their image formation against the backdrop of a modernity that seemed to threaten their high social position is vital to our consideration of cultural categorisation. So too is an understanding of the way in which such singers interacted, or were perceived to interact, with performers from other fields of entertainment during this period. Star singers were the public face of opera: attitudes towards them therefore shaped attitudes towards the art form as a whole. In highbrow terms, they were problematic because of their similarity to stars from 'lesser' cultural spheres, and because of the way in which they were not autonomous artists, owing their prominence largely to the intervention of money-minded

8. See, for example, the negative comparison of Alfred Piccaver with Caruso in H. J. K., 'Singers of the Month', *MT*, 66/987 (1 May 1925), 447–8.

9. 'It is the fashion with certain "superior" persons to sneer at the *prima donna*. To ridicule her status and pretension, to lament her influence, minimize her attainments, and, in every way, endeavour to deprive her of the *éclat* which, for centuries, she has enjoyed. They make it their business to do so, though nobody knows why. They tell us that she can and does sing, and sometimes can and does act, yet she is "no musician"'. Francesco Berger, 'The Prima Donna', *The Monthly Musical Record*, 52/617 (1 May 1922), 101–2, 101.

10. See, for example: Susan Rutherford, *The Prima Donna and Opera, 1815–1930* (Cambridge: Cambridge University Press, 2006); Rachel Cowgill and Hilary Poriss (Eds.), *The Arts of the Prima Donna in the Long Nineteenth Century* (New York: Oxford University Press, 2012); Karen Henson, *Opera Acts: Singers and Performance in the Late Nineteenth Century* (Cambridge: Cambridge University Press, 2015); and Karen Henson (Ed.), *Technology and the Diva: Sopranos, Opera, and Media from Romanticism to the Digital Age* (Cambridge: Cambridge University Press, 2016).

middlemen. They were doubly problematic because of the way in which they adopted and embraced the new media of the age: modern advertising techniques and the latest technologies for sonic reproduction. They were triply problematic because of their sheer popularity with a mass audience, a phenomenon antithetical to the highbrow modernist mindset. Despite the 1920s being the era of the prima donna's supposed social decline, we shall see that she still exerted considerable sufficient clout to disturb as well as to divert.[11] The battle over opera's uncomfortable position within the 1920s' cultural divide would be as hard fought over personalities as it was over works.

THE CULT OF PERSONALITY

The question of 'personality' was a key point in debates about opera stardom and cultural categorisation. The way in which the star singer allowed his or her persona to be exploited within the expanding modern culture of celebrity in much the same way as film stars, jazz band leaders, or popular novelists situated him or her comfortably within the middlebrow. For highbrow commentators, such singers' celebrity status was incompatible with any sense of serious artistry.

It was still common during this period for a 'mania' to build up around individual opera singers, just as it still does occasionally around singers such as Jonas Kaufmann. Many people with a passing rather than a specialist interest in opera were far more interested in the performer than in the music they performed, leading one critic to remark that 'some men and women collect personalities just as others collect postage-stamps'.[12] The press often noted that hero worship had a tendency to get out of control and must be reined in, advising audiences to temper their enthusiasm for opera stars. Even the populist *Musical Mirror* cautioned its readers thus: 'It is a pardonable weakness to desire to gaze at celebrated people, but that desire needs to be kept within bounds of reason. To make an idol of a popular performer may be excellent for the artist's bank balance, but art is very little served thereby'.[13] Such hysteria was, of course, being fuelled by the fact that managers and publicists were finding new and ever more

---

11. For further reading on the decline of the prima donna, see Rutherford, *The Prima Donna and Opera.*

12. Anon., 'Temperament Without Brains', *The Saturday Review*, 129/3370 (29 May 1920), 495–6, 495. Figaro argued that 'there is nothing wrong with opera, except its incomparable capacity to create every now and again mass mania. There is no drug so potent'. Figaro, 'The Operatic World', *MO*, 49/586 (July 1926), 993–5, 993.

13. Anon., 'Music Today: Celebrity Concerts', *MM*, 8/2 (February 1928), 29.

excessive ways of promoting star singers. Indeed, such was the hype surrounding some singers visiting from abroad that they could scarcely live
up to it: Galli-Curci could not; Aureliano Pertile (who appeared in *Aida* at
Covent Garden in 1927) was a rare exception who did.[14]

One of the problems with the public idolisation of opera stars, insofar as
the highbrows were concerned, was the fact that it was seen as an American
phenomenon, and thus inherently lowbrow. The American composer
Laurence Powell argued that artist worship was rife in the United States
and that there was a celebrity-loving audience that had 'an utter lack of discrimination as to good and bad'.[15] Indeed, the excessive adulation of stars
had wreaked havoc in the American opera house, turning productions at
the Met and the Chicago Civic Opera into 'splendidly engineered stage
concerts—fancy dress concerts', in which it sometimes seemed as though
neither performers nor audience members were interested in drama or
plot.[16]

Of course the relationship between the British and American systems
prompted anxiety at a number of levels during this decade. Many members of the musical establishment were concerned about the fact that after
the War the difficulties in attracting leading international singers to Covent
Garden—who had flocked to London in droves between 1880 and 1914—
became acute. Because it was no longer easy to afford star singers' fees,
London was becoming a backwater: European operatic stars were 'skip-
ping' London and going straight to New York.[17] This was a blow to national
pride. Furthermore, it aggravated the perceived problems surrounding the
so-called celebrity singer. The fact that London was no longer able to attract
the international singers of genuine artistic quality, at least at the start of
the 1920s, meant that the visits by commercially minded celebrity singers
loomed ever larger in the public consciousness.

By the second half of the decade, fine singers from overseas would start
to return to Britain. The serious opera critics welcomed the arrival of a new
generation at Covent Garden but were keen to see the demise of the star
system of old, regarding it as an impediment to improving musical taste
and stimulating public interest in orchestral and choral music.[18] Yet singers
continued to dictate repertory in the egregious way that they had in the

---

14. Figaro, 'The Operatic World', *MO*, 50/598 (July 1927), 967–9, 968.

15. Laurence Powell, 'Gumchewers and Music', *The British Musician*, 3/1 (May 1927),
19–21, 20.

16. Ibid., 21.

17. Figaro, 'The Operatic World', *MO*, 46/541 (October 1922), 33; Herman Klein, 'Our Lost
Operatic Lead', *MT*, 63/947 (1 January 1922), 20–1.

18. See, for example, Sydney Grew, *Favourite Musical Performers* (Edinburgh and London: T.
N. Foulis, Ltd., 1923), pp. 131–2.

nineteenth century—and indeed as they still do today—prompting disapproval from high-minded critics who persisted in playing upon the
stereotype of the demanding, ignorant prima donna.[19] Reporting upon
a production of *Fedora* put on 'as a means of displaying' Maria Jeritza at
Covent Garden in 1925, Eric Blom of *The Manchester Guardian* noted
that despite the fact that the opera was abysmal, that Jeritza's performance
was well below par, and that the production as a whole was a lamentable
failure, one came away with the impression of a huge triumph.[20] The cult of
personality, in other words, was all, and artistic integrity be damned.

Four years later, Covent Garden put on *Norma* and *La Gioconda* especially to showcase the American soprano Rosa Ponselle.[21] While critics admired her vocal talents greatly, considered her worthy of the hype and were
even surprised by how much they enjoyed *Norma*,[22] they condemned *La
Gioconda* as a boring work with no opportunity for subtle characterisation,
which even surpassed 'the average operatic absurdity'.[23] Furthermore, although Ponselle was acknowledged to have sung the opera extremely well,
she was criticised for turning it into a 'dress parade', changing her clothes
five times during the less than twenty-four hours of action in which the
opera was supposed to take place.[24] This phenomenon of allowing the
singer's real-life sartorial taste to intrude upon the action was problematic
not only in terms of disrupting the dramatic flow of the opera but because
it brought to mind more popular types of entertainment, such as variety
theatre where, by and large, the performer appeared onstage 'as themselves'
rather than in character.[25] The perception was presumably exacerbated in
Ponselle's case because she had a background in vaudeville. Furthermore,
her constant dress changes drew attention to a troubling connection with
film: Gundle and Castelli argue that many early films 'either incorporated

---

19. Colson, for instance, argued that repertoire 'should not be chosen by the prima donnas,
whose intelligence is often extremely limited'. Percy Colson, 'Music News and Notes', in
R. Sydney Glover (Ed.), *Apollo: A Journal of the Arts, Vol 2 July to December 1925* (Nendeln,
Liechtenstein: Kraus Reprint, 1976), pp. 120–2, p. 121.

20. E. B., '*Fedora* at Covent Garden', *The Manchester Guardian*, 25 June 1925, 7.

21. HMV made a point of advertising her recording of 'Casta diva' to coincide with her performances in *Norma*. Anon., 'Gems of Recordings on "His Master's Voice"', *The Manchester
Guardian*, 20 June 1929, 8.

22. In praise of Ponselle's Norma, see Anon., 'The Operatic World', *MO*, 52/622 (July 1929),
905–7, 905; W. J. Turner, 'The World of Music: The Italian Season at CG', *ILN*, 8 June 1929,
1020; Anon., 'Opera at Covent Garden', *The Manchester Guardian*, 2 June 1929, 14.

23. Anon., 'Music of the Week', *The Observer*, 9 June 1929, 14.

24. Schaunard, 'Stray Musings', *MO*, 52/622 (July 1929), 903–5, 904.

25. Double, *Britain Had Talent*, p. 1.

fashion shows or were little more than a sequence of episodes linking display set pieces.[26]

Star vehicles were of course largely a Covent Garden problem: the touring companies, run on repertory lines, rarely used singers of international calibre. However, on the few occasions when they secured a big name they too came in for criticism for using a singer whose starry presence undermined the cooperative efforts of the rest of the ensemble. When the BNOC hired Melba to sing Mimì in 1923, Harvey Grace wrote: 'We cannot be expected to regard opera as a serious musical form when a single performer is put forward as being of more importance than all the rest of the cast, the orchestra, and the composer.'[27] Singer licence had long been criticised and was one of the reasons why opera both sat so uneasily within the parameters of the organic musical 'work' and was so difficult to categorise.[28]

PUBLICITY STRATEGIES

Although star singers remained household names during the 1920s, there was growing speculation that they were gradually being eclipsed in the public eye by new types of celebrity. The composer Percy Colson observed retrospectively that 'By the mid twenties great singers and stage celebrities had been replaced in popular favour by film stars and lawn-tennis "aces"; at any rate with the semi-literate people of which London society is now chiefly composed and with the general public.'[29] Melba, for instance—whose comments about shabbily dressed opera-goers cited earlier demonstrate a sense of arrogant complacency about the prima donna's ability to command respect, even deference—was reported to have been furious at having to share the limelight at a society luncheon with Suzanne Lenglen, the first female tennis celebrity.[30]

Doubtless in response to the threat to their long-held high social status, singers of the 1920s became increasingly adept at exploiting the new, significantly more sophisticated and powerful publicity tactics of the post-War

---

26. Stephen Gundle and Clino T. Castelli, *The Glamour System* (Basingstoke: Palgrave MacMillan, 2006).

27. 'Feste', 'Ad Libitum', *MT*, 64/965 (1 July 1923), 465–8, 467.

28. As Mary Ann Smart writes: 'Sopranos are routinely demonized in operatic history as greedy and ambitious, willing to sacrifice the aesthetic balance of a masterwork to satisfy their vanity with an additional showpiece aria, a few more gaudy ornaments'. Mary Ann Smart, 'The Lost Voice of Rosina Stoltz', in Corinne E. Blackmer and Patricia Juliana Smith (Eds.), *En Travesti: Women, Gender Subversion, Opera* (New York: Columbia University Press, 1995), pp. 169–89, p. 171.

29. Colson, *Those Uneasy Years*, pp. 28, 32.

30. Ibid., p. 32; Collier and Lang, *Just the Other Day*, p. 106.

age that were used by rival types of celebrity. In the early 1920s, music promotion was still in its infancy in Britain. While a few stars from the world of music had been promoted well—notably the pianists Paderewski and Pachmann and violinist Kreisler—the practice was still generally regarded in the arts as something rather 'immodest'.[31] Most singers had to do their own promotion and were not particularly efficient at it: concert agents' offices were piled high with identikit circulars that consisted of little more than a photograph and some poorly arranged and badly selected complimentary reviews. Over the course of the decade, singers and their managers would become more adept in their publicity strategies. But this was of course a factor that further underlined their connection with commerce and materialism in the eyes of the highbrows. Opera was beginning to be promoted during this period using the same hard salesman-like techniques as any number of everyday products. Charles B. Cochran—a theatre manager and impresario who managed everything from wild west shows and boxing to celebrated actors—argued that 'Selling opera to the public involves the same technique as selling a new brand of soap. The opera-house has got to be presented in pretty much the same way as a Selfridge's'.[32] A highbrow vision of opera this certainly was not.

Celebrity—the selling of notable people to a mass public—was widely accepted as a 'thing of the moment' and new types of activity or success qualified one to become a celebrity and offered an entrée into high society. Percy Colson observed that 'Now, anyone who had written a successful play or a popular book; who had been involved in a *cause célébre* [sic], or had speculated in a big way without getting into gaol, was to be met everywhere'.[33] Some musical highbrows hoped that it would be merely a passing fad. In his book *Orpheus, or the Music of the Future* (1926), W. J. Turner prophesied that in five generations, 'the people will have forgotten that it is interesting to know whether a celebrity drinks de-caffeined coffee or dehydrogenated water because there will be no "people" and no celebrities. The age of vulgarity will have passed'.[34]

But for now the age of vulgarity was in full swing (and would, of course, only intensify with the passing of the decades). The celebrity interview had first emerged as a British phenomenon in the 1880s and 1890s, with the intention of uncovering public figures' supposed 'real selves'.[35] The human

31. A. Corbett-Smith, 'Music and Salesmanship', *MO*, 46/541 (October 1922), 49.

32. Charles B. Cochran, 'Opera and Showmanship', *MILO*, 1/3 (Christmas 1929), 18.

33. Colson, *Those Uneasy Years*, p. 28.

34. W. J. Turner, *Orpheus, or the Music of the Future* (London and NY: Kegan Paul, Trench, Trubner and Co. Ltd./E. P. Dutton & Co., 1926), pp. 93–4.

35. Salmon, 'Signs of Intimacy', 160.

interest story fostered since the turn of the century by Lord Northcliffe in *The Daily Mail* and Lord Beaverbrook in *The Daily Express* and targeted particularly at female readers had found its way into a wide range of types of newspaper and magazine, and journalistic profiles of singers going about their everyday lives also abounded.[36] For the tabloid press, the arrival or departure in the UK of a star singer was big news and fodder for the gossip columns, with a focus upon her high fees, the audience numbers she attracted, and her hobbies.[37] There was often a nationalistic focus to such reports—calculated to diffuse the protectionist resentment often expressed towards foreign singers—with stars such as Galli-Curci and Jeritza repeatedly quoted as saying how much they loved England and being appropriated as honorary Brits.[38]

Society magazines also published photographs and human interest stories about the latest noteworthy prima donnas, such as a photograph published in *Tatler* in 1920 of 'Madame Kousnietzoff' (Mariya Kuznetsova), then appearing in *La bohème*, who had been imprisoned by the Bolsheviks two years earlier and made her way to Britain disguised as a boy and hidden in a trunk.[39] Large photographs of star singers appeared in illustrated newspapers aimed at members of Society, either as themselves or in role, although the distinction between the two was not always particular clear. A photograph of Jeritza in *The Sketch* in costume as Maliella from *I gioielli della Madonna*, for example, showed her wearing a simple white silk dress, crown, and jewels, with her hair fashionably curled. Again, the singer's persona and fashion choices loomed large: there is little to tell the character apart from the real-life prima donna.[40]

Sales-hungry newspapers and magazines were quite happy to devote copious pages to star singers' every activity, to what serious-minded critics considered to be a disproportionate degree. Schaunard of *Musical Opinion* mused over whether some publications employed a team of dedicated staff whose sole duty was to report on celebrity singers' extra-musical activities.[41] Not only were such columns trivial, but they also had troubling

36. For further reading, see John Carey, *The Intellectuals and the Masses: Pride and Prejudice Among the Literary Intelligentsia, 1880–1939* (London: Faber and Faber, 1992), pp. 7–8.

37. For singers promoted on the front page of the tabloids, see Anon., 'Mme. Galli-Curci's Goodbye', *The Daily Mirror*, 18 Dec 1924, 1 and Anon., 'Mme Jeritza in London', *The Daily Mirror*, 16 June 1925, 1.

38. See, for instance, 'Galli Curci Loves Us', *The Daily Mirror*, 18 December 1924, 2.

39. 'Madame Kousnietzoff', *Tatler*, No. 987, 26 May 1920, n.p. [V&A Theatre and Performance Collections, production box: Covent Garden Theatre, 1920]. On Kuznetsova see Macy (Ed.), *The Grove Book of Opera Singers*, p. 261.

40. Clipping from *The Sketch*, 9 June 1926 [V&A Theatre and Performance Collections, Maria Jeritza file].

41. Schaunard, 'Stray Musings', *MO*, 48/573 (June 1925), 905–7, 906.

implications for the integrity of serious music criticism. Publications that were in the habit of hyping operatic stars in advance then found themselves in an awkward position of not being able to be impartial when reviewing those stars' performances: *The Musical Times* criticised *The Daily Mail* and *The Evening News* for their 'hysterical boosting' of Melba as Mimì in 1924 and the fact that they had to send their critics 'bound and gagged' to the actual performance.[42]

Singers courted the attention of the popular press, however much they might have denied the fact. Jeritza, for instance, claimed that 'I shrink from attracting attention outside my own legitimate sphere of action—the opera stage', yet such modesty was patently false, given that she wrote of her daily routine including countless interviews with press representatives.[43] Indeed, Mabel Wagnalls, in her book of interviews with celebrity singers, recalled the difficulties of getting an appointment to interview Jeritza in New York and of the sycophantic kowtowing of the entire staff of the St Regis Hotel.[44] In London Jeritza was considered a prima donna of suitable clout to have a dessert created in her honour at the Savoy Hotel—the Salambô Voilé Jeritza—for an evening when she dined with John McCormack and Antonio Scotti.[45]

The press often embellished the material it was given in order to fit the public perception of the typical prima donna. The circulation of particular mythic tropes were tricks of the trade, wheeled out over centuries as a way of advertising the prima donna: the story of the bare-footed, hungry child singer who was discovered by a nobleman; the story of the singer whose jewels or furs were stolen when she was out undertaking charitable good works; or the story of the star who was forced to continue singing after being financially ruined by the gambling of her fourth husband.[46] Luisa Tetrazzini exposed the tactics of the gossip journalist when explaining that interviewers had wanted from her a clichéd story of a rise from rags to riches, which she had steadfastly refused to provide. Journalists tried to put words in her mouth so that she would endorse the nationalistically driven stories that they wanted to tell, encouraging her, for instance, to make the

42. 'Feste', 'Ad Libitum', *MT*, 65/975 (1 May 1924), 409–11, 410.

43. Jeritza, *Sunshine and Song*, pp. 179, 176.

44. Wagnalls, *Opera and its Stars*, pp. 55–6.

45. The dessert consisted of an immense sugar lyre filled on one side with fruit and on the other with salambo (small sugar shells, like marzipan, filled with ice cream). It stood upon a block of ice 6ft by 3ft, the base illuminated by electricity, and the whole was draped in spun sugar. Anon., 'Opera Stars' Menu: A First-Meeting Dinner', *The Daily Mail*, 20 June 1925, 7.

46. Berger, 'The Prima Donna', p. 102.

case for opera in English or to argue that England could produce composers as great as those from Italy.[47]

Singers may have complained about the ways in which the press manipulated them, but some were shameless about using the press for their own ends. Tetrazzini herself was regarded as a particularly cynical exploiter of all publicity methods. She was a dangerous phenomenon: an old style, self-regarding diva in possession of modern marketing tools. Grace, outraged at the attention given to her over high-quality orchestral concerts, sarcastically called her 'the Great One', and mocked the fact that she was met at Victoria Station for her 1919 visit to London by a military band, 'like a returning conqueror', when in fact 'To the musician there can be no more depressing phenomenon than the recent London success of Tetrazzini'.[48]

Modern promotional materials were problematic in terms of cultural categorisation because they actively worked against the establishment of clear hierarchies within the listener's own mind. That is to say, extravagant publicity reports about singers misled the public and made it more difficult for them to distinguish between what was artistically good and bad. As some highbrow critics observed, there was a public that was totally naïve and susceptible to being influenced by irresponsible advertising. For the modernist composer Kaikhosru Sorabji, who despised what he regarded as the vulgarity of the masses, it was understandable 'that the "uncooked" . . . who absorb their opinions as they do their food, with complete lack of taste, discernment, intelligence, or even a moderate amount of rationality, should believe and hear what they are told to hear'.[49] Insofar as members of the serious musical establishment were concerned, the problem was largely attributable to a divorce in the press between specialist arts columns and the more general arts news pages, usually written by sub-editors who lacked the expertise to write knowledgeably about music.[50] (Precisely the same divide continues to exist in the broadsheet press today.) The public couldn't tell the difference between an error-ridden 'news story' written by a press agent and a serious review written by a professional critic.[51] Newman called in 1920 for a thoroughgoing overhaul of music criticism, insisting that in this

47. Luisa Tetrazzini, *My Life of Song* (London, New York, Toronto, and Melbourne: Cassell, 1921), p. 209.

48. 'Feste', 'Interludes', *MT*, 60/921 (1 November 1919), 600–2, 601. Figaro noted the success with which Tetrazzini —who was, he argued, years past her vocal best —was 'borne triumphantly on the wings of her press agents' vivid imagination'. Figaro, 'The Operatic World' *MO*, 46/541 (October 1922), 33.

49. Sorabji, 'Galli-Curci Mania', 32. Scaife ('British Music Criticism in a New Era', p. 34) describes Sorabji as 'a composer-critic who firmly believed in the aristocratic principle'.

50. Figaro, 'The Operatic World', *MO*, 49/586 (July 1926), 993–5, 995.

51. Figaro, 'The Operatic World', *MO*, 49/578 (November 1925), 137–8, 138.

field, as in others 'the only people who have a right to talk on a specialised subject are the specialists'.[52] But gatekeeping of this kind was no longer really possible in an era of mass media, with its countless diverse types of musical publication. Such cries would nevertheless continue to echo on down the decades, of course, reaching a crisis of anxiety about critical 'authority' in the free-for-all of the internet age.

It was the focus upon irrelevant and often entirely banal non-musical anecdotes in promotional materials that particularly vexed highbrow commentators. Figaro wondered at the numerous press stories about Tetrazzini's 'attempts to reduce her weight, her cooking, her housekeeping and her dusting, and above all her amazing geniality of spirits'.[53] Similarly, a great deal of space was devoted to Amelita Galli-Curci's interests and pursuits, both before and during her visit to London in 1924, in what Sorabji called 'a press-boosting campaign of, perhaps, unprecedented extent and duration and surely unprecedented offensiveness and vulgarity'.[54] Tabloid newspapers such as *The Daily Mirror* published numerous pictures of her during her British visit, engaged in such pursuits as carving her initials into the trunk of a tree in a London park for posterity.[55]

Singers were not always in control of their own image, but Galli-Curci is an example of a singer managing to exploit the media adeptly to her own ends. Figaro—with some sarcasm—depicted her as the author of her own promotional narrative (see Figure 6.2), writing: 'Galli-Curci may be a great soprano: they say she is coming in October, but the Galli-Curci I love is the journalist who is apparently already here—a supreme mistress of the English language and of the art of getting her "Copy" past critical editors. G-C may earn a mere £5,000 or so by an hour or two of concert work in America, but she is never too busy to sit down and start "banging the buttons" (as they call type-writing in the USA) while thumbing a dictionary of synonyms and antonyms'.[56] Ironically, Galli-Curci made great play of the fact that she was keen not to reveal too much about herself, telling *Opera* magazine that 'All of a singer's ideas and opinions should not be aired. And the only way she may be assured of immunity from haphazard broadcasting of her views is to refrain from making confidants'.[57] Such false modesty and feigned humility was, of course, all part of the spin.

52. Ernest Newman, 'First Aid for Critics', *The Sunday Times*, 14 November 1920, in Ernest Newman, *More Essays From The World of Music: Essays from The Sunday Times Selected by Felix Aprahamian* (London: John Calder, 1958), p. 145.

53. Figaro, 'The Operatic World', *MO*, 46/541 (October 1922), 33.

54. Kaikhosru Sorabji, 'Galli-Curci Mania', *MNH*, 68/1711 (10 January 1925), 32–3, 32.

55. *The Daily Mirror*, 10 October 1924, 12.

56. Figaro, 'The Operatic World', *MO*, 48/565 (October 1924), 31–2, 31.

57. Amelita Galli-Curci, 'Thoughts on Facing a London Audience', *Opera and the Ballet*, 2/8 (autumn 1924), 28.

Figure 6.2 Amelita Galli-Curci typing (date unknown). George Grantham Bain Collection (Library of Congress)/Wikimedia Commons. No permission needed.

Once Galli-Curci arrived, Figaro speculated about whether over-exposure could have backfired, leading to boredom on the part of readers and potential audience members. Galli-Curci had lost all mystique, and was allowing herself to be exploited in much the same manner as a rather down-market drink: 'She has seemingly taken up a permanent position in the columns along with announcements of "Nicholson's Gin", and we feel that we no longer wish to hear her sing, any more than we wish to hear our dear sister Jane thump the piano'.[58] Galli-Curci's concerts were poorly received

58. Figaro, 'The Operatic World', *MO*, 48/566 (November 1924), 143–4, 144.

in the event, and Basil Maine argued that the heralding of her as though she were a film star had done her no favours. He argued that the hype had prejudiced the critics against Galli-Curci, who were 'revolted by this shameless-ness' and came to the Albert Hall with pens poised ready to fix upon and magnify every little imperfection.[59] It was possible, therefore, for singers to be sabotaged by their managers' ever more creative publicity efforts.

The 1920s was a boom era for the publication of singer autobiographies— some of them ghostwritten and highly unreliable—both by stars of the 'golden age' and by new stars.[60] Such publications were a strategic form of promotion. Tetrazzini's arrival in Britain in 1921 was timed to coincide with the publication of her autobiography, *My Life of Song*, bringing a flood of publicity.[61] Sections of her book were, for instance, serialised in *The Strand Magazine*, prefaced by an audaciously hyperbolic foreword, calling her 'the greatest living soprano' and boasting that 'wherever she has gone she has been publicly feted and lionized as one of those divine songstresses who appear but once in a century'.[62] The foreword not only hyped Tetrazzini's musical significance and lineage (including an anecdote in which Adelina Patti had supposedly declared her to be her successor) but boasted of her adventures all over the world, her meetings with royalty, and her earnings of more than a million pounds. Stereotypical diva behaviour was hinted at, with references to spats with impresarios and managers, and enmities and jealousies that had been aroused by her 'astonishing successes'.

Once again we find a connection with popular fiction: Tetrazzini's 'literary adviser'—presumably her ghostwriter—was A. J. Russell, who wrote serialised short stories for *The Daily Mirror*, including some on an operatic theme ('The Mystery Husband', for example, was about an impresario). *The Strand* itself was a mass-market general-interest magazine, full of adverts for products such as Bovril and cigarettes, which published popular fiction in short, easily digestible chunks.[63] The excerpts from Tetrazzini's book were accompanied by romanticised pen and ink illustrations suggestive of high drama, similar to those used throughout this popular fiction magazine

---

59. Basil Maine, 'Galli-Curci: An Appreciation', *MT*, 66/983 (1 January 1925), 35–6, 35. Maine himself believed that the critics had seriously underestimated Galli-Curci and that her voice was clear, smooth, and sweet throughout its range (p. 36).

60. See Nellie Melba, *Melodies and Memories* (London: Butterworth, 1925); Luisa Tetrazzini, *My Life of Song* (London: Cassell, 1921); Blanche Marchesi, *Singer's Pilgrimage* (London: Grant Richards, 1923); Jeritza, *Sunshine and Song*.

61. Anon, 'Tetrazzini's Publicity', *MNH*, 61/1539 (24 September 1921), 305.

62. Luisa Tetrazzini, 'My Life of Song', *The Strand Magazine*, 61/364 (April 1921), 330–40, 330.

63. For further reading on *The Strand*, see Mike Ashley, *The Age of the Storytellers: British Popular Fiction Magazines 1880–1950* (London: The British Library and Oak Knoll Press, 2006), pp. 10–11.

for short stories by bestselling novelists of the day. Memoir was thus presented as genre fiction, and the publisher of the autobiography played up the 'adventure' angle in its promotional material, stating in an advert in *The Bookman* that 'Madame Tetrazzini has had innumerable adventures in all parts of the globe, and here she tells in racy language, full of quiet humour, the fascinating story of her amazing career as an international prima donna'.[64] The book was widely panned: it offered plenty of fodder for the gossip columns but was of negligible importance either as a piece of biography or of music history.[65]

Tetrazzini's autobiography also exposes the way in which singers were being used to promote a vast array of commercial products. She wrote of turning down invitations to endorse voice pastilles, cold cures, face cream, and cigarettes but reckoned that 'if I had agreed to the propositions that were made to me by business houses at that time my name and photograph would have figured in most of the advertisements of that day'.[66] In fact, Tetrazzini did not turn them all down—her name appeared regularly on advertisements for such products as Pond's Vanishing Cream and Amplion Wireless Loudspeakers that appeared in populist publications like *The Daily Mirror*.

Promoting commercial products was testimony to the status prominent international singers held as full-blown celebrities. It is, of course, a practice that has endured to the present. The difference, however, is that today's leading singers are typically hired to promote luxury goods in advertisements that will appear either in upmarket magazines or in specialist publications such as opera house programmes; they are rarely deemed recognisable enough to feature in mass-market publications. Rolex, in particular, has used opera singers, including Plácido Domingo, Cecilia Bartoli, Renée Fleming, and Jonas Kaufmann, to act as 'ambassadors' for its watches (as well as leading figures from the world of sport such as David Beckham and Roger Federer). During the 1920s, however, opera singers were not used merely to promote objects associated with 'class' but a much wider variety of everyday goods, in a more diverse range of publications.

As well as promoting products, which undermined their claim to being considered serious artists, singers of the 1920s were themselves becoming commodities. In a study of contemporary film, Ernest Betts observed that the cinematograph had swiftly become a 'sound article of commerce', which had been swiftly exploited 'like a new soap or cheese or prima donna or

64. Advertisement for The House of Cassell, *The Bookman* (October 1921), 45.

65. See, for example, Anon., 'A Singer's Memories', *The Saturday Review* (22 October 1921), 488–9.

66. Tetrazzini, 'My Life of Song', pp. 212, 213.

political war-cry by men with cigars and limousines and no time to waste'.[67] According to this reading, the star singer was a product to be sold, no different from a new soap, and this commodification clearly, in the eyes of the highbrows, disturbed any claim that opera might be classified as high art.

Recordings, it goes without saying, acted as a vital form of self-promotion for singers, together with the publicity that went with them through new specialist magazines such as *Gramophone*. A visit to a recording studio by a first-rank celebrity singer was very much an event: according to an anonymous studio official, such occasions 'demanded a certain amount of ceremony, and were more or less in the nature of a reception'.[68] And the flashier and more virtuosic the recording the better. Writing about the rash of recordings by popular prima donnas in 1924, Herman Klein noted: 'The more dazzling the "fireworks" the better the record seems to sell. The loftier the flights of scales, arpeggios, and cadenzas into the *altissimo* region, the stronger the fascination seems to grow'.[69] But again, the gramophone record was a promotional tool that could backfire in unexpected ways. Such was the perfection of Galli-Curci's studio recordings—the products, as audiences clearly did not yet really understand, of multiple takes—and the hype with which she had been billed that when she sang live in concert at the vast and acoustically unforgiving Albert Hall in 1924, only disappointment could result.[70]

Galli-Curci was also often characterised as a sort of automaton, her rise to prominence through recordings and her media-savvy manger having undermined her credibility. Sorabji, for example, wrote 'This singer is mechanical and perfunctory—everything seems sung by rote, lifeless, without either a distinction or charm—and one has the feeling of listening to some very marvellous marionette made vocal'.[71] Figaro, similarly, expressed distaste at the fact that 'we are now in an era when reputations may be, to some extent, what may be called "machine-made"'.[72] This idea of the modern creation

67. Ernest Betts, *Heraclitus, or the Future of Films* (London: Kegan Paul, Trench, Trubner, and Co. Ltd./New York: E. P. Dutton & Co., 1928), p. 13.

68. A Studio Official, 'Secrets of the Recording Room: Fads and Foibles of Famous Artists', *MM*, 9 (January 1929), 5–28, 5.

69. Herman Klein, 'The Gramophone and the Singer', *The Gramophone*, 2/2 (July 1924), 40–3, 40.

70. I discuss this further in Alexandra Wilson, 'Galli-Curci Comes to Town: The Prima Donna's Presence in the Age of Mechanical Reproduction', in Cowgill and Poriss (Eds.), *The Arts of the Prima Donna*, 328–48.

71. Sorabji, 'Galli-Curci Mania', 32.

72. Figaro, 'The Operatic World', *MO*, 51/602 (November 1927), 143–4, 143. For further reading on references during the 1920s to mechanical prima donnas, see Alexandra Wilson, 'Modernism and the Machine Woman in Puccini's *Turandot*', *Music & Letters*, 86/3 (2005), 432–51.

of both artificial voices—particular voices that were well adapted to the new recording medium—and artificial public personae is important. At the heart of the anxiety about star singers lay a crucial distinction between singers who were considered to be genuine artists and those whose fame had been fabricated. (The same debate, of course, plays out today about 'authentic' rock stars versus commercial pop bands.) Highbrow commentators did not loathe *all* opera singers, or even all foreign singers, then. They recognised that there were many genuinely talented and modest singers who were being overlooked because they tended not to seek out opportunities to market themselves via the new advertising methods or were less adept at it.[73] It was, emphatically, the capricious star singer who was the problem.

A 'THING APART'

The focus upon singers' daily lives and personal habits was a popularising ploy to erase the distance between them and the reader, a tactic that has been used from the earliest days of mass journalism to the present and that endeared singers to a wide range of readers. Yet sometimes the popular press caricatured opera stars in such a way as to emphasise the notion of opera as 'a thing apart', and to a certain extent this contributed to the public perception that it was too highbrow. Of course, the star's special talents, their ability to do something beyond the capabilities of the man in the street, have—at least until the age of reality TV—been a key strategy of celebrity formation. However, in the case of opera, the perceived 'difference' of the opera singer had, by the interwar period, become simultaneously a selling point and something that aroused hostility and suspicion. The impulsive prima donna was a stereotype of popular culture who popped up in an array of music hall parodies and popular plays, such as Gilda Varesi's and Dolly Byrne's *Enter Madame*, performed at the Royalty Theatre in 1922. The play, which had transferred from Broadway and would also be made into a silent film, charted the relationship of a couple whose marriage was at breaking point because 'The wife is an opera singer, full of the whims and caprices which stage tradition assigns to the prima donna; the husband has grown tired of playing second fiddle to "Madame"'.[74]

---

73. Figaro admired the 'mighty performance' by Frida Leider in a much praised production of *Götterdämmerung* at Covent Garden in 1926, observing that 'Certainly, she is the most considerable of the German singers in the company, and easily the poorest in the matter of press publicity'. Figaro, 'The Operatic World', *MO*, 49/586 (July 1926), 993–5, 993.

74. Anon., 'The Playhouses', *ILN*, 25 February 1922, 272.

Josephine O'Donnell, reflecting upon her period working as secretary to Colonel Blois at Covent Garden from 1925, noted that the press wrote with monotonous regularity about the whims and eccentricities of star singers, to the extent that 'the notion that they are something of a race apart has developed almost into an article of belief'.[75] She conceded that some singers had unusual personalities, erratic tempers, and 'original manners'—surely code for the rumours of diva-like behaviour that still circulate around certain high-profile singers today—but asserted that most were quiet, polite, sensible, and hard-working. O'Donnell explained that it was imperative for singers to adhere to a straight and narrow lifestyle, ostensibly for the good health of their voices, although one detects behind this statement an attempt to defend singers against a long-standing suspicion of theatrical types as being of dubious morality.[76]

Periodicals that represented opera companies, such as the BNOC's *Opera* magazine, emphasised singers' credentials as ordinary, hard-working people, again trying to maximise their appeal to the mass market. And even the starriest of names were at pains to promote themselves in similar terms, playing into an enduring Victorian value system that positioned hard work as an indicator of good morals. Tetrazzini, for example, advised the aspiring singer to follow the maxims 'Work! Work! Work!' and 'Faith, Hope, and Charity'.[77] Singers continued the long tradition of using their autobiographies to demonstrate their respectability and philanthropic work.[78] This was also the forum in which to assert one's traditional feminine virtues: Jeritza, for example, waxed lyrical in her autobiography about how much she preferred cooking to playing 'a horrible character in an ultramodern opera'.[79] Such claims to good character were somewhat undermined in Jeritza's case by her reputation as a temperamental diva of the worst sort. Much publicity was given in 1925, for instance, to a fracas in Vienna where she had been talking so loudly and insultingly in the wings about the private life of her co-star, Maria Olczewska, that the latter spat at her from the stage, missing and hitting another member of the cast.[80] All of this personal trivia,

75. Josephine O'Donnell, *Among the Covent Garden Stars* (London: Stanley Paul, 1936), p. 9.
76. Ibid., p. 10.
77. Luisa Tetrazzini, *How to Sing* (London: C. Arthur Pearson, 1923), p. 20.
78. For further reading on the tradition of singer philanthropy, see Hilary Poriss, 'Prima Donnas and the Performance of Altruism', in Cowgill and Poriss (Eds.), *The Arts of the Prima Donna*, pp. 42–60.
79. Jeritza, *Sunshine and Song*, p. 181. For further reading, see Alexandra Wilson, 'Prima Donnas or Working Girls? Opera Singers as Female Role Models in Britain, 1900–1925', *Women's History Magazine*, 55 (2007), 4–12.
80. Our own correspondent, 'Prima Donna Dismissed For Spitting at Mme Jeritza', *The Daily Mail*, 15 May 1925, 9.

entertaining as it was for readers, further served to undermine the case of such singers as serious musicians.

Other sectors of the press were quick to seize upon examples of singers whose habits were not respectable, although such singers tended not to be found among the first rank. Here journalists tapped into a long-standing British suspicion of theatrical types as morally suspect. The drunken prima donna who indulged in much performer licence became a particular trope: a drunken Lancashire-Irish leading lady with a fatal liking for Irish whiskey who sang with the J. W. Turner Company, for instance, or a British soprano who, having drunk several foaming tankards of beer during a rehearsal of *Faust*, announced that she would cling to a cross in the final scene while singing 'Abide with me'.[81] Foreign singers' colourful private lives were also subject to much disparaging public comment, such as Luisa Tetrazzini's brief marriage to a much younger man of lower social status: Pietro Vernati (32 to her 53), the son of a linen draper. In April 1929 *The Musical Mirror* reported her honeymoon in London, only to announce three months later that she had been granted a separation on the grounds of 'incompatibility of temperament and interests'.[82]

But if the 'apartness' of musicians was something that was regarded with suspicion by guardians of public respectability, there is no denying that it was simultaneously a selling point for audience members or potential audience members. The public didn't want opera stars to be 'just like us': they wanted them to be exotic, glamorous, different, both in habits and in terms of physical appearance. Jennifer R. Sheppard has argued that it was becoming imperative around the turn of the century—at a time when the Wilde trial provoked a fear of artistic decadence—for male musicians to cast off any suggestion of bizarre dress or effeminacy and to take an interest in outdoor activities and exercise.[83] And yet it would appear that by the 1920s, stereotypes about singers' eccentricities of appearance lingered on, and were even taking on positive connotations as personal 'branding' became central to the new advertising methods of the age.[84] The fact that the

---

81. Cecil, *The History of Opera in England*, pp. 3–4; Anon., 'Operatic diehards: heroes and heroines who sing pages when they are supposed to be dead', *MM*, 5/3 (March 1925), 48. On James Turner's operatic troupe, which toured from 1886, see Rodmell, *Opera in the British Isles*, pp. 136–7.

82. Piacevole, 'Heard in the interval', *MM*, 9/4 (April 1929), 87; Anon., 'Tetrazzini separated', *MM*, 9/7 (July 1929), 172.

83. Sheppard, 'Sound of Body', 363.

84. In a 1925 study of school music, schoolmaster Thomas Wood explained that it was important to alert children early to the fact that 'music has suffered too long from a public which imagines that an artist to be great must be eccentric, and from performers who imagine that they must be eccentric to please the public; and that both parties in their stupidity disregard good taste'. Thomas Wood, *Music and Boyhood: Some Suggestions on the Possibilities of Music*

new stars of popular culture had an instantly recognisable look was making it ever more important for increasingly publicity-savvy musicians to follow suit. The middlebrow, gossip-mongering *Musical Mirror*, for example, observed that long hair was the virtuoso musician's 'familiar trade mark'. Audiences would feel short-changed if he cut it because 'The long hair of a virtuoso is as much the property of the public as Charlie Chaplin's bowler hat'.[85]

During the late Victorian and the Edwardian era, certain star sopranos had consciously created an aura of glamour that set them apart from everyday life. Landon Ronald, who was Nellie Melba's accompanist for fourteen years, wrote that 'To those who are not in the habit of travelling with Royalty, a short tour with a famous prima donna is strongly recommended as the next best thing!'[86] Such a tour was characterised by huge crowds, thunderous applause, autograph hunters, and a great deal of sycophancy from polite officials, policemen, and hotel servants. The association of star singers with luxury and great wealth persisted during the 1920s, and some were keen to emphasise an ongoing association with royalty, as seen, for instance, in a chapter in Jeritza's autobiography entitled 'The Hapsburgs as I knew them', which contained anecdotes about eating iced cakes with archduchesses after performances at the Hofoper.[87] Jeritza set herself on a plane with aristocrats, playing upon the title she had acquired upon marriage (Baroness Popper) and arriving in London with an entourage of servants and pets.[88]

The high sums that star singers were paid in comparison with jobbing singers naturally compromised their status as real artists in the eyes of the highbrows. Wild rumours abounded of celebrity singers' fees that seemed to go up by the month.[89] The tabloids were fixated on star singers' pay, but

---

in *Public, Preparatory and other Schools* (Oxford/London: Oxford University Press/Humphrey Milton, 1925), p. 29.

85. Symphonicus, 'Heard in the Interval', *MM*, 2/11 (November 1922), 325. In an article in the same periodical in April 1924, however, the Austrian operetta composer Leo Fall advised musicians to do precisely the opposite. First in his list of ten tips for getting rich quick in music was 'If you have long hair, have it cut!' Leo Fall, 'How to Get Rich Quick on Music', *MM*, 4/4 (April 1924), 64.

86. Landon Ronald, *Variations on a Personal Theme* (Toronto, London, and New York: Hodder and Stoughton, 1922), p. 53.

87. Jeritza, *Sunshine and Song*, p. 95.

88. Phillips-Matz, *Rosa Ponselle*, p. 235.

89. On Galli-Curci's concert fees, see Anon., 'Heard in the Interval', *MM*, 4/3 (March 1924), 43; Cover, *MM*, 4/11 (November 1924); Figaro, 'The Operatic World', *MO*, 47/560 (May 1924), 785–6, 785. For operatic performances proper, Rosa Ponselle was paid $9,800 for seven performances (two in *Norma*, two in *L'amore dei tre re*, three in *La traviata*) in 1929–30. Mary Jane Phillips-Matz, *Rosa Ponselle: American Diva* (Boston: Northeastern University Press, 1997), p. 234. A letter to Ponselle from Blois stated: 'I am sure, dear Rosa, that we are paying

were also, interestingly, the least critical of it. For them, it was just another type of sensational story, a way to garner interest and sell papers. So far as the more serious music commentators were concerned, the attention paid by the tabloids and by popular music magazines to singers' wealth rather than anything remotely artistic was, in itself, an embarrassment. But in fact the more serious publications were in a sense *more* exercised about the issue of foreign singers working in Britain and being well paid for it, precisely because they cared more about stimulating British musical activity than the popular press did.

Reports of the high earnings and extravagant lifestyles of a small number of celebrity singers were met by the general public with a complex mixture of fascination and resentment (yet did not compromise the performers' perceived artistry). Figaro argued that the public was fascinated by star singers for the same reason that it enjoyed reading gossip columns about high society or novels about dukes and duchesses: because it seemed glamorous.[90] Moreover, some members of the opera audience actually took pride in singers being paid better than, say, music hall artists, because this seemed to legitimise their own superior taste. But if there was a certain appeal to the idea of the wealthy singer, so too was there a romance to the idea of the starving artist in the garret, whose poverty enhanced his or her artistic integrity. *Musical Opinion* reported in 1922 that musicians were struggling to afford both concert dress and food: 'The average man or woman who attends an occasional concert or opera performance has no conception of the straits to which music artists have been reduced.'[91]

THE CELEBRITY CONCERT

For those few singers with a high enough profile there was a quick buck to be made from the celebrity concert, a phenomenon that anticipated what we would call the 'crossover' repertoire today and was often held up by more anxious members of the musical establishment as evidence of the moribund state of British musical culture.[92] Some stars were increasingly

you more than we ever paid anybody, except Chaliapin; but I know the expense you are put to in coming here'.

90. Figaro, 'The Operatic World', MO, 47/560 (May 1924), 785–6, 785. Sean Latham observes that by the turn of the twentieth century 'the English middle classes had long been obsessed with the fashions and manners of the aristocracy'. Sean Latham, *Am I a Snob? Modernism and the Novel* (Cornell: Cornell University Press, 2003), p. 44.

91. A. Corbett-Smith, 'Stop Tinkering!', MO, 45/538 (July 1922), 853–4, 853.

92. See, for example, H., 'Music: the Better Way', *The Saturday Review*, 143/3721 (19 February 1927), 271.

to be found gravitating away from Covent Garden and towards the concert hall, which placed fewer demands upon them and did not require them to share the stage with any potential rivals. Eric Blom revealed that the same singer was capable of taking on two completely different guises, depending upon whether he or she was performing in an opera or singing in a concert. Recalling attending Melba's farewell performances at Covent Garden and the Royal Albert Hall, he wrote that he had come away from the first 'as arrant a sentimentalist as anybody' but was left cold by the second, which he saw as having no artistic value.[93] In the concert hall one was presented with the celebrity rather than the artist: 'at Covent Garden we heard Melba, at the Albert Hall only Dame Nellie'.

Blom's comments need to be placed within the context of a more widespread highbrow snobbery about the Royal Albert Hall, home of boxing matches and balls.[94] This venue was widely loathed on acoustic grounds: prior to the installation of acoustic diffusers, or 'mushrooms', in the 1950s, audiences were troubled by a strange echo effect that was created by the cove of the ceiling.[95] Turner barked in 1922 that 'It is a crime against the art to perform music in such a building. It is only fit for an Armageddon of brass bands'.[96] The Albert Hall also prompted embarrassment because it had gained a reputation as the last-chance saloon of the fading star who refused to retire. Edward Dent wrote: 'To serious lovers of music it is almost always a matter of regret when famous singers or players reach that point in their career when they give concerts in the Albert Hall. No doubt it is quite possible for a great artist to remain a great artist when singing in that place, though there are probably many people who would deny this altogether'.[97] And finally, of course, the Albert Hall was suspect because it played host to a wide variety of different types of entertainment. Similarly, its present-day programme of events juxtaposes performances by the world's leading orchestras at the BBC Proms with populist 'classical spectaculars', amplified operas in the round, gigs by high-profile pop stars, and even tennis matches.

Some concerts at the Albert Hall were one-offs but others formed part of the international celebrity concert series put on in the mid-1920s by the agents Lionel Powell and Holt. Well-known foreign names—sometimes

93. Eric Blom, 'Singers' Farewells', *MNH*, 71/1791 (7 August 1926), 114–15, 115.

94. The first professional boxing tournament was staged at the Albert Hall on (appropriately) Boxing Day 1919. John B. Geale, *A Short History of the Royal Albert Hall London*, 2nd edn (London: n.p., 1949), p. 22.

95. https://www.royalalberthall.com/about-the-hall/our-history/explore-our-history/building/acoustic-diffusers-mushrooms/ (accessed 25 October 2017).

96. W. J. Turner, 'The World of Music: English Choral Singing', *ILN*, 7 January 1922, 12.

97. E. J. Dent, 'The World of Music: The Performer and the Public', *ILN*, 14 October 1922, 600–1, 601.

singers, sometimes virtuoso pianists or violinists—would embark upon extensive UK tours, covering towns and cities from Southampton to Glasgow, often with an additional leg to Dublin.[98] Richard Terry, formerly organist at Westminster Cathedral, and latterly editor of *The Musical News and Herald* and an outspoken voice against operatic stardom, set the instrumentalists apart from the singers. He argued: 'It is the vocalists—males, females, and old women of both sexes, who are the real problem. More than any other type of executant, they are petted and spoiled by a thoughtless public. Unlike instrumentalists they are not always artists'.[99] The 'thoughtless public' of which Terry despaired was to be found in its largest numbers in the north, and here we see a pronounced snobbery about the provinces and the lower middle classes. The agent Lionel Powell himself, unsurprisingly, defended these listeners, telling *The Daily News* that 'There is no doubt about the north being more musical than the south': audiences for stars such as Chaliapin, McCormack, and Tetrazzini tended to be particularly large in cities such as Liverpool, Edinburgh, and Glasgow.[100]

The repertory for the celebrity concerts was mixed, unadventurous, and not always terribly well performed. The typical programme featured a mixture of old-fashioned showy operatic arias, Victorian ballads, and popular showpieces chosen to demonstrate particular vocal 'effects'. (Galli Curci, for example, sang Henry Bishop's 'Pretty Mocking Bird' on her 1924 tour, a song that ends with an extended cadenza of cheeping and chirruping.) Such songs were well suited to the eclectic tastes of what would later be defined as middlebrow audiences, which enjoyed any music that roused a sense of wonder, whether that be serious music or—conversely—laughing choruses for brass bands, devil's tricks on the piano or violin, or semi-religious ballads.[101] Highbrow critics looked with particular disdain upon prima donnas' propensity for singing showy arias from the then highly unfashionable *bel canto* repertoire. Part of the problem with this body of

98. Powell and Holt's clients included Melba, Tetrazzini, Galli-Curci, Butt, Hempel, McCormack, Hislop, and many other singers foreign and British, together with numerous instrumentalists and conductors. Advert in Programme, Galli-Curci Recital, Alexandra Palace, 22 November 1924 [V&A Theatre and Performance Collections, performer file: Amelita Galli-Curci].

99. Anon., 'Celebrity Concerts', *MNH*, 67/1698 (11 October 1924), 306. The author pondered: 'Why wind players of international reputation should never be exploited is one of life's little mysteries which so far has eluded solution'.

100. Some northern cities such as Leeds and Sheffield were unable to afford 'expensive musical taste', owing to trade depression, but the least musical towns were undoubtedly in the south: 'Southampton, Portsmouth and other Southern towns are terrible'. Anon., 'The Most Musical Town? Liverpool, Edinburgh, and Glasgow Lead the Way in Number of Celebrity Concerts', *MM*, 5/11 (November 1925), 214.

101. 'Devana', 'The "Popular" Audience', *MM*, 2/6 (June 1922), 170.

works, so far as the highbrows were concerned, was the fact that Rossini, Bellini and Donizetti had been far too interested in playing to the crowd.[102] The singers who performed this repertory were undiscriminating crowd pleasers too: in Figaro's words, 'the coloratura has always had the power to thrill even the non-musical in a nation of fast bowlers, centre forwards, sprinters and gymnasts'.[103]

As William Weber has shown, concerts with *pot-pourri* programmes had been the norm during the eighteenth and early nineteenth centuries, but serious and less serious musics were increasingly being separated out by the mid-nineteenth century.[104] And whereas the term 'miscellaneous' had had positive connotations in the eighteenth century, it was increasingly ideologically marginalised by critics eager to 'shore up their newly claimed professional authority'.[105] The drive towards specialised types of concerts continued in the early twentieth century. By the 1920s, what we might call 'pick-and-mix' concerts were therefore also problematic from the highbrow perspective because they were old-fashioned in format: an embarrassing throwback to Victorian tastes.[106]

Celebrity concerts, then, were distinctly middlebrow, arguably even verging on the lowbrow at times. The promotional tactics that celebrity singers used in this context, the hybrid repertory that they sang, and their tendency to milk the audience for applause blurred the boundaries with other sorts of entertainment.[107] Pick-and-mix concerts were reminiscent of the eclectic array of acts performed in the music halls and the new variety halls. Indeed, one of the reasons why the operatic star system was so reviled by early twentieth-century highbrows is because the music hall also had its own star system from the 1860s onwards.[108] Several critics suggested explicitly that Galli-Curci ought to be performing in the music hall when she visited in 1924. After seeing promotional pictures of her nursing a lamb while picking flowers in Hyde Park, Figaro proposed that audiences would rather see her as a rustic music-hall turn, milking a cow and chasing

102. Eric H. Thimann wrote that 'Rossini, Donizetti and Bellini all worked hard to produce exactly what the public wanted, and also perhaps to give our prima donnas and queens of song something to sing nowadays when they fill the Albert Hall'. Eric H. Thimann, 'The Growth of Opera (Part 2)', *MM*, 4/12 (December 1924), 229–30, 229.

103. Figaro, 'The Operatic World', *MO*, 48/569 (February 1925), 478–9, 478.

104. William Weber, *The Great Transformation of Musical Taste: Concert Programming from Haydn to Brahms* (Cambridge: Cambridge University Press, 2008), pp. 1, 35.

105. Ibid., p. 14, 103.

106. For further reading on the problem of mixed programmes, see Tunbridge, 'Frieda Hempel and the Historical Imagination', 440–1 and 443–5.

107. 'To the critically minded, this aggressive "platform manner" is odious; but the general public evidently loves it'. Edward J. Dent, 'The World of Music', *ILN*, 30 December 1922, 1084.

108. Scott, *Sounds of the Metropolis*, p. 35.

chickens, than they would as a performer in grand opera.[109] And Terry, also writing about Galli-Curci, argued that 'Your trick vocalist has a fine commodity for sale—his or her vocal tricks. His or her proper sphere is therefore the music-hall'.[110] Diverting the star singer to the music hall made good economic sense: singers would be paid equally high salaries but the bill would be picked up by the music halls, leaving opportunities open in concert halls for 'real' musicians.

Celebrity singers were castigated not only by highbrow critics antipathetic to opera per se such as Grace and Terry but by others including Figaro, Edward Dent, and Herman Klein, who were enthusiastic about opera within its proper context of the opera house but objected to virtuosity for virtuosity's sake. Serious critics routinely drew analogies between celebrity singers and circus acts or even performing animals, dismissing them for performing 'vocal trapeze acts',[111] for being 'capering creatures of no more importance in the scheme of musical affairs than performing Pomeranian pups',[112] and for appealing to an audience incapable of distinguishing an opera singer from a conjurer.[113] Celebrity concerts were problematic because they were all about spectacle, a spectacle that audiences were only too happy to lap up.

Such concerts were also held responsible for attracting and encouraging the sort of listener who did not really know how to listen 'properly', something for which the celebrity did not care a jot, since they came to Britain to 'seek a crowd, irrespective of its nature'.[114] Serious music critics derided the audience for celebrity concerts as well as the stars themselves. It is striking that some went so far as to use the word 'mob'—a highly loaded term. Terry, for instance, declared that celebrity singers 'set the mob agape' with their vocal 'stunts'.[115] The late nineteenth-century fear of crowd psychology was still current in the interwar period—witness the popularity in Britain of Gustave Le Bon's study of the subject, *The Crowd*, which had been reprinted twelve times by 1920—but the terminology was changing somewhat.[116] The nineteenth-century concept of the mob was tending to

109. Figaro, 'The Operatic World', *MO*, 48/566 (November 1924), 143–4, 144.

110. Anon., 'Celebrity Concerts', 306.

111. Figaro, for instance, noted that Tetrazzini had been succeeded by many 'rivals in the line of vocal trapeze acts', citing Hempel, Bossetti, Pareto, Mabel Garrison, and Galli-Curci. Figaro, 'The Operatic World' *MO*, 46/541 (October 1922), 33. Frieda Hempel was also likened to a circus artist or music hall performer, as discussed in further detail in Laura Tunbridge, 'Frieda Hempel and the Historical Imagination', *Journal of the American Musicological Society*, 66/2 (2013), 437–74, 465.

112. Anon., 'Half a Million for Opera!', *MNH*, 69/1755 (14 November 1925), 437–8, 437.

113. Edward J. Dent, 'The World of Music', *ILN*, 30 December 1922, 1084.

114. Anon., 'Half a Million for Opera!', *MNH*, 69/1755 (14 November 1925), 437–8, 437.

115. Anon., 'Celebrity Concerts', *MNH*, 67/1698 (11 October 1924), 306.

116. LeMahieu, *A Culture for Democracy*, p. 108.

be replaced in the early twentieth century by the term 'mass', the difference between the two being literacy: the mass was literate where the mob was wild, unruly, and illiterate.[117] Terry therefore reduces the audience for celebrity concerts to pre-literate levels, while Dent's reference to the popular audience's 'herd instincts' renders them little better than cattle.[118] That said—and not insignificantly in this context of discussing opera's closeness to popular culture—the idea of the 'frenzied mob' was a stereotype that would remain current throughout much of the twentieth century within the context of film fandom.[119] It is hard to ignore a certain degree of class snobbery here, similar to that discussed earlier (see Chapter 3) in the context of fragmented listening.

To conclude, the hostility towards star singers from highbrow commentators was motivated by many factors: their overt commercialisation and readiness to allow themselves to be commodified, their prioritisation of personality over artistry, and their old-fashioned concerts that blurred the boundaries with various forms of popular culture and pleased the unsophisticated crowd. At the same time, anxieties about star singers' 'foreignness' cropped up again and again: as ever, concerns about the brows and concerns about identity politics went hand in hand, as I shall explore in greater detail in the next chapter. Many commentators expressed concern about the fact that foreign star singers were 'over here' while many British musicians were 'over there', forced through lack of job opportunities to seek out work on the continent. This was a point that was expressed not only by the populist press but by musicians themselves, most notably Landon Ronald, who as Principal of the Guildhall School had a vested interest in protecting the interests of home-grown singers.[120] Star singers, moreover, were widely perceived to be draining money away from local musical enterprise. There is a marked sense throughout this period of there being a finite audience for music and a finite amount of money to be spent on concerts.[121] Anecdotes abounded of towns that had previously been rich in musical activity, with local choral societies, flourishing amateur orchestras, and lively church choirs, all now declining as local audiences handed their money

117. Carey, *The Intellectuals and the Masses*, p. 5.

118. 'This behaviour is due largely to *herd instinct*, and to a pleasure which certain types of mind derive from being in a crowd and doing what the crowd does'. Dent, 'The World of Music', *ILN*, 30 December 1922, 1084.

119. Samantha Barbas, *Movie Crazy: Fans, Stars, and the Cult of Celebrity* (New York and Basingstoke: Palgrave, 2001), p. 3.

120. Landon Ronald, *Myself and Others: Written Lest I Forget* (London: Sampson Low, Marston & Co., 1931), pp. 200–1.

121. Ibid., p. 166.

over to celebrity concerts.[122] Richard Terry went so far as to liken celebrity 'raids' on provincial towns to a flight of locusts, crippling local musical activity to devastating effect.[123]

There was, furthermore, widespread disapproval from critics about the fact that audiences would flock to hear musicians whether or not they were talented, simply on the basis that they had foreign names.[124] *The Musical Mirror* commented in 1928: 'The truth is that the fetish of a foreign reputation still finds its worshippers here, regardless of merit, and provided a singer has a non-British name, he is greeted with frantic applause, and his shouting and his tremolo are hailed as singing with dramatic intensity. Perhaps one of these days we shall know better.'[125] Singers with British names, in comparison, suffered, and there was still a perception that a British name was a handicap. Occasionally, singers adopted quasi-foreign stage names, a by then old-fashioned practice that had been common during the 1870s.[126] The Australian singer Elsa Fischer was introduced to British audiences in 1919 as having adopted the alias Elsa Stralia, a tribute to her motherland but also a name that sounded vaguely Italian.[127] And Thomas Beecham contrived to point out the hypocrisy of audiences by promoting a new star called Lisa Perli—generating great excitement—who turned out in the event to be a British singer by the name of Dora Labbette, with whom he was having an affair. Figaro, with tongue only half in cheek, warned that the policy was still advisable: 'the advice to all who contemplate opera as a profession today must be ... either change your name to something with a very foreign sound and graduate in Italy, or,—sell soap over the counter of a grocer's shop'.[128] It was of course paradoxical that the press was often hostile towards 'greedy' foreign performers yet the public and tabloids expected performers to 'act foreign' by, as noted above, adopting an exotic look. But this was just one of many contradictions in the complicated, nationalistically fraught relationship between 1920s Britons and opera.

122. See, for instance, Da Capo, 'Celebrity Concerts', *MNH*, 67/1696 (27 September 1924), 257.

123. Anon., 'Celebrity Concerts', *MNH*, 67/1698 (11 October 1924), 306.

124. See, for instance, Anon., 'The Foreign Name Mania', *MM*, 2/11 (November 1922), 332.

125. Anon., 'Music Today: Our English Singers', *MM*, 8/7 (July 1928), 169.

126. Rodmell, *Opera in the British Isles*, p. 8.

127. Anon, 'Biographies of the artists', Royal Opera, Covent Garden, *Stories of the Operas and the Singers*, Official Souvenir, Season 1919, pp. 85–104, p. 86.

128. Figaro, 'The Operatic World' *MO*, 46/552 (September 1923), 1128–9, 1128.

CHAPTER 7

❧

Identities

It all came down, in the final assessment, to a conversation about identity.[1] Arguments in the 1920s about cultural categorisation—whether these applied to opera, literature, or any other field—were underpinned by competing visions of what it meant to be British. By the end of the decade there were still many commentators who believed opera's cause—or even music's cause—in Britain to be hopeless. In his 1930 history of opera in English, for instance, George Cecil wrote: 'In the proper sense of the word, England is not musical, for the affections of those who are by way of "liking music" usually are set upon unmusical rubbish'.[2] However, those who genuinely believed there to be a large potential audience for opera invested time, energy, and funds in concerted publicity campaigns for the art form, even if some expressed concern at attempts to promote opera using modern advertising methods.[3]

---

1. The section of this chapter concerning Thomas Beecham and the Imperial League of Opera reuses some material from Alexandra Wilson, 'Gender', in Helen Greenwald (Ed.), *The Oxford Handbook of Opera* (New York: Oxford University Press, 2014), pp. 774–94, reproduced by permission of Oxford University Press, https://global.oup.com/academic/product/the-oxford-handbook-of-opera-9780195335538?cc=gb&lang=en&.

2. Capt. George Cecil, *The History of Opera in English* (Taunton: Barnicott and Pearce, the Wessex Press, 1930), p. 1. Cecil was dismissive about the working- and middle-class taste for musical comedy and claimed that the well-to-do members of the opera audience didn't understand what they were listening to.

3. See W. J. Turner in *Variations on the Theme of Music* (London: Heinemann, 1924), pp. 74–5. Percy Colson complained that the rhetoric employed in a National Opera Trust circular campaigning for money in 1926 was unequalled in 'blatant vulgarity' and that while it might have been effective for selling cheap toothpaste, it would discourage potential subscribers of 'the cultivated class'. Percy Colson, 'Music News and Notes', in R. Sydney Glover (Ed.), *Apollo: A Journal of the Arts, Vol 3 January to June 1926* (Nendeln, Liechtenstein: Kraus Reprint, 1976), 121–2, 121.

Many commentators of the 1920s argued that opera was something that a civilised nation ought to be promoting, drawing particular comparison with the vibrant operatic culture in Germany, where the art form was generously supported by the state. The image of England as a utilitarian nation of shopkeepers—in contrast with Germany as a land of culture—was widely entrenched in Britain by this time.[4] Writing to *The Times* in support of the proposed British opera subsidy in 1930, Ralph Vaughan Williams argued that 'music as well as the other arts is not a luxury but a necessity of life, and is as vital to the well-being of the community as our motor-roads, our street lighting and our sanitation, on which public money is at present being unhesitatingly spent'.[5] On the other hand, some highbrows envisaged a more austere cultural future for the nation, in which opera should not pay a significant part.

The prospect of a subsidy for opera that was raised at the end of the decade prompted widespread discussion in national and local newspapers about whether Britain was an operatic nation, with polarised responses on both sides. *The Times* noted in 1928 that 'Englishmen made up their minds quite early that the larger forms of opera are something which foreigners do best, and having made that decision they stubbornly refused to revise it'.[6] Yet many within the musical establishment were determined to counter such perceptions of opera and developed strategies for promoting it that played into quintessential notions of Britishness.

This question of national identity was intertwined with the battle of the brows: as Collini notes, middlebrows gloried in 'their four-square, middle-of-the-road, downright English status', which they set up in opposition to the 'bloodless refinement' and European affectations of the highbrows.[7] The identification of a cosmopolitan sensibility with the highbrow is fundamental to the 1920s opera debate. Discussions about whether the British were an operatic race and about how opera ought to be categorised therefore became entangled not only with each other but also with broader debates about how to define the post-War cultural identity. This chapter considers the way in which opera was promoted during the 1920s

---

4. John F. Porte of *Opera* magazine reported: 'It is interesting to observe how the tradition of Germany being the home of culture and England "a nation of shopkeepers" still comes to some people's mind where music is concerned'. However, Porte himself challenged the notion, asserting that England simply had a broader view of music, welcoming the 'widely embracing and broad minded' concert programmes that were to be found in Britain, in contrast with the narrowly nationalistic programmes (supposedly) to be found in Germany. John F. Porte, 'Those Musical Germans', *Opera*, 2/4 (April 1924), 31.

5. RVW, letter to *The Times*, 6 December 1930, cited in *MMR* (1 January 1931), 7–8, 8.

6. Anon., 'English Musical Taste: Attitude Towards Opera', *The Times*, 21 January 1928, 8.

7. Collini, *Absent Minds*, pp. 112–13.

by reference to non-musical phenomena that were widely understood to be particularly 'British', such as sport and empire, and explores how such debates played into nationalistic and gendered rhetoric, and into the highbrow-middlebrow debate itself.

OPERA AND SPORT

The regularity with which commentators drew analogies between music and sport is one of the most striking aspects of the operatic discourse of the 1920s. Somehow the two just happened to come up time and again in the same conversations.[8] Sport and opera were often presented as polar opposites: either/or options, as epitomised by Francesco Berger's observation in 1928 that 'The average Briton has hitherto shown himself supremely indifferent about opera, neither rejoicing when he had it nor grieving when he had it not. Given the option of hearing an opera or attending a football or cricket match, he will certainly select the latter.'[9] But there had long been a parallel discourse that argued that the two spheres were not really so very far apart. As Jennifer R. Sheppard has shown, numerous attempts had been made in Britain during the late nineteenth century to present music and sport as comparable activities, partly to counter the threat that sport was already at this early stage posing to the popularity of music, but also to stress music's health-giving, character-building properties in an age concerned about moral and physical degeneration.[10] Members of the 1920s musical establishment who were well disposed towards opera were, therefore, able to tap into well-established discourses about the common ground between music and sport in order to make the case for their art form.

The opera propagandists adopted four principal approaches. The first was pragmatic. There was a boom in sporting activities as a pursuit for both men and women during the 1920s, stimulated by increased leisure time, changing attitudes towards fitness and body image, and effective modern publicity methods. Reflecting back from 1932, Collier and Lang wrote:

> sport became in the 1920s a far more important element in daily life than it ever had
> been ... The games-mania of Imperial Rome was, by comparison, a parochial excitement,

8. Harvey Grace even compared the act of ranking the Great Composers with choosing a cricket team for a Test Match: critics would agree on Bach, Beethoven, and Wagner as quickly as the Test team would select Hobbs, Sutcliffe, and Hendren. Harvey Grace, 'Music and Musicians', *Yorkshire Post and Leeds Intelligencer*, 8 December 1924, 7.

9. Francesco Berger, 'Opera in England: The Native Form', *The Times*, 6 October 1928, 10.

10. Sheppard, 'Sound of Body', 362–3.

lacking newspapers, broadcasting stations, and cinemas to spread the fame of champions across a world many times larger than the Romans knew.[11]

Both spectator sport and participatory sport were perceived to be taking audiences away from opera, as well as musical and theatrical events more generally. Thus opera's advocates used references to sport as a strategy for bringing opera-goers back into the fold, encouraging them that it was socially acceptable to be both a sports enthusiast and an opera enthusiast.

Secondly, drawing analogies between opera and sport was a way of assertively 'masculinising' opera. Even though this was the era in which women's sport began to take off in earnest, operatic propaganda more typically played upon a particular type of hearty masculinity. Centuries-old anti-operatic rhetoric had attempted to posit the art form as 'feminine' and the stereotype was hard to dislodge. Yet if the masses were really to be mobilised into loving opera, it was clear that such perceptions would have to be overturned. Sport was not only threatening music in the market place but was perceived as ostensibly more 'masculine'. As Sheppard argues, the early twentieth-century discourse about correlations between music and sport was 'a self-interested move to boost music's position in a culture increasingly obsessed with sport, muscularity, masculinity and racial degeneration.'[12] Making opera manly was yet another way of trying to re-categorise it.

Likening opera to sport was also a way of making it seem more British. Sport's relationship with national identity was far more straightforward than that of music: for example, Jack Williams goes so far as to argue that 'Between the wars cricket was celebrated as a metaphor for England and for Englishness', and that it was held up as 'a distillation of English moral worth.'[13] Numerous articles from the period made the point that sport was an inherently British pursuit and opera an inherently foreign phenomenon. Surprisingly, this notion was often taken as read in specialist music publications as much as in the daily press. As a writer for *The Sackbut* observed in 1928, 'To many nations on the Continent—not all, by any means—an instinctive and general interest in music is as great as the Englishman's unquestioned general interest in sport', and went so far as to suggest that 'The English equivalent to subsidized opera would be subsidized race-meetings

---

11. Collier and Lang, *Just the Other Day*, p. 103. As David Trotter states: 'By the mid-1920s, sport had become a major fashion and mass-media event'. David Trotter, *Literature in the First Media Age: Britain Between the Wars* (Cambridge, MA and London: Harvard University Press, 2013), p. 105.

12. Sheppard, 'Sound of Body', 368.

13. Jack Williams, *Cricket and England: A Cultural and Social History of the Interwar Years* (London and Portland, OR: Frank Cass, 1999), pp. 1, 5.

and sports grounds'.[14] However, commentators acknowledged that a certain exchange of ideas was starting to take place: the British were throwing off some of their artistic timidity and reserve and the 'Latins' were becoming 'enthusiastic votaries of outdoor sports', with positive benefits for both.[15]

Finally, and particularly importantly for our purposes, drawing a connection between opera and sport was a way of rendering opera middlebrow, by counteracting perceptions of opera as an intellectual art form. Sport, after all, was rarely perceived as lofty, despite Mendl's view that there could be highbrows in any field of endeavour. Quite the opposite, indeed: a 1929 editorial in *The Listener* argued that 'It is sometimes assumed that the world is divided into "highbrows" and "lowbrows", with a fixed dividing line between them . . . on the one side the thin bespectacled bookworm, on the other the jolly careless sportsman.[16] Those hoping to promote opera to a wide new audience understood that in order to capture this market it was essential to promote opera as entertainment rather than as art. Perceval Graves, the Publicity Manager for the BNOC, argued that 'Unless, and until, opera in England becomes subsidized, propaganda should avoid all references to "culture" and "the uplift". Tell the music-lover and would-be music-lover that it is recreational rather than educational, and the battle is half-won.[17] Similarly, Percy Colson observed in *Apollo* that it was foolish and useless to try to promote opera by talking about 'moral uplift' and 'educative and civilizing powers'—terms in which variety shows or football matches would never be presented—because the average opera-goer did not care about such matters, but simply wanted to see opera well done.[18]

Those making the case for opera frequently used passing sporting analogies in order to give opera-going an exciting allure. To cite a typical example, Figaro of *Musical Opinion* argued that reading about the summer's new productions and casts provided a greater thrill than dog or horse racing and that 'Booking a seat for one particular night during every week in the season provides to the connoisseur as great a thrill as betting on horses.[19] Yet bold claims that opera could rival sport's popularity sometimes met with sarcasm in other sectors of the press—including the music press—and provided fodder for humorous articles which played upon the stereotypical clash between 'highbrow' music and 'populist' sport. In 1926, for example,

14. W. H. Kerridge, 'Music and the People', *The Sackbut*, 9 (December 1928), 171–4, 172.

15. Mrs Albert de Belleroche, 'Permanent British Opera in London', *MT*, 67/1006 (1 December 1926), 1094–5, 1094.

16. Cited in Napper, *British Cinema and Middlebrow Culture*, p. 114.

17. Perceval Graves, 'Opera in Town and on Tour', *The Sackbut*, 8 (June 1927), 332–4, 334.

18. Percy Colson, 'Music News and Notes', in R. Sydney Glover (Ed.), *Apollo: A Journal of the Arts, Vol 3 January to June 1926* (Nendeln, Liechtenstein: Kraus Reprint, 1976), 121–2, 121.

19. Figaro, 'The Operatic World', *MO*, 52/620 (May 1929), 719–20, 719.

The Sunday Post gleefully reported a curious anecdote about a Dutch boxer called Joop Liet (known as the Singing Dutchman) who had sung excerpts from *Pagliacci* before knocking the stuffing out of his opponent during a fight at the Blackfriars Road Ring.[20]

Particularly amusing was a satirical article in the middlebrow *Musical Mirror*, which imagined a future when music would have 'become sufficiently popular to replace football or even racing in the public mind'.[21] The magazine presented a lengthy spoof concert report from fifty years in the future (an imagined 1978), covering a recital by the pianist 'Schweinhund', in which more than 900 people were treated in hospital for minor injuries, and which concluded with the audience storming the concert platform and the musician being lifted shoulder high.[22] This was followed by a far shorter report about a football match, in which a fictional manager, Sir Miles Platting, argued that it was scandalous that football 'instead of being, like music, a great national sport, was merely the pursuit of the cultured few'. Platting argued that there was nothing highbrow about football and that there was no reason why a cup final should not one day become as popular as a symphony concert, and establish itself as firmly as in Germany and Italy, even if the average man found football 'heavy' and 'academic' and preferred to relax with a Schoenberg sextet. The interview concluded 'When I see business men on tramcars and omnibuses immersed in miniature scores of Debussy or Stravinsky, and once-famous footballers kicking in the gutter for a mere pittance, I feel inclined to cry out, "What is England coming to?" '

The more 'highbrow' forms of orchestral, instrumental, and chamber music are the real targets of satire here. But opera, although not mentioned explicitly, is alluded to in the comparison with Germany and Italy, and in references to funding: much of the report was devoted to a dreary appeal for subscriptions towards the establishment of a permanent football team and ground. The idea that football—the ultimate proletarian sport during this era—should ever be in the position of having to appeal to the public purse must have seemed farcical, resolutely ridiculing the attempts of those who were trying to promote opera by claiming its appeal to be the same as sport and placing all classical music firmly into a box marked 'highbrow'.[23]

It is harder to judge the tone of an open letter published a few years earlier in the same publication, which made direct reference to the issue of

20. Anon., 'The Comments of Claude. Some News Items of the Week', *The Sunday Post*, 10 January 1926, 5.

21. R. S. W. 'Concert Thrill of the Future. Music Ousting Football from Favour', *MM*, 8/10 (October 1928), 265–267, 265.

22. Ibid., 265–7.

23. On football's working-class status during this period, see Pugh, *'We Danced All Night'*, pp. 294–5.

trying to popularise opera by masculinising it. The letter was addressed by a correspondent signing himself 'G.B.' to 'an unmusical nephew: the modern youth who regards opera and such things as "high-brow muck"'. The uncle observed that 'Matters are better now, but the average boy still leaves school with a sneaking suspicion that to like music is "effeminate"'.[24] Whether seriously or satirically, G.B.'s strategy for convincing his nephew that this was 'rot' was to stress the macho image, interests, and demeanour of the great composers, of whose lives his young relative knew nothing. He asserted that 'Wagner himself was one of the most virile, pugnacious characters in recent history; mentally, he would have been a fine "scrum half"; then there was Puccini, who looked like a stockbroker, and talked like one'.

The organisation of the sporting year was something that was often referenced when commentators discussed methods for popularising opera. In 1927 Ethel Smyth wrote an article about the means by which a thoughtful, critical audience for opera might be built. Although the answer was not entirely clear, Smyth was sure that audiences needed something more regular than 'snacks and snippets of opera' from a touring opera company who visited for one week during the year, arguing 'No one would be mad enough to believe you could make an unsporting nation take to hunting by touring the country with a pack of hounds'.[25] Fox hunting was both seasonal and aristocratic. Rather, people had to develop a taste for opera that they could not drop, just as they had for their weekly local football match.

To this end, using sport as a publicity mechanism was a tactic that was employed regularly by the most important touring opera company of the era, the BNOC. This is particularly significant in the context of debates about opera, sport, and identity, given that the company positioned itself as *the* national opera company. The BNOC's *Opera* magazine did not initially make its connection to the company overt—billing itself as an organ of operatic current events and an educational publication—but the magazine had been acting as a mouthpiece for the company all along, featuring articles by and about BNOC staff and using articles by supposedly neutral correspondents to sing the company's praises.[26] It also regularly employed

24. G. B., 'Open Letter to an Unmusical Nephew. The Modern Youth Who Regards Opera and Such Things as "High-brow Muck". An Uncle's Straight Talk', *MM*, 5/11 (November 1925), 218.

25. Smyth, 'An Iron Thesis on Opera', 159.

26. See, for example, claims of very successful seasons, many memorable performances, an orchestra that was 'one of the finest bodies of players which London had ever heard in grand opera', and 'brilliant new singers'. A Special Correspondent, 'British National Opera: Fifth London Season', *Opera and the Ballet*, 2/6 (June 1924), 17–18/20, 17. Only from around the middle of 1924 was the connection between the magazine and the company made absolutely explicit, when the editor declared 'We have the privilege of recording in these pages the

sporting analogies when it wanted to make the patriotic case for British performers and opera in English: the two defining hallmarks of the BNOC itself.

Railing in *Opera* against criticism of opera in English elsewhere in the press, the outspoken bass Robert Radford played upon populist concerns about economic and cultural protectionism. He argued that the old model of international opera had made a handful of foreign singers extremely rich but 'did little for the cause of native music', demanding 'why should the fact of being British be used against us as a reproach? Why should not the cosmopolitan singer come and sing under our conditions and in our language?'[27] Likening opera to a game of football, he argued:

> Nobody wishes to put nationality before everything, but we can place a team of composers, conductors, orchestras, producers and singers in the field which can hold its own with any other country, so why should we not be glad about it and do all we can to help our own team? The position is almost hopeless for our youngsters unless we begin to make our own traditions and give them a worthy field to play in.[28]

Perceval Graves and his colleague Germaine Chevreau—joint Publicity Managers for the BNOC—spent much time devising a marketing campaign for the company and finally decided that associating opera with sport would provide an excellent photo opportunity. They invited the South African cricket team to come to a 'Wagner evening' after a day's play at Lord's. Many members of the team 'came, saw, heard, and were conquered' and the team's vice captain was quoted as saying that he would be ashamed to return to South Africa without being able to say that he had attended at least one opera in Britain.[29] It was symbolic that the sport Graves and Chevreau selected was cricket: it was a sport capable of binding people together across the nation and indeed across the Empire, just as they sought to do with opera.

progress of the first British opera organisation to work on a co-operative basis. Its ideals are our ideals'. Anon., 'Editorial', *Opera and the Ballet*, 2/6 (June 1924), 5.

27. Robert Radford, 'The Future of Opera in England', *Opera*, 1/1 (January 1923), 6–8, 6.

28. Radford, 'The Future of Opera in England', 6. Similarly, Richard Capell of *The Daily Mail* discussed European operatic endeavour as though it were a game of sport: 'Those countries naturally produce teams of singers who can face the world, as we face cricket teams. What figure should we cut in international sport if we had at home but a couple of cricket or football clubs to draw on for players?' RC, 'Brilliant New Singers We Shall Hear', *The Daily Mail*, 22 April 1929, 12.

29. Perceval Graves, 'Opera in Town and on Tour', *The Sackbut*, 8 (June 1927), 332–4, 332. Williams writes: 'Cricket played between teams from Britain and other parts of the Empire was seen as a highly effective means of strengthening imperial loyalties'. Williams, *Cricket and England*, p. 12.

Comparisons and confrontations between opera and sport are of course alive and well today. More often than not, they are negative and hinge upon financial debates that started to emerge during the interwar period. There has been much discussion in recent decades, for example, about opera's need for public subsidy versus sport's ability to thrive without it. (The significant investment of public funds in maximising the performance of Olympic athletes is often conveniently overlooked.) One also still frequently hears arguments about the comparative cost of the two activities: the media continues to reinforce the prohibitive cost of attending the opera, and the counter-argument that it is often cheaper to attend an opera than to watch a Premier League football match seemingly falls on deaf ears.[30] The routine use of sporting allusions in articles about opera and references to musicians as if they were sportsmen or women has subsided. However, refreshingly, there seems to have been a re-emergence in recent years of endeavours to popularise opera by reference to sport, as seen perhaps most notably in Opera Holland Park's short film 'From Footy to Verdi'.[31]

POLITICS, CHARACTER, AND HEALTH

As well as popularising opera and attempting to make it seem more British by reference to sport, the BNOC went to some lengths to draw correlations with wider debates about the national character and public health and well-being. *Opera* magazine's editor, Gordon Beckles Willson, was a journalist hailing originally from Canada, who had a background in the world of advertising.[32] The articles he contributed to the magazine were politically impassioned and often pugnacious, and it is clear that he saw the BNOC's remit as being to cultivate good citizens through the promotion of music. Particularly powerful was an article published in autumn 1924 in the run up to a general election (the third in under two years), in which he complained, after seeing the streets emblazoned with political posters, of the 'tremendous pity that no party leader had ever declared any programme of the arts'.[33] He lamented the fact that 'in all the countless columns of electioneering balderdash there was never any mention of those things which make life worth the living, which distinguish the soul of the man

---

30. For further reading see Andrew Mitchell, 'It's Time to Scotch the Cliché that Opera Tickets are too Expensive': *The Guardian* music blog, 3 November 2015, https://www. theguardian.com/music/2015/nov/03/opera-tickets-expensive-cliche-john-humphrys (accessed 27 October 2017).

31. https://www.youtube.com/watch?v=6QxaLMiHsUU (accessed 27 October 2017).

32. Bohun Lynch, 'Youth and the Editor of "Opera"', *Opera*, 2/1 (January 1924), 9.

33. G. B., Editorial, *Opera and the Ballet*, 2/8 (autumn 1924), 7.

from the brain of the beast', and even went so far as to praise the Soviet government for keeping open theatres, concert halls, and galleries at times of great stress, recognising that economic insecurity could be alleviated by aesthetic pleasure. Beckles Willson argued that the priorities of the British governing class were, and always had been, wrong in placing empire building and sport above art, for they could never 'represent the full glory of life'. Yet he clearly understood that in order to promote opera to the British, one had to tap into these particularly British enthusiasms. As we shall see later in this chapter, Thomas Beecham and his circle would go even further in attempting to harness empire and sport in the cause of opera.

The connection between music, health, and national character was also strongly emphasised in the pages of *Opera* by regular contributor Agnes Savill, a self-declared opera convert who allied herself with the magazine's target readers as an interested amateur. Savill was the author of a book entitled *Music, Health and Character*, in which she recounted her journey to becoming a music enthusiast: after having been 'actively antagonistic' towards music for more than thirty years, she gradually came to find it a source of consolation when stationed in France as a doctor during the War. Savill encouraged others to follow 'the path of [her] own initiation', indeed went so far as to argue that music could improve the health, increase the working capacity, provide companionship, strengthen the character, and enrich the mind.[34] Like Beckles Willson's, Savill's stance was at times a politicised one: she too made the case that the Bolshevik regime in Russia had made opera available to all at low prices and that in most European countries the provision of good opera was state-subsidised because it was seen as necessary for the well-being of the people.[35]

Savill was also an important voice in presenting opera as something for the everyman and something inherently British. In 1924 she contributed an article to *Opera* comparing the international season at Covent Garden and the recent BNOC summer season. Despite claiming to have a supposedly impartial stance towards the two organisations, Savill made her bias crystal clear: she claimed that the BNOC had the 'greater array of fine voices' and that its season had a heart, whereas the Covent Garden season might have been 'brilliant' but was not 'spiritual'.[36] More interesting are Savill's observations about physicality, masculinity, and national identity: she praised the healthy, brown, athletic limbs of the British male singers in the BNOC, deeming them more suitable for bringing to life the Wagner roles

34. Savill, *Music, Health and Character*, viii.
35. Agnes Savill, 'Opera and the People', *The English Review* (September 1928), 327–31, 329.
36. Dr Agnes Savill, 'Why not *Parsifal* on Sundays?', *Opera and the Ballet*, 2/8 (autumn 1924), 13–15, 13, 14.

(ironically) than the 'pale and pasty' German singers at Covent Garden.[37] As in so many contemporary articles about opera, this one was coloured by cultural protectionism, but Savill was also asserting an argument of national superiority and attempting to distance 'manly' British musicians from the stereotype of the sickly foreign musician.

Making the case for opera for everyone, Savill argued elsewhere that a taste for it could have a profound effect upon the national character. She claimed that the Italian working man in the street and peasant in the field tramped long miles to hear opera when a troupe visited the nearest town and that the songs that they sang as they worked were operatic arias rather than the popular ragtime tunes that prevailed in England.[38] The difference in cultural 'nourishment' provided by the two types of music was likely to have long-lasting social consequences, which Savill expressed in emphatic, even alarmist terms: 'The emotions of mankind must be given healthy food which nourishes the spirit; the State which neglects this duty will reap an evil harvest of perverted emotionalism, expressing itself in sensational and ugly living, even crime.'[39] She expressed disbelief that the case for opera was even having to be made, putting its necessity down to ignorance on the part of the general public, and argued that—with the assistance of the gramophone, the pianola, and the wireless—there would be no excuse, other than sheer apathy, for the parents of the future not to introduce their children to an art form that should be their 'consolation and chief delight'. And for those more inclined to be persuaded by material rather than ideological arguments, she proposed that lending support to the cause of a national opera would bear dividends: today's financial speculation would become tomorrow's 'gilt-edged investment'.

SCHOOLBOY OPERA

Cultivating a taste for opera among children was clearly an important priority for Beckles Willson, who expressed a utopian vision of his magazine's remit: '*Opera* is a magazine of youth, and those whose privilege it is to direct its welfare believe, heart and soul, that art makes the world a more beautiful place to live in.'[40] Much was made in *Opera* of the company's special

37. Ibid., 14.

38. Savill, 'Opera and the People', 330–1.

39. Ibid., p. 331. Matt Houlbrook observes that by the 1920s, crime had become 'a key battleground in the newspaper circulation wars of the period' and that it seemed to many people that 'the number and nature of crook life stories were spiraling out of control' (*Prince of Tricksters*, pp. 116, 123).

40. G. B., Editorial, *Opera and the Ballet*, 2/8 (autumn 1924), 7.

performances for school children—2,000 children had the opportunity to watch *Hansel and Gretel* in Bradford, for example, in February 1923.[41] The children were required to write an essay about the opera afterwards and the authors of the best ones were presented with a copy of a book entitled *Opera at Home*. Perceval Graves called the young critics' frankness 'alarming, but disarming', but the excerpts that were published in *Opera* were carefully chosen so as to serve as further propaganda for the BNOC's own enterprise, the winner having apparently written 'Everything at the opera was perfect, there was not a hitch. Every player played his or her part in an effective, impressive manner. The scenery was the best I have ever had the privilege of seeing'.[42]

We might draw a comparison between the efforts of the 1920s touring opera companies to build new audiences and the many laudable efforts still made by opera company outreach departments to engage children and young people today. It is more depressing, however, to reflect on the disparity between attitudes in the 1920s and today towards opera within formal educational settings. In the present, music has to fight hard to maintain any sort of presence in British schools, with cuts to instrumental lessons and many schools no longer offering it as a subject for examination at the higher levels. And where music is offered, popular music is often prioritised, with classical music relegated to the sidelines and regarded with suspicion by a younger generation of teachers reared (in some cases) on the idea of opera, in particular, as elitist. This then perpetuates a vicious circle of hostility, as a perceptive anonymous 17-year-old wrote in a blog for *Gramophone* magazine in 2016: 'This reluctance to discuss classical music (let alone hear it) at young ages generates the stigma against the form in later life; the labels so frequently attached to classical music as lacklustre, upper-class, and unendurable exist only because people have failed to listen to classical music in the first place'.[43]

By contrast many schools in the 1920s used gramophone recordings in order to introduce opera to schoolchildren early and to present it as something commonplace. Writing in the BNOC's *Opera* magazine, music teacher Mabel Chamberlain praised the growing use of gramophones to familiarise primary school children with opera and the fact that music publishers

---

41. Our Unsophisticated Critic, 'February', *Opera*, 1/3 (March 1923), 24.

42. Perceval Graves, 'Opera in Town and on Tour', *The Sackbut*, 8 (June 1927), 332–4, 334; Anon, 'Leeds Essay Competition', *Opera*, 1/4 (April 1923), 27–8, 27. The winning author was 15-year-old C. H. Schofield of Boyd's Modern School.

43. Anon, 'Why Are our Schools Pushing Classical Music to the Margins?', *Gramophone*, 23 August 2016, https://www.gramophone.co.uk/blog/gramophone-guest-blog/why-are-our-schools-pushing-classical-music-to-the-margins?__prclt=bPMFchKQ (accessed 27 October 2017).

were sending out the scores of operatic excerpts to be played by school orchestras.[44] Chamberlain advocated that teachers might also talk about the stories of operas in English classes. However, some 'policing' of listening and learning would be required here too: the obvious caveat was that many opera plots were unsuitable for young minds and would need to be presented with discretion. Chamberlain used this argument in order to make a predictable patriotic plea: 'This difficulty makes it all the more desirable that there be a production of British operas about British life which *can* be studied by young people'. For the time being, *The School Music Review* published a list of works it deemed particularly suitable, including (among vocal works): 'Casta diva'; 'The Steersman's Song' and 'Erik's Song' from *The Flying Dutchman*; 'Ch'ella mi creda libero' from *The Girl of the Golden West*; the Toreador's Song from *Carmen*; 'Spiegel' from *Tales of Hoffmann*; the trio of the Masks from *Turandot*; and 'Bella figlia dell'amore' and 'La donna è mobile' from *Rigoletto*.[45]

Percy Scholes published a course-book for schools to use in teaching music appreciation via the gramophone.[46] The book, published (with a clear vested interest) by the Gramophone Company, specified listening programmes and provided pupil and teacher notes and worked its way chronologically from folksongs to Elgar. Operatic excerpts featured included Dido's lament, the overture to *The Marriage of Figaro*, 'Ah, my pretty brace of fellows' from *The Seraglio*, and the funeral march from *Siegfried*. *The Illustrated London News* reported in 1922 that:

> The educational function of the gramophone is now recognised, and children are being taught to appreciate and know what is good in music, and, thus being caught at the most receptive age, leave school with a wholesome taste, and not a little knowledge of the subject.[47]

The point about 'wholesome taste' is an important one. It is reflective of the ongoing Victorian ethos of self-improvement that classical music should have appeared upon the curriculum, for purposes of both instruction and

44. Mabel Chamberlain, 'Opera; It's [sic] Place in the Primary Schools', *Opera*, 1/2 (February 1923), 16–17, 17.

45. Anon., 'The Gramophone in School and College by One Who Uses It', *The School Music Review*, 38/446 (15 July 1929), 62–4, 64.

46. Percy Scholes, *Learning to Listen by Means of the Gramophone: A Course in the Appreciation of Music for Use in Schools* (London: The Gramophone Co. Ltd., 1921). The gramophone had several potential applications in the classroom. H. G. Wells, for example, advocated its use as a tool in language teaching. H. G. Wells, *The Salvaging of Civilization* (London, New York, Toronto and Melbourne: Cassell and Company, 1921), pp. 160–1.

47. Stylus, 'The Talking Machine', *ILN*, 13 May 1922, 724.

entertainment (and indeed music had been far more prominent in general on the school curriculum since the War).[48] Yet there is an apparent paradox here in the choice of opera specifically, given the suspicion with which it had not long before been regarded by puritanical educationalists: opera would appear, then, to be losing its 'immoral' status by the 1920s. In certain cases we can see an explicit attempt to use opera to form a positive national character, even to help young people to avoid the temptation of crime. For instance, the use of operatic gramophone records in schools was extended to institutions that taught disaffected and troubled youngsters. The Manchester Guardian reported in 1925 that the practice had been introduced in 'London County Council industrial schools in Surrey, Herts, Sussex and London'.[49] These schools were institutions for juvenile delinquents that placed an emphasis upon the reform and retraining of young criminals.

A teacher called Charles T. Smith at the Glengall Road L. C. C. Elementary School in Poplar, on the Isle of Dogs—then a working-class area of East London—used gramophones to particularly imaginative effect in the 1910s and 1920s, with important consequences for male character formation. He played his pupils excerpts from *Tannhäuser*, talked through the plot of the opera (with props), and got the children singing arrangements of sections of the score in three- and four-part harmony.[50] This led to an even bolder experiment: children from the school put on a run of performances of, first, Gounod's *Faust* in 1914 (with a mixed cast), followed in 1920 by *The Magic Flute* (with boys only), which was described as 'the height of ambitiousness in school music', despite the fact that the costumes were home-made by the school art department and the accompaniment provided on a piano.[51] The opera was performed almost in full, with some small adjustments to the score to make it suitable for the voices of twelve- and thirteen-year-olds, but with all of Mozart's harmonies preserved. Smith was realistic about adapting the opera so that it fell within the capabilities of his cast: he believed that the Queen of the Night's coloratura passages could

48. W. H. Kerridge, 'Music and the People', *The Sackbut*, 9 (December 1928), 171–4, 172.

49. Anon., 'Opera for Children— By Gramophone', *The Manchester Guardian*, 6 June 1925, 5.

50. Charles T. Smith, *The School of Life: A Theatre of Education* (London: Grant Richards, Ltd., 1921), p. 61.

51. Anon., 'Mozart's *The Magic Flute*: School-Boy Performance', *The School Music Review*, 28/ 334 (March 1920), 171. The programme for the school's two performances of *Faust* in 1914 contained the words: 'This performance of Grand Opera has been undertaken as an educational experiment and with the hope of inculcating an intelligent appreciation of, and genuine interest in, the highest forms of entertainment'. Charles T. Smith, *The Music of Life: Education for Leisure and Culture, With Curricula Evolved By Experiment in an Elementary School*, 2nd edn (London: P. S. King and Son, 1919), p. 121.

be taught to a cathedral chorister, but his challenge was to make them sing-able by the sort of boy who spent his free time selling newspapers.[52]

Smith invited Edward Dent to give a pre-performance talk on Mozart to the local, working-class residents who attended, which ensured that a number of high-profile critics, from *The Observer*, *The Telegraph*, and *The Express*, amongst others, were in attendance.[53] According to Ernest Newman, 'the results were extraordinary' and the boys had 'an amazing knowledge of their music, and an excellent idea of the opera'; indeed, he imagined that this production, lacking vocal sophistication but rich in character psychology, might have been similar to the first performances, capturing the fun intended by Schikaneder.[54] Bernard Shaw, meanwhile, ar-gued that Mozart was invariably made 'shabby and tedious and out-of-date' when performed at Covent Garden, whereas the schoolboys from the Isle of Dogs succeeded in bringing out everything that was unique, modern and immortal in Mozart's work.[55] Schoolboy opera was hailed as the way for-ward, an artistically worthy counterbalance to the prevailing star system.

The endeavour was a demanding one—the time involved in rearran-ging the work for children's voices had been considerable, and depended upon the ability and initiative of a really committed music teacher—and so the idea never took off on a large scale.[56] Nevertheless, a few other schools followed suit in putting on full-scale operatic performances by children. For instance, a Mr Cunliffe of Todmorden, in Calderdale, West Yorkshire, undertook a similar experiment in the mid 1920s, staging *The Magic Flute* with his pupils, followed by performances of Rimsky Korsakov's *Le Coq d'Or*, Wolf-Ferrari's *Il segreto di Susanna*, and *Pagliacci*.[57]

Smith was pursuing a rigorous, practical programme of music and drama at his school and hoped these subjects would have benefits for the rest of the curriculum. He took serious music seriously and believed that children were perfectly capable of appreciating it on its own terms. Furthermore, his

---

52. Smith, *The School of Life*, p. 70.

53. Ibid., p. 66.

54. Ernest Newman, *The Observer*, cited in Charles T. Smith, *The School of Life: A Theatre of Education* (London: Grant Richards, Ltd., 1921), p. 53. See also Anon., 'Mozart's *The Magic Flute*: School-Boy Performance', *The School Music Review*, 28/334 (March 1920), 171. The ex-periment was repeated at Stanhope Street School, St Pancras.

55. Cited in Smith, *The School of Life*, p. 14.

56. The challenges of arranging the opera are discussed in Ibid., pp. 67–73.

57. Reported in H. S. Gordon, 'The Supersession of the Star', *The Sackbut*, 6 (February 1926), 190–1, 191. Gordon suggested that the movement for boy operas opened great possibilities, including 'the assigning to boys of certain parts which, hitherto, have been made ridiculous by women singers'.

expectations of what children could achieve in performance were high.[58] There is a sense of a real team effort in his endeavour: the pupils decided among themselves who would be most suitable to play each part, and Smith saw no reason to override their decisions. The boys 'got well into the skin of the characters'—even throwing themselves with gusto into playing female roles—and were able to sing one another's parts if so required.[59] Smith argued that 'They enter into their parts so intensely simply because they are happy', and his descriptions of the individual personalities of the boys and their transformation as a result of taking on their roles is a joy to read.[60] Parents were astonished and Smith observed that 'It is almost sad to think that children should ever mask such blithesome mirth under cheerless, saddened exteriors'.[61]

Smith's aim that operatic performances could be regular events in ordinary schools, attended by ordinary children was a resolutely democratic one, issuing a challenge to the idea of opera as a highbrow thing apart. Normalising opera in this way was an important strategy for audience building: children used to performing in operas and other types of school plays would form the 'intelligent interested audience' of the future.[62] Furthermore, Smith viewed his endeavour as being rewarding and of educative value not only to the schoolboy participants, but also to the parents and other members of the local community, who were previously unfamiliar with opera and responded with such comments as 'Grand', 'Lovely', 'Comin' agen', and 'Bin three times'.[63] Smith had outlined his broader manifesto for encouraging a love of music, with the aim of 'developing the moral and aesthetic faculties' in a book published in 1919.[64] He aimed to turn around the lives of his deprived pupils: a boy who had spent his evenings shoplifting out of boredom had, after following Smith's curriculum, become a reformed character, standing up to his abusive father and spending his day off going to hear *Cavalleria rusticana* and *Pagliacci*.[65] (The boy attended performances by the Beecham Company; a similar, roughly contemporaneous production by the Carl Rosa Company is shown in Figure 7.1.) Smith's

58. He wrote: 'Mount an opera and give it a chance. No-one need say of a school that an opera cannot be performed owing to a lack of good singers or actors; it would not be true'. Smith, *The School of Life*, p. 87.

59. Ibid., p. 85, p. 66, p. 74. The programme for the performances stated 'Many of the performers know each other's parts, and the chorus singers may have to sing solo passages'. Ibid., afterpages.

60. Ibid., p. 87.

61. Ibid., pp. 91, 93.

62. Ibid., p. 55.

63. Ibid., p. 54.

64. Smith, *The Music of Life*, p. 7.

65. Ibid., pp. 8–9.

Figure 7.1 Pietro Mascagni, *Cavalleria rusticana*: 1921 production by the Carl Rosa Opera Company, with Eva Turner as Santuzza and Booth Hitchen as Alfio. © Lebrecht Music and Arts/Lebrecht.

productions, then, overturned stereotypical assumptions about the morally dubious nature of opera and about it being 'difficult': they endeavoured to foster both good citizenship and enquiring minds, but remained resolutely good fun.

IMPERIALISM AND MASCULINITY

Finally we come to Thomas Beecham himself, a key figure in the contemporary musical scene. Even though the Beecham Opera Company, so significant during the 1910s in introducing British audiences to new works, had collapsed at the turn of the 1920s, and despite the fact that Beecham had himself fallen on financial hard times, he remained, throughout the 1920s, one of the most powerful advocates of opera in Britain.[66] During the late 1920s, Beecham concentrated his efforts upon his new Imperial League of Opera (ILO), a funding scheme launched in 1927 to attract subscriptions for a new national opera company. Beecham acknowledged the decline of traditional patronage, believed that opera could never pay its way and was pessimistic about the likelihood of state subsidy for opera ever coming to fruition. The solution he proposed was to ask opera lovers and opera propagandists to put their money where their mouths were and invite them to contribute to a subscription scheme (five years in the first instance) that would fund a new company and ultimately a permanent opera house. He spoke of appealing to a 'small but astonishingly faithful minority of people who regularly supported the opera',[67] but in reality the number of donors he believed he would be able to find was ambitious: 150,000 at a conservative estimate and perhaps as many as 250,000.[68]

Beecham approached the task of drumming up support for the ILO with great energy, frequently being likened by the press to a missionary, or 'a political leader making an appeal to the country'.[69] He toured around the country giving talks and putting on concerts and fundraising balls, with an orchestra and a troupe of British singers in order to give a practical demonstration of his ambitions for the company. Many operatic commentators pinned their hopes upon the scheme in the final years of the 1920s, but like so many similar endeavours before it, such as Isidore de Lara's National Opera Scheme of 1924, the ILO was doomed to failure and in 1934 was finally forced to return money to those who had bought shares.

Despite the fact that the scheme was unsuccessful, the terms in which Beecham made his case are interesting from the perspective of considering endeavours to link opera with national identity. The ILO produced a short-lived magazine, *MILO*, edited by Philip Heseltine (using the pseudonym Peter Warlock), which conspicuously sought to 'reinvent' opera in terms that would appeal to men. *MILO* attempted to masculinise opera not only as a strategy for expanding its audience but also as a way of mobilising men to *fund* opera, since some of the most active operatic patrons of the period

---

66. Colson wrote, 'It is, perhaps, not too much to assert that during the 'twenties the word *music* was spelt BEECHAM'. Colson, *Those Uneasy Years*, p. 85.

67. Anon., 'The Future of Opera', 10.

68. Anon., 'Imperial League of Opera: Big Initial Response', *The Times*, 17 November 1927, 12.

69. Anon., 'Opera: "But" and "If". Explainers Wanted', *The Times*, 26 November 1927, 12.

were wealthy women, Mrs Courtauld and Emerald, Lady Cunard being notable examples.

Like *Opera* magazine, then, *MILO* was a magazine with a vested interest, affiliated with, if not an existing opera company, then a would-be one, and it made the association explicit from the start. The magazine was established at the ILO's Regent Street headquarters in the July of 1929, with the first issue appearing in the October, and Beecham gave a more or less free rein to its editor.[70] *MILO* was sent free of charge to all members of the League and one of its stated aims was to attract new members and keep readers abreast of the League's progress. However, the magazine also sought 'to interest and educate the public generally in all matters pertaining to opera'.[71] Beecham made much of the fact that he wanted to raise taste as well as raise money and *MILO* was an important organ to that end.

MILO was somewhat less overtly about 'opera for the people' than *Opera* magazine but it was still keen to combat stereotypes about opera being the preserve of the idle rich. Both publications had a social and cultural agenda deeply intertwined with notions of Britishness, but the course *MILO* steered between presenting opera as highbrow or middlebrow was a less clear-cut one. Its contributors included well known writers on music such as J. H. Fuller-Maitland, Edwin Evans, and Cecil Gray, together with the composers Constant Lambert and Kaikhosru Sorabji. The stance of these writers on opera's placement within the battle of the brows was somewhat eclectic, as we have seen. Lambert was positive about popular opera but Evans, Gray, and Sorabji displayed marked highbrow tendencies, being highly antipathetic to Covent Garden-style 'luxurious' opera, so-called grand opera, star singers, and supposedly 'ignorant' audiences.

MILO strongly promoted the aims of the ILO and criticised the competition, as *Opera* had done before it. The ILO was conceived as a consciously 'democratic' outfit and Warlock dismissed Covent Garden, conversely, as 'the most undemocratic . . . theatre in London'.[72] *MILO* criticised Covent Garden for its two months of opera per year with 'hastily collected casts', albeit ones featuring some fine singers.[73] Beecham's ambition was to expand the British repertory, as he had done previously in the 1910s.[74] The ILO promised a six-week season in May 1930 (which would not, in the event, come to fruition) of operas that were, by and large, 'quite unknown to

70. Barry Smith, *Peter Warlock: The Life of Philip Heseltine* (Oxford and New York: Oxford University Press, 1994), p. 259.

71. Anon., editorial, *MILO*, 1/1 (October 1929), 2.

72. The Editor (Peter Warlock), 'Contingencies', *MILO*, 1/1 (October 1929), 12–19, 16.

73. Ibid., 14.

74. Ibid., 18.

present-day England': *The Trojans* and *The Damnation of Faust, Prince Igor, A Village Romeo and Juliet, Così fan tutte, The Tales of Hoffmann, The Snow Maiden, The Italian Girl in Algiers, The Thieving Magpie,* and *The Bartered Bride*.[75]

MILO was, of course, an acronym for 'Magazine of the Imperial League of Opera' but it also symbolically evoked the name of the great hero of ancient Rome, Milo of Croton, a many times Olympic victor who was supposedly capable of feats of extreme strength. Milo was also a military leader who led a legendary campaign against the much larger army of the neighbouring Sybarites.[76] In associating itself with this manly hero, *MILO* posited opera in terms that drew reference to militarism, classicism, imperialism, physical strength, national vigour, and civilisation.[77] The ILO thus consciously tried to reclaim opera from those who had long derided it as feminine and foreign, and to counter the Victorian and Edwardian view of music as an ungentlemanly pursuit.[78]

Beecham sought to fight a war on two fronts: against the apathy of Britons who cared little for serious music on the one hand and against Britain's cultural rivals on the Continent on the other. The first editorial of *MILO* set an overtly hard-hitting tone: 'The modern descendants of the Sybarites are those who are indifferent to the claims of art and beauty. A vigorous offensive that shall rouse them from this condition is being launched, and it is suggested that each member of the Imperial League of Opera should be a modern "Milo" and a soldier in the great army of intellectual progress'.[79] Such militaristic rhetoric was not limited to *MILO*. In 1926, Figaro had written in *Musical Opinion* that 'the undoubted sharpened appetite for opera is the inevitable reaction from years of war strain; and there *must* be a vast army of "potential" opera-lovers'.[80] When reporting upon Beecham's campaign, this critic also emphasised its quasi-military characteristics: Beecham had 'almost militant optimism' and was 'vivacious ... almost pugnacious', and would 'combat the mental musical laziness which the "talkies" will infallibly develop'.[81]

75. Ibid., 12. The magazine published articles on some of these works, together with general interest pieces on such topics as 'humour in opera' and Verdi's debut.

76. For further reading on Milo, see Michael B. Poliakoff, *Combat Sports in the Ancient World: Competition, Violence, and Culture* (New Haven and London: Yale University Press, 1987), pp. 117–19.

77. This discussion about *MILO* and masculinity is developed in greater detail in Wilson, 'Gender' in Greenwald (Ed.), *The Oxford Handbook of Opera*, pp. 774–94.

78. For further reading see Corissa Gould, 'Aspiring to Manliness: Edward Elgar and the Pressures of Hegemonic Masculinity', in Ian Biddle and Kirsten Gibson (Eds.) *Masculinity and Western Musical Practice* (Farnham and Burlington, VT: Ashgate, 2005), 161–81.

79. Anon., editorial, *MILO*, 1/1 (October 1929), 2.

80. Figaro, 'The Operatic World', *MO*, 49/581 (February 1926), 471–2, 471.

81. Figaro, 'The Operatic World', *MO*, 52/616 (January 1929), 331–2, 331.

'War-talk' was still a routine part of the national conversation about all manner of topics only a decade after the armistice. *MILO* built upon a growing campaign in associating opera with masculinity and physical strength; however, the language used in *MILO* was more jingoistic than in most other music publications, adding into the mix an overtly imperialist zeal. The magazine posited Britain's lack of a permanent opera company or opera house as 'a national disgrace'.[82] Improving Britain's culture was, for the ILO, a way of restoring the nation's threatened international supremacy. Beecham was rather reticent about the extent to which the ILO would promote British opera but adopted a protectionist attitude towards casting: the singers performing in ILO productions would be drawn exclusively from the Empire.[83] Others involved with the ILO wanted to go further still: the designer Edward Gordon Craig wrote an open letter to *The Observer* offering to design a *mise en scène* and stage sets for a British opera, on condition that 'the entire scheme be British and be allied to no foreign persons or purposes whatever'.[84]

Whereas *Opera* magazine focused more on opera as a source of enjoyment for ordinary people—potential customers for the BNOC's own business—*MILO* spoke more overtly about intellectualism and taste formation. It was in some ways a more ideological publication, while lacking the vision of a socialist utopia that one sometimes finds in *Opera*. It was Britain's place on the world stage that interested Beecham the most. In his fundraising speeches and articles in the press, he betrayed a profound fear of cultural decline, in line with the comments by many other observers that Britain was becoming an operatic backwater. *MILO* became a vehicle through which he could assert a bold, confident message about how Britain could use opera to reclaim its 'rightful' place among the civilised nations of the world. By the 1920s, faith in the imperial project was starting to waver in intellectual circles but *MILO* played upon a more old-fashioned, Edwardian model of imperialism, based on ideals of sporting prowess, militarism, and derring-do. This concept of popular imperialism continued to be disseminated to popular audiences via film, popular journalism, children's adventure stories, school textbooks, memorabilia, postcards, and cigarette cards, and not least through the extravagant Empire Exhibitions held at Wembley in 1924 and 1925.[85] Beecham tapped into a widespread fear that British

---

82. Ibid., 18
83. Thomas Beecham, 'The Future of Opera', *The Times*, 5 November 1927, 10.
84. As reported in Anon., 'Interesting Musical Discoveries: Craig and British Opera', *MM*, 8/11 (November 1928), 286.
85. John M. MacKenzie, *Propaganda and Empire: The Manipulation of British Public Opinion, 1880–1960* (Manchester: Manchester University Press, 1984), pp. 10, 17, 26.

civilisation (as exported via its empire) and Britain's status as the hub of the Western world were under threat.[86]

Beecham hoped to shame the nation out of its cultural apathy by comparing it to regions untouched by British imperial rule, as imagined in the crudest terms. Chiming with extensive debates then current in the press about whether Britain was constitutionally an operatic nation, Beecham lamented in the inaugural issue of *MILO* that 'The State of England has never taken one step in the way of forming or elevating the taste of the people. It has ever shown a singular indifference to things intellectual and spiritual, worthy only of a great barbarian country'.[87] In the next issue he went further, writing in a capital-centric article entitled 'London and the League' that 'In many parts of the Kingdom I have discovered less knowledge of the subject than I should expect to find in the middle of Africa'.[88]

References to savages and barbarians might seem to hark back to the simplistic jingoism of the Edwardian classroom and *MILO* did indeed at one point use a schoolboy as a mouthpiece for its ideals. *MILO*, like the BNOC, adopted the strategy of organising an essay-writing competition for schoolchildren (in this case at King Edward's School, a grammar school in Birmingham), publishing the winning entry in its pages. Here too there was a difference in emphasis between the two magazines: whereas the BNOC favoured essays that praised their own performances, the essay that won the *MILO* prize was far more ideological, reflecting the magazine's own preoccupation with cultural imperialism and national pride. Its author asserted that 'There is no getting out of the fact that our national form of entertainment has risen no higher than the cinema. To put it frankly, it is a crime. All countries are agreed that such things as opera cannot be left out of the programme of a civilized nation . . . The average Frenchman, German and Italian can enjoy opera as cheaply as the average Englishman can enjoy the picture house'.[89] Such comments epitomise the complicated stance *MILO* took upon the brows: opera here is presented as something civilised that needed to be differentiated from more populist forms of entertainment—ostensibly something highbrow. And yet there was nothing exclusive about the desired audience for opera: the schoolboy mouthpiece, with his references to the average man, seems to voice the idea that high culture should be accessible to all.

86. Overy, *The Morbid Age*, p. 4.
87. Anon., 'A Message from Thomas Beecham', *MILO*, 1/1 (October 1929), 4–6, 6.
88. Thomas Beecham, 'London and the League', *MILO*, 1/2 (November 1929), 2–3, 2.
89. N. J. F. Craig, 'The Need for Opera in England' (The Prize Essay on Sir Thomas Beecham's Recent Address to the Boys of King Edward's School, Birmingham), *MILO*, 1/3 (Christmas 1929), 34–5.

But what sort of readership were Beecham and Warlock trying to reach, or likely to reach with their classical references? Milo as a historical figure embodied the ideal of the 'sportsman soldier' that had particular resonance for an elite readership who had attended British public schools. In this context, sport was elevated to a cult, associated with ideals of courage and heroism, and regarded as essential training for those destined to become future leaders of empire. This readership would also have been highly familiar with the legend of Milo, since a knowledge of ancient history was central to the public school curriculum. In couching *MILO* in terms of references to ancient Rome, Beecham (who attended Rossall School in Lancashire) and Warlock (an alumnus of Eton) might at first glance appear to have been aiming their campaign at a privileged minority for whom classical models of civilisation were still very much a guiding point of reference.[90]

What is interesting here is the way in which the two men attempted to bring music into the mix of the public school character-building project, by associating it with sport and classical allusions. Music, as we have already seen, had historically been widely regarded in Britain as a foreign, feminised pursuit.[91] *MILO*, however, chimes with a recently published book entitled *Public Schools and Their Music* by A. H. Peppin, formerly Director of Music at Mill Hill School, Clifton College, and Rugby School. Peppin argued that the most important objective of education was to develop character, but what was unusual about his book was its focus on the role of music—both performing it and listening to it—in creating such 'men of character'.[92] Peppin was rather dismissive of the expression 'music appreciation', arguing that understanding music demanded 'severe and concentrated mental effort' and rigorous, quasi-militaristic discipline.[93] But after the application of such discipline, the study of music would develop mind, spirit, and body, fostering perfectionism, intellectual ambition, and

90. Theodore Ziolkowski argues that 'When thoughtful Europeans in the twenties looked to the ancient past for a sense of continuity and stability, their gaze focused most often on ancient Rome' and writes that 'In England . . . the Roman tradition constituted a steadfast part of the cultural atmosphere'. Theodore Ziolkowski, *Classicism of the Twenties: Art, Music, and Literature* (Chicago and London: The University of Chicago Press, 2015), p. 60.

91. When a group of boys from Abbotsholme School in Staffordshire paid a visit to the studios of Rudall Carte, Britain's most important flute manufacturer, Ursula Greville quipped sarcastically in *The Sackbut* 'What is England coming to? Playing-fields of Europe and all that. Some one ought to write to *The Times* about it? Terrible thing for the country's morale? Why, if that sort of thing spreads the whole atmosphere of England will change!' Ursula Greville, 'Excursions', *The Sackbut*, 10/2 (September 1929), 29–31, 29. For context on the flute company, see Robert Bigio, *Rudall, Rose and Carte: The Art of the Flute in Britain* (London: Tony Bingham, 2011).

92. A. H. Peppin, *Public Schools and Their Music* (Oxford and London: Oxford University Press and Humphrey Milford, 1927), p. 7.

93. Ibid., p. 15.

teamwork, the last being an important mechanism by which public schools fostered individual character.[94]

MILO's cultural references therefore spoke with particular eloquence to public school alumni, but it is unlikely that these were the only readers Beecham and Warlock sought to reach. Quintessential public school values had been disseminated via adventure stories to a large audience of middle-class boys during the early decades of the century, including—it would appear—*MILO*'s grammar schoolboy correspondent. The public at large, meanwhile, were now encountering figures from the ancient world on a daily basis via the mass media: popular novels, circus acts, advertising, and films such as Fred Niblo's 1925 *Ben Hur*. Indeed, the classical strongman was targeted deliberately at a male, working-class audience.[95]

Interestingly, Milo himself was (unlike most ancient athletes) of humble rather than aristocratic origins,[96] and clearly the ILO's great army had a need for foot soldiers as well as generals. It is noteworthy that Heseltine/Warlock had previously founded and edited *The Sackbut*, a music journal that explicitly sought to be accessible, despite the elite social and intellectual background of its contributors; indeed, he expressly described the journal as one in which 'composers, critics, and plain men-in-the-street can meet on equal terms'.[97] Beecham, meanwhile, appeared to adopt a populist tone in depicting music as 'the great popular art, the one art in which everyone can have a share',[98] but the messages he sent to the public were contradictory. References to the need to 'purify' people's tastes emanated superiority, a sense of looking down, patrician-style, upon 'the masses'. This stance contrasted sharply with *Opera*'s repeated assertions that it was a co-operative venture, in which readers themselves had a stake.

Furthermore, Beecham was sometimes prone to gaffes, offending those people to whom he ostensibly desired to reach out. When giving a speech about his fundraising scheme at a reception at the Mayfair Hotel in November 1927 (put on in his honour by the Music Club), he stated, apparently to much laughter, that the general public could be left out of the equation when attempting to raise funds because it had not the smallest knowledge of art and was 'savage and barbarous'.[99] He positioned the provinces, furthermore, as an uncultivated hinterland, giving a speech at the Leeds Luncheon Club in which he talked about English culture being

94. Ibid., p. 49.
95. On the classical muscle men of early film, see Maria Wyke, *Projecting the Past: Ancient Rome, Cinema, and History* (New York and London: Routledge, 1997).
96. Poliakoff, *Combat Sports in the Ancient World*, p. 118.
97. Collins, '"Never Out of Date and Never Modern"', pp. 406, 418.
98. Anon., 'A message from Sir Thomas Beecham', *MILO*, 1/1 (October 1929), 4–6, 4.
99. Anon., 'The Future of Opera', *The Times*, 5 November 1927, 10.

immeasurably below the standard of other civilised countries and said 'In Leeds you have never heard of opera done well, not once'.[100] Members of the Leeds opera audience, who were particularly committed to opera and sophisticated in their tastes, as we have seen in Chapter 5, must have been gravely offended.

By the beginning of 1929, the ILO was faltering, partly as a result of the repercussions of the collapse of the American stock market, and Beecham wrote to Warlock dispensing with his services, brusquely informing him that he did not intend to proceed further with *MILO*.[101] Warlock would commit suicide in December 1930. (According to *MILO* contributor Cecil Gray, 'the more lucrative sources of his income had dried up entirely, and the subsequent collapse of *Milo* and the indefinite suspension of the opera scheme had given the final blow'.[102]) The ILO was effectively wound up that same year (although repeated attempts were made to prop it up in the early 1930s), collapsing before it even got off the ground as a performing venture, following hot on the heels of the BNOC, which had itself ceased operating in 1929. In the assessment of Figaro, the ILO had not known where to position itself in the market. The ILO had stressed its democratic ambitions at the outset but the viability of the entire operation had hinged ultimately upon soliciting and accepting donations from rich people. Moreover, the proposed 1930 season was, for Figaro, a frustrating mish-mash, 'which would neither please the opera-loving masses, nor the cultured patrons of opera'.[103] By the end of the 1920s, then—for all the laudable efforts to create an operatic public—opera's position in British society remained an uncertain one.

One of the really heartening things about the 1920s opera debate was the way in which members of the musical establishment, political figures, and others took active steps to build a larger audience for opera and were not afraid to make the case for it. There is little evidence of social or cultural elites attempting to 'protect' opera from democratisation or to keep opera for themselves (unlike, arguably, Modernist literature). The initiatives to promote opera, as we have seen, were many and varied, as were people's motivations for promoting it. Although one might question the wisdom of children performing complete operas from a vocal point of view, there is no doubt that initiatives such as Charles T. Smith's were well-intentioned and

---

100. Anon., 'Music in England: Sir Thomas Beecham's Criticism', *The Times*, 2 October 1928, 11.

101. Smith, *Peter Warlock*, p. 266.

102. Cecil Gray, *Peter Warlock: A Memoir of Philip Heseltine* (London: Jonathan Cape, 1934), p. 289.

103. Figaro, 'The Operatic World', *MO*, 53/625 (October 1929), 23–4, 24.

yielded positive results, both in terms of giving the children involved enjoyment and shaping their future cultural outlook. Some opera propagandists were motivated by a spirit of political one-upmanship and concerned primarily with Britain's reputation in the world, but it is hard to dispute the sincerity of many in believing that opera was something of benefit both to individuals and to society. These were cultural politics that were underpinned with conviction, and they offered a sharp riposte to anyone who might be inclined to assume that opera was elite or highbrow.

Epilogue

I n the years after the First World War, all those who were involved in producing, performing, writing about, and listening to opera were forced
to reassess its cultural status and its position in British society. Changes
in operatic institutions and practices, in the ways in which opera was disseminated, and in the audiences for it led to a major re-slanting of critical
debates surrounding the art form. These discussions—sparked by a sense
of disorientation, if not crisis—intensified long-standing anxieties about
opera's very legitimacy as a form of British entertainment, as well as becoming entangled with broader discussions about cultural categorisation
that were emerging at that moment in response to the expansion of mass
culture. This was an important moment of reflection that would shape the
way in which British people thought, talked, and wrote about opera for
decades—in some respects, right up to the present.

Analysing the battle of the brows through the lens of a single facet of
culture—opera—can help us to understand that there was in fact no clear
consensus in the 1920s, among intellectuals, critics, or the public at large,
about what the new cultural categories actually meant. The terms highbrow, middlebrow, and lowbrow carried many different connotations, not
only about the artworks in question and their properties but also about
the audiences by which they were received and consumed. In other words,
some of the anxieties contemporary commentators felt about opera were
aesthetic; others were social. Critics couldn't even agree among themselves whether the word highbrow was an insult, a compliment, or a badge
of honour. When applied to opera, it was used variously to mean something too exclusive, too expensive, too cosmopolitan, or too intellectual.

Our operatic case study also stretches to the limit the notion of any sim-plistic cultural 'Great Divide' during this period. As all the evidence pre-sented here demonstrates, opera could not comfortably be categorised as either highbrow or lowbrow. Sectors of the populist press certainly *pre-sented* opera as highbrow, in a bid to perpetuate stereotypes about its sup-posed social exclusivity or out of a suspicion of its foreignness. And those who sought to popularise opera were aware that acknowledging such per-ceptions was a necessary step in combating them. Paget Bowman, legal adviser to the British National Opera Company and one of its founder fig-ures, argued in the company's house magazine in 1923 that opera had an image problem: 'Opera is regarded by thousands as high-brow, difficult-to-understand entertainment, performed by people with enormous voices and nothing else to recommend them, which it is only given to musical people to enjoy'.[1] And yet, as we have seen, opera did remain a form of popular en-tertainment for many so-called 'unmusical' people, while being disdained by some of the most 'musical' people (professional musicians and critics).

Of all art forms, opera was *particularly* difficult to pigeonhole: more so than instrumental music, more so than film. Opera was, in a sense, ultim-ately uncategorisable, partly because it was performed and encountered in so very many different settings during this period: in theatres both elite and humble, in fragments on gramophone recordings, in the concert hall, in restaurants and cafés. It could be highbrow, middlebrow, or lowbrow, depending upon whom you asked; it also took on different associations in different contexts. Opera's resistance to categorisation prompted un-easiness. Its 'slipperiness' within the new categories was a problem both for those highbrows who wanted to take ownership of the canon and for those populists who wanted to sneer at anything that appeared—at least superficially—to be socially or intellectually superior.

Although opera failed to slot neatly into any one cultural category, one might, on balance, make a compelling case that its position in the new clas-sifications was closer to the emerging middlebrow than to the highbrow. This might seem surprising, yet opera was an art form that had for centuries been demonstrating its ease with the ideas of boundary-crossing, genre-crossing, and multiple authorship. During the 1920s it continued to attract large mixed audiences, to be accepted as a form of entertainment like any other, causing a great deal more anxiety in self-styled highbrow snobs than in ordinary people who were content to go to an opera on a Friday and a film on a Saturday. If we detach it from its negative connotations, middlebrow

---

1. Paget Bowman, 'On Broadcasting', *Opera*, 1/6 (June 1923), 18–9, 18. On Paget Bowman's role in setting up the BNOC, see an article in the later journal of the same name: Cedric Wallis, 'The British National Opera Company', *Opera* (January 1955), 20–24.

(as a mindset) becomes a useful term, in that it denotes a certain breadth of taste and allows personal preferences—rather than a deference to cultural hierarchies or critical norms—to dictate cultural choices.

Part of the argument of this book is, of course, to warn against the perils of attempting to pigeonhole artworks. It might, therefore, seem odd to be arguing the case for the middlebrow label within the operatic context. Nevertheless, the impulse to classify and to categorise remains extremely powerful in the present day, and if labels must be applied, then reframing opera as 'middlebrow' could be a useful way of resisting the prevailing assumption that opera is and always has been 'elitist'—a consciously pejorative expression suggestive of social exclusion that has emerged with particular vehemence in recent decades. The elitism rhetoric—often perpetuated by hostile journalists who have never seen an opera—hinges upon stereotypes about expense, class, exclusivity, and pretension that not only misrepresent the diversity of present-day operatic culture but are also entirely blind to the nuances of operatic history. My 1920s case study provides a refreshing counterblast to current anti-operatic prejudices, demonstrating that in the not-so-distant past, opera was accepted as a form of entertainment with numerous connections to popular culture.

There are, of course, many ways in which operatic culture has changed since the 1920s—both for good and for ill. On the positive side, standards of performance are now almost universally higher than they were in the 1920s, with the quintessentially British habit of 'making do' of that era being replaced by an industry that is now professional, as highly esteemed as any in the world, and that has excellent systems in place for the training of singers. On the negative side, live opera has become more of a curiosity than it once was because of a relative decline in touring opera. Notwithstanding the valiant efforts of Opera North, Scottish Opera, Welsh National Opera, English Touring Opera, and others, a visit from a touring opera company no longer has the prominence in a local social calendar that it once did, and many towns and cities receive no visits at all. British operatic discourses have also evolved considerably since the 1920s, in response to changes in funding, cultural policy, institutions, and performing practices.

And yet for all these differences, it is worth pointing to a number of distinct similarities between the operatic culture of the present day and that of the 1920s, with its vivid connections to popular culture and 'everyday life'. New opera companies continue to form, and to find innovative ways of performing opera to diverse audiences in a multiplicity of everyday spaces: witness, for example, the recent trend for scaled-down performances in London pubs. Excerpts from operas are used frequently in film soundtracks, advertising, even occasionally via appropriation into popular song, and opera's most famous performers—if only those of an older generation, such as Pavarotti, Domingo, and Carreras—are household names. High-profile opera singers still combine 'serious' repertory with performances (whether live or on disc) of popular arias and sometimes even pop songs or show tunes. These phenomena demonstrate that opera continues to interact fruitfully with a wide variety of forms of popular culture. They also prompt a certain degree of hand-wringing from some sectors of the opera-loving community.

Indeed, many of the arguments that people were having about opera during the 1920s continue to rumble on today. There are still debates, just as there were a century ago, about whether opera is a socially important or relevant art form and anxieties remain about the 'proper' relationship between opera and various forms of mass culture. The opera audience was never entirely 'poached' by film (nor by the other forms of technological media that would follow), yet those invested in opera remain concerned today about the threat posed to live performance by cinema relays. The refrain about opera becoming a museum culture has only intensified, and the death of the art form continues to be regularly heralded. Questions about the funding of opera have not gone away, and painfully those advocating on behalf of opera have to make the case for its legitimacy, even for its existence, even more strongly than they did during the 1920s. Yet opera as an institution has shown great robustness, and new and imaginative works continue to be written, even if they struggle to enter the performing canon.

Perhaps, in considering the challenges that face opera today—and in particular anxieties about audience diversity or the lack of it—we can take a few seeds of hope from reflecting upon the debates of the 1920s. Undercurrents of snobbery from above and suspicion from below swirled around opera in 1920s Britain, and yet it is equally important to recognise that there were also many sincere attempts to get more people listening to it and to educate people about it. In demonstrating the historical fluidity between so-called 'high art' and popular culture, I hope that my research will challenge present-day assumptions that opera is and always has been 'elitist'. Opera has meant different things in different historical periods: its status has changed many times in the past and could, if we are determined enough, change again.

I also hope that my findings about the cultural eclecticism of an earlier age and opera's resistance to reductive labelling will provide opera companies with inspiration for creative ways of engaging new audiences. Presenting opera as something everyday, restoring its 'normality' and arguing persuasively that opera is not 'a thing apart', is the strongest tool operatic outreach departments have, and they would be well advised to find strategies to make this point.[2] There is much else that needs to change: public broadcasters could go further in putting cultural programming centre stage, governments could recognise the importance of the arts in the school curriculum, public figures could attend and talk about cultural events more openly. Opera is not, to return to Basil Maine's pithy maxim, 'a luxury', nor need it be 'absurd', but if future audiences are to stand a chance of encountering its musical beauty, its political bite, and the many consolations it offers in difficult times it does need, once more, to become 'a habit'.

2. Referring to drama rather than opera specifically (although the same approach could be used), McColvin advised in 1926: 'Tell him . . . that *Twelfth Night* is a good farce and *Macbeth* a good melodrama—as they undoubtedly are; rid his head of the idea that Shakespeare is primarily something else, something much more "brainy" and stodgy'. McColvin, *Euterpe, or the Future of Art*, p. 44.

BIBLIOGRAPHY

PRIMARY SOURCES
Archival collections

BBC Written Archives Centre

    BBC Written Archives Centre R27/326/1 Music Gen—Opera—General Memos 1929–34; WAC R27/375/1 Opera General Policy April 1930–December 1938, file 1.

Oxford University Opera Club programmes

    Oxford University Opera Club Programmes, Bodleian Library, University of Oxford shelf-mark 17405 d. 27 (boxes 1–2).

Victoria & Albert Theatre and Performance Collections

    Production boxes for Covent Garden, the Old Vic, the Scala Theatre; performer boxes for Amelita Galli-Curci, Maria Jeritza.

Newspapers and periodicals

APOLLO.
The Athenaeum.
The Bookman.
The British Musician.
The Daily Express.
The Daily Mail.
The Daily Mirror.
The Daily Telegraph.
Dancing Times.
The Dominant.
The Dundee Courier.
The English Review.
The Era.
Femina.
The Financial Times.
The Gloucester Journal.
The Graphic.
The Hull Daily Mail.
The Illustrated London News.
The London Mercury.
Magazine of the Imperial League of Opera (MILO).
The Manchester Guardian.
The Midland Musician.
Music & Letters.
The Musical Mirror.

Musical Opinion.
The Musical Standard.
The Musical Times.
The Nottingham Evening Post.
The Old Vic. Magazine.
Opera.
The Portsmouth Evening News.
The Queen.
The Sackbut.
The Saturday Review.
The School Music Review.
The Stage.
The Strand.
The Sunday Post.
Tatler.
Time.
The Times.
The Western Daily Press.
The Yorkshire Evening Post.
The Yorkshire Post.
Yorkshire Post and Leeds Intelligencer.

Articles and books

Anon., Royal Opera, Covent Garden, *Stories of the Operas and the Singers*, Official Souvenir, Season 1919.

Anon., *Opera at Home* (London: The Gramophone Company, 1921).

Anon., *Orpheus: A Story in Music by Claudio Monteverde* (Oxford: The Holywell Press, 1925).

Anon., Royal Opera, Covent Garden, *Stories of the Operas and the Singers*, Official Souvenir, Season 1926.

Beecham, Thomas, *A Mingled Chime: Leaves from an Autobiography* (London, New York and Melbourne: Hutchinson, 1944).

Benjamin, Walter, 'The Work of Art in the Age of Mechanical Reproduction', in Hannah Arendt (Ed.), *Illuminations* (London: Pimlico, 1999), 211–44.

Betts, Ernest, *Heraclitus, or the Future of Films* (London and New York: Kegan Paul, Trench, Trubner and Co. Ltd. and E. P. Dutton & Co., 1928).

Blom, Eric, *Stepchildren of Music* (London: G. T Foulis and Company, 1925).

Bonavia, F., *Verdi* (London: Oxford University Press, 1930).

Boughton, Rutland, *The Glastonbury Festival Movement* (London: Somerset Folk Press, 1922).

Brimley Johnson, R., *Moral Poison in Modern Fiction* (London: A. M. Philpot Ltd., 1923).

Broadley Greene, K., *How to Listen to Good Music and Encourage the Taste in Instrumental and Vocal Music* (London: William Reeves, 1923).

Busenello, Giovanni Francesco, *The Coronation of Poppaea* (Oxford: The Holywell Press, 1927).

Calvocoressi, M. D., *The Principles and Methods of Musical Criticism* (London: Oxford University Press, 1923).

Calvocoressi, M. D., *Musician's Gallery: Music and Ballet in Paris and London* (London: Faber and Faber, 1933).

Capell, Richard, *Opera* (London: Ernest Benn, Ltd., 1930).

Cardus, Neville (Ed.), *Samuel Langford: Musical Criticisms* (London: Oxford University Press, 1929).

Cecil, Captain George, *The History of Opera in England* (Taunton: Barnicott and Pearce, the Wessex Press, 1930).

Collier, John, and Iain Lang, *Just the Other Day: An Informal History of Great Britain since the War* (London: Hamish Hamilton, 1932).

Colson, Percy, *Those Uneasy Years. 1914–1939: A Medley* (London: Sampson Low, Marston & Co., 1948).

Demuth, Norman, *An Anthology of Music Criticism* (London: Eyre and Spottiswoode, 1947).

Dent, Edward J., *Terpander; or, Music and the Future* (London and New York: Kegan Paul, Trench, Trubner and Co. Ltd. and E. P. Dutton & Co., 1926).

Dent, Edward J., *Foundations of English Opera: A Study of Musical Drama in England During the Seventeenth Century* (London: Cambridge University Press, 1928).

England, Paul, *50 Favourite Operas: A Popular Account Intended as an Aid to Dramatic and Musical Appreciation* (London: Harrap, 1925).

Evans, Edwin, *The Margin of Music* (London: Oxford University Press/Humphrey Milford, 1924).

Flügel, J. C., *The Psychology of Clothes* (London: The Hogarth Press, 1930).

Forsyth, Cecil, *Music and Nationalism: A Study of English Opera* (London: Macmillan, 1911).

Foss, Hubert J., *Music in My Time* (London: Rich and Cowan Ltd., 1933).

Fuller-Maitland, J., *The Spell of Music: An Attempt to Analyse the Enjoyment of Music* (London: John Murray, 1926).

Geale, John B., *A Short History of the Royal Albert Hall, London* (London: F. J. Milner, 1944).

Geale, John B., *A Short History of the Royal Albert Hall London*, 2nd edn (London: n.p., 1949).

Grace, Harvey, *The Organ Works of Bach* (London: Novello, 1923).

Graves, Robert, and Alan Hodge, *The Long Weekend: A Social History of Great Britain, 1918–1939* (London: The Folio Society, 2009; first published Faber and Faber, 1940).

Gray, Cecil, *A Survey of Contemporary Music*, 2nd edn (London: Oxford University Press/ Humphrey Milford, 1927).

Gray, Cecil, *Peter Warlock: A Memoir of Philip Heseltine* (London: Jonathan Cape, 1934).

Grew, Sydney, *Favourite Musical Performers* (Edinburgh and London: T. N. Foulis, Ltd., 1923).

Hempel, Frieda, *My Golden Age of Singing* (Portland, Oregon: Amadeus Press, 1998).

Hussey, Dyneley, *Eurydice, or the Nature of Opera* (London and New York: Kegan Paul, Trench, Trubner and Co. Ltd. and E. P. Dutton & Co., 1929).

Huxley, Aldous, *Music at Night and Other Essays* (London: Chatto and Windus, 1931).

Jeritza, Maria, *Sunshine and Song: A Singer's Life* (New York and London: D. Appleton, 1924).

Kennedy, Margaret, *The Constant Nymph* (London: Vintage, 2014) [originally William Heinemann, 1924].

Klein, Herman, *Musicians and Mummers* (London, New York, Toronto, and Melbourne: Cassell and Company, 1925).

Klein, Herman, *Great Women Singers of my Time* (London: Routledge and Sons, Ltd., 1931).

Klein, Herman, *The Golden Age of Opera* (London: George Routledge and Sons, Ltd., 1933).

Leavis, F. R., *Mass Civilisation and Minority Culture* (Cambridge: The Minority Press, 1930).

Leavis, Q. D., *Fiction and the Reading Public* (London: Chatto and Windus, 1932).

McColvin, Lionel R., *Euterpe, or the Future of Art* (London and New York: Kegan Paul, Trench, Trubner and Co. Ltd. and E. P. Dutton & Co., 1926).

Mackenzie, Compton, *My Record of Music* (London: Hutchinson, 1955).

Mackenzie, Compton, *My Life and Times: Octave Five, 1915–1923* (London: Chatto and Windus, 1966).

Mackenzie, Compton, *My Life and Times: Octave Six 1923–30* (London: Chatto and Windus, 1967).

Maine, Basil, *Behold These Daniels: Being Studies of Contemporary Music Critics* (London: H. & W. Brown, 1928).

Marchesi, Blanche, *Singer's Pilgrimage* (London: Grant Richards, 1923).

Margrie, William, *A Cockney's Pilgrimage: In Search of Truth* (London: Watts & Co., 1927).

Melba, Nellie, *Melodies and Memories* (London: Butterworth, 1925).

Melitz, Leo, *The Opera-Goers' Complete Guide: Comprising 268 Complete Opera Plots, with Musical Numbers and Casts* (London and Toronto: Dent, 1925).

Mendl, R. W. S., *From a Music Lover's Armchair* (London: Philip Allan and Co., 1926).

Mendl, R. W. S., *The Appeal of Jazz* (London: Philip Allan and Co., 1927).

Myers, Rollo H., *Modern Music: Its Aims and Tendencies* (London and New York: Kegan Paul, Trench, Trubner and Co. Ltd. and E. P. Dutton & Co., 1923).

Newman, Ernest, *A Musical Critic's Holiday* (London: Cassell, 1925).

Newman, Ernest, *From The World of Music: Essays from The Sunday Times Selected by Felix Aprahamian* (London: John Calder, 1956).

Newman, Ernest, *More Essays from the World of Music: Essays from The Sunday Times Selected by Felix Aprahamian* (London: John Calder, 1958).

Newman, Vera, *Ernest Newman: A Memoir By His Wife* (London: Putnam, 1963).

Nicolson, Nigel (Ed.), *A Change of Perspective: The Letters of Virginia Woolf, 1923–1928* (London: Chatto & Windus, 1977).

Norris, Herbert, *Costume and Fashion: The Evolution of European Dress* (London and Toronto: J. M. Dent and Sons, 1924).

Norris, Herbert, *Costume and Fashion: Volume Two Senlac to Bosworth, 1066–1485* (London and Toronto: J. M. Dent and Sons, 1927).

O'Donnell, Josephine, *Among the Covent Garden Stars* (London: Stanley Paul, 1936).

Peppin, A. H., *Public Schools and Their Music* (Oxford and London: Oxford University Press and Humphrey Milford, 1927).

Phillips, Henry, *Musical and Personal Recollection During Half a Century*, Volume II (London: Charles J. Skeet, 1864).

Ponsonby, Robert, and Richard Kent, *The Oxford University Opera Club: A Short History 1925–1950* (Oxford: The Potter Press, 1950).

Poucher, W. A., *Eve's Beauty Secrets* (Chapman and Hall, Ltd.: London, 1926).

Priestley, J. B., *Open House: A Book of Essays* (London: William Heinemann Ltd., 1927).

Ronald, Landon, *Variations on a Personal Theme* (Toronto, London and New York: Hodder and Stoughton, 1922).

Ronald, Landon, *Myself and Others: Written Lest I Forget* (London: Sampson Low, Marston & Co., 1931).

Rosenthal, Harold, *Two Centuries of Opera at Covent Garden* (London: Putnam, 1958).

Russell, Henry, *The Passing Show* (London: Thornton Butterworth Ltd., 1926).

Savill, Agnes, *Music, Health and Character* (London: John Lane, The Bodley Head, 1923).

Scholes, Percy A., *Learning to Listen by Means of the Gramophone: A Course in the Appreciation of Music for Use in Schools* (London: The Gramophone Co. Ltd., 1921).

Scholes, Percy A., *The First Book of the Gramophone Record* (London: Oxford University Press, 1924).

Scholes, Percy A., *Everybody's Guide to Broadcast Music* (London: Oxford University Press/ Hodder and Stoughton, 1925).

Scholes, Percy A., *The Second Book of the Gramophone Record* (London: Oxford University Press, 1925).

Scholes, Percy A., *A Miniature History of Opera: For the General Reader and the Student* (London: Oxford University Press, Humphrey Milton, 1931).

Sherson, Erroll, *London's Lost Theatres of the Nineteenth-Century, With Notes on Plays and Players Seen There* (London: John Lane, The Bodley Head, 1925).

Simnett, W. E., *Books and Reading* (London: George Allen and Unwin, 1926).

Smith, Charles T., *The Music of Life: Education for Leisure and Culture, With Curricula Evolved By Experiment in an Elementary School*, 2nd edn (London: P. S. King and Son, 1919).

Smith, Charles T., *The School of Life: A Theatre of Education* (London: Grant Richards, Ltd., 1921).

Strauss, Rita, *The Beauty Book* (London, NY, Toronto and Melbourne: Cassell, 1924).

Tetrazzini, Luisa, *My Life of Song* (London: Cassell, 1921).

Tetrazzini, Luisa, *How to Sing* (London: C. Arthur Pearson, 1923).

Toye, Francis, *The Well-Tempered Musician: A Musical Point of View* (London: Methuen and Co., 1925).

Toye, Francis, *Giuseppe Verdi: His Life and Works* (London: William Heinemann, 1930).

Trewin, J. C., with pictures by Raymond Mander and Joe Mitchenson, *The Gay Twenties: A Decade of the Theatre* (London: MacDonald, 1958).

Turner, W. J., *Variations on the Theme of Music* (London: Heinemann, 1924).

Turner, W. J., *Orpheus, or the Music of the Future* (London and New York: Kegan Paul, Trench, Trubner and Co. Ltd. and E. P. Dutton & Co., 1926).

Wagnalls, Mabel, *Opera and Its Stars: A Description of the Music and Stories of the Enduring Operas and a Series of Interviews with the World's Famous Sopranos* (New York and London: Funk and Wagnalls, 1924).

Wagner, Charles L., *Seeing Stars* (New York: G. P. Putnam's Sons, 1940).

Waugh, Evelyn, *Brideshead Revisited* (London: Penguin Classics, 2000; first published London: Chapman and Hall, 1945).

Wells, H. G., *The Salvaging of Civilization* (London, New York, Toronto, and Melbourne: Cassell and Company, 1921).

Wood, Thomas, *Music and Boyhood: Some Suggestions on the Possibilities of Music in Public, Preparatory and other Schools* (Oxford and London: Oxford University Press/Humphrey Milton, 1925).

Woolf, Leonard, *Hunting the Highbrow* (London: The Hogarth Press, 1927).

SECONDARY SOURCES

Ashley, Mike, *The Age of the Storytellers: British Popular Fiction Magazines 1880–1950* (London: The British Library and Oak Knoll Press, 2006).

Aspden, Suzanne, *Rival Sirens: Performance and Identity on Handel's Operatic Stage* (Cambridge: Cambridge University Press, 2013).

Ayers, David, *English Literature of the 1920s* (Edinburgh: Edinburgh University Press, 2004).

Barbas, Samantha, *Movie Crazy: Fans, Stars, and the Cult of Celebrity* (New York and Basingstoke: Palgrave, 2001).

Barker, Clive, and Maggie B. Gale (Eds.), *British Theatre Between the Wars, 1918–1939* (Cambridge: Cambridge University Press, 2000).

Baxendale, John, *Priestley's England: J. B. Priestley and English Culture* (Manchester: Manchester University Press, 2007).

Bigio, Robert, *Rudall, Rose and Carte: The Art of the Flute in Britain* (London: Tony Bingham, 2011).

Bloom, Clive, *Bestsellers: Popular Fiction Since 1900*, 2nd edn (Basingstoke: Palgrave Macmillan, 2008).

Bracco, Rosa Maria, *Merchants of Hope: British Middlebrow Writers and the First World War, 1919–1939* (Providence and Oxford: Berg, 1993).

Brantlinger, Patrick, *The Reading Lesson: The Threat of Mass Literacy in Nineteenth-Century British Fiction* (Bloomington and Indianapolis: Indiana University Press, 1998).

Bribitzer-Stull, Matthew, *Understanding the Leitmotif: From Wagner to Hollywood Film Music* (Cambridge: Cambridge University Press, 2015).

Brooker, Peter, and Andrew Thacker (Eds.), *The Oxford Critical and Cultural History of Modernist Magazines, Vol. 1, Britain and Ireland, 1880–1955* (Oxford: Oxford University Press, 2009).

Brown, Erica, and Mary Grover (Eds.), *Middlebrow Literary Cultures: The Battle of the Brows, 1920–1960* (Basingstoke: Palgrave Macmillan, 2012).

Brown, Julie, 'Framing the Atmospheric Film Prologue in Britain, 1919–1926', in Julie Brown and Annette Davison (Eds.), *The Sounds of the Silents in Britain* (New York: Oxford University Press, 2013), pp. 200–21.

Burdekin, Russell, 'The Failure to Establish English Opera in the Nineteenth Century', unpublished MA dissertation, Oxford Brookes University, 2015.

Burrows, Jon, *Legitimate Cinema: Theatre Stars in Silent British Films, 1908–1918* (Exeter: University of Exeter Press, 2003).

Carey, John, *The Intellectuals and the Masses: Pride and Prejudice Among the Literary Intelligentsia, 1880–1939* (London: Faber and Faber, 1992).

Chanan, Michael, *Repeated Takes: A Short History of Recording and its Effects on Music* (London and New York: Verso, 1995).

Chowrimootoo, Christopher, 'Bourgeois Opera: *Death in Venice* and the Aesthetics of Sublimation', *Cambridge Opera Journal*, 22/2 (2010), 175–216.

Collini, Stefan, *Absent Minds: Intellectuals in Britain* (Oxford and New York: Oxford University Press, 2006).

Collini, Stefan, *Common Reading: Critics, Historians, Publics* (New York: Oxford University Press, 2008).

Collins, Sarah, ' "Never Out of Date and Never Modern": Aesthetic Democracy, Radical Music Criticism and *The Sackbut*', *Music and Letters*, 95/3 (2014), 404–28.

Cormac, Joanne, 'From Satirical Piece to Commercial Product: The Mid-Victorian Opera Burlesque and its Bourgeois Audience', *Journal of the Royal Musical Association*, 142/1 (2017), 69–108.

Cuddy-Keane, Melba, *Virginia Woolf, the Intellectual and the Public Sphere* (Cambridge: Cambridge University Press, 2003).

Davies, J. Q., 'Veluti in Speculum: the Twilight of the Castrato', *Cambridge Opera Journal*, 17/3 (2005), 271–301.

DiMaggio, Paul, 'Cultural Boundaries and Structural Change: The Extension of the High Culture Model to Theater, Opera, and the Dance, 1900–1940', in Michèle Lamont and Marcel Fournier (Eds.), *Cultivating Differences: Symbolic Boundaries and the Making of Inequality* (Chicago and London: University of Chicago Press, 1992), pp. 21–55.

Dizikes, John, *Opera in America: A Cultural History* (New Haven and London: Yale University Press, 1993).

D'Monté, Rebecca, *British Theatre and Performance, 1900–1950* (London: Bloomsbury, 2015).

Doctor, Jennifer, *The BBC and Ultra-Modern Music, 1922–1936: Shaping a Nation's Tastes* (Cambridge: Cambridge University Press, 1999).

Double, Oliver, *Britain Had Talent: A History of Variety Theatre* (Basingstoke: Palgrave Macmillan, 2012).

Dzamba Sessa, Anne, *Richard Wagner and the English* (London: Associated University Presses, 1979).

Fauser, Annegret, 'The Scholar Behind the Medal: Edward J. Dent (1876–1957) and the Politics of Music History', *Journal of the Royal Musical Association*, 139/2 (2014), 235–60.

Federico, Annette R., *Idol of Suburbia: Marie Corelli and Late-Victorian Literary Culture* (Charlottesville and London: University Press of Virginia, 2000).

Fillion, Michelle, *Difficult Rhythm: Music and the Word in E. M. Forster* (Urbana, Chicago and Springfield: University of Illinois Press, 2010).

Fryer, Paul, *The Opera Singer and the Silent Film* (Jefferson, N. C. and London: McFarland, 2005).

Gale, Maggie B., *West End Women: Women and the London Stage, 1918–1962* (London and New York: Routledge, 1996).

Gilbert, Susie, *Opera for Everybody: The Story of English National Opera* (London: Faber and Faber, 2009).

Glixon, Beth, 'Private Lives of Public Women: Prima Donnas in Mid Seventeenth-Century Venice', *Music & Letters*, 76/4 (November 1995), 509–31.

Gould, Corissa, 'Aspiring to Manliness: Edward Elgar and the Pressures of Hegemonic Masculinity', in Ian Biddle and Kirsten Gibson (Eds.), *Masculinity and Western Musical Practice* (Farnham and Burlington, VT: Ashgate, 2005), 161–81.

Gumbrecht, Hans Ulrich, *In 1926: Living at the Edge of Time* (Cambridge, MA and London: Harvard University Press, 1997).

Gundle, Stephen, and Clino T. Castelli, *The Glamour System* (Basingstoke: Palgrave MacMillan, 2006).

Guthrie, Kate, 'Democratizing Art: Music Education in Postwar Britain', *The Musical Quarterly*, 97/4 (Winter 2014), 575–615.

Hall-Witt, Jennifer, *Fashionable Acts: Opera and Elite Culture in London, 1780–1880* (Lebanon, NH: University of New Hampshire Press, 2007).

Hamberlin, Larry, *Tin Pan Opera: Operatic Novelty Songs in the Ragtime Era* (Oxford and New York: Oxford University Press, 2011).

Hand, Richard J., and Michael Wilson, *London's Grand Guignol and the Theatre of Horror* (Exeter: University of Exeter Press, 2007).

Haywood, Ian, *The Revolution in Popular Literature: Print, Politics and the People, 1790–1860* (Cambridge: Cambridge University Press, 2004).

Henson, Karen, *Opera Acts: Singers and Performance in the Late Nineteenth Century* (Cambridge: Cambridge University Press, 2015).

Henson, Karen (Ed.), *Technology and the Diva: Sopranos, Opera, and Media from Romanticism to the Digital Age* (Cambridge: Cambridge University Press, 2016).

Holt, Richard, *Sport and the British: A Modern History* (Oxford: Clarendon Press, 1992).

Houlbrook, Matt, *Queer London: Perils and Pleasures in the Sexual Metropolis, 1918–1957* (Chicago and London: The University of Chicago Press, 2005).

Houlbrook, Matt, *Prince of Tricksters: The Incredible True Story of Netley Lucas, Gentleman Crook* (Chicago and London: Chicago University Press, 2016).

Howard, Diana, *London Theatres and Music Halls 1850–1950* (London: The Library Association, 1970).

Huggins, Mike, *Horseracing and the British, 1919–1930* (Manchester: Manchester University Press, 2003).

Hughes, Meirion, and Robert Stradling, *The English Musical Renaissance, 1840–1940: Constructing a National Music*, 2nd edn (Manchester: Manchester University Press, 2001).

Humble, Nicola, *The Feminine Middlebrow Novel, 1920s to 1950s: Class, Domesticity, and Bohemianism* (Oxford: Oxford University Press, 2001).

Hurd, Michael, *Rutland Boughton and the Glastonbury Festivals* (Croydon: The Rutland Boughton Memorial Trust, 2014).

Huyssen, Andreas, *After the Great Divide: Modernism, Mass Culture, Postmodernism* (Basingstoke: Macmillan, 1988).

Joe, Jeongwon, and Sander L. Gilman (Eds.), *Wagner and Cinema* (Bloomington: Indiana University Press, 2010).

Joncus, Berta, 'A Star is Born: Kitty Clive and Female Representation in Eighteenth-Century English Musical Theatre', unpublished doctoral dissertation, University of Oxford, 2004.

Julius, Anthony, *Trials of the Diaspora: A History of Anti-Semitism in England* (Oxford and New York: Oxford University Press, 2010).

Kerman, Joseph, *Opera as Drama*, new and revised edn (London: Faber and Faber, 1989).

Kift, Dagmar, *The Victorian Music Hall: Culture, Class and Conflict* (Cambridge: Cambridge University Press, 1996).

Kilburn, Mike, *London's Theatres* (London: New Holland Publishers, 2002).

Kreuzer, Gundula, *Verdi and the Germans: From Unification to the Third Reich* (Cambridge: Cambridge University Press, 2010).

Latham, Sean, *Am I a Snob? Modernism and the Novel* (Cornell: Cornell University Press, 2003).

LeMahieu, D. L., *A Culture for Democracy: Mass Communication and the Cultivated Mind in Britain Between the Wars* (Oxford: Clarendon Press, 1988).

Leonardi, Susan J., and Rebecca A. Pope, *The Diva's Mouth: Body, Voice, Prima Donna Politics* (New Brunswick, NJ: Rutgers University Press, 1996).

Levi, Erik, *Music in the Third Reich* (Basingstoke: Macmillan, 1994).

Levine, Lawrence W., *Highbrow/Lowbrow: The Emergence of Cultural Hierarchy in America* (Cambridge, MA: Harvard University Press, 1988).

Light, Alison, *Forever England: Femininity, Literature and Conservatism Between the Wars* (London and New York: Routledge, 1991).

Littau, Karin, *Theories of Reading: Books, Bodies and Bibliomania* (Cambridge: Polity Press, 2006).

Lucas, John, *Thomas Beecham: An Obsession with Music* (Woodbridge: The Boydell Press, 2008).

McAllister, Annemarie, *John Bull's Italian Snakes and Ladders: English Attitudes to Italy in the Mid Nineteenth Century* (Newcastle upon Tyne: Cambridge Scholars, 2007).

MacDonald, Hugh, *Music in 1853: The Biography of a Year* (Woodbridge: Boydell, 2012).

Macdonald, Kate (Ed.), *The Masculine Middlebrow, 1880–1950: What Mr Miniver Read* (Basingstoke: Palgrave Macmillan, 2011).

MacKenzie, John M., *Propaganda and Empire: The Manipulation of British Public Opinion, 1880–1960* (Manchester: Manchester University Press, 1984).

McKibbin, Ross, *Classes and Cultures: England 1918–1951* (Oxford: Oxford University Press 1998, repr. 2013).

Macy, Laura (Ed.), *The Grove Book of Opera Singers* (New York: Oxford University Press, 2008).

Martin, George, *Verdi at the Golden Gate: Opera and San Francisco in the Gold Rush Years* (Berkeley, Los Angeles, and Oxford: University of California Press, 1993).

Martin, George W., *Opera at the Bandstand: Then and Now* (Plymouth: Scarecrow Press, 2014).

Martin, Steven Edward, 'The British "Operatic Machine": Investigations into the Institutional History of English Opera, c. 1875–1939', unpublished PhD dissertation, University of Bristol (2010).

Marvin, Roberta Montemorra, 'Verdian Opera Burlesqued: A Glimpse into Mid-Victorian Theatrical Culture', *Cambridge Opera Journal*, 15/1 (2003), 33–66.

Mays, Kelly J., 'The Disease of Reading and Victorian Periodicals', in John O. Jordan and Robert L. Patten (Eds.), *Literature in the Marketplace: Nineteenth-Century British Publishing and Reading Practices* (Cambridge: Cambridge University Press, 1995), pp. 165–94.

Melman, Billie, *Women and the Popular Imagination in the Twenties: Flappers and Nymphs* (Basingstoke: Macmillan, 1988).

Milestone, Rachel, '"A New Impetus to the Love of Music": The Role of the Town Hall in Nineteenth-Century English Musical Culture', unpublished doctoral thesis, University of Leeds, 2009.

Morra, Irene, *Twentieth-Century British Authors and the Rise of Opera in Britain* (Aldershot: Ashgate, 2007).

Napper, Lawrence, *British Cinema and Middlebrow Culture in the Interwar Years* (Exeter: University of Exeter Press, 2009).

Nicholson, Steve, *The Censorship of British Drama 1900–1968. Volume 1: 1900–1932* (Exeter: University of Exeter Press, 2003).

Nott, James J., *Music for the People: Popular Music and Dance in Interwar Britain* (Oxford and New York: Oxford University Press, 2002).

Nott, James, *Going to the Palais: A Social and Cultural History of Dancing and Dance Halls in Britain, 1918–1960* (Oxford: Oxford University Press, 2015).

Overy, Richard, *The Morbid Age: Britain and the Crisis of Civilization* (London: Penguin Books, 2009).

Paz, Lina María, 'Crinolines and Bustles: The Reign of Metallic Artifices', in Denis Bruna (Ed.), *Fashioning the Body: An Intimate History of the Silhouette* (New Haven and London: Yale University Press, 2015), pp. 177–97.

Phillips-Matz, Mary Jane, *Rosa Ponselle: American Diva* (Boston: Northeastern University Press, 1997).

Poliakoff, Michael B., *Combat Sports in the Ancient World: Competition, Violence, and Culture* (New Haven and London: Yale University Press, 1987).

Poriss, Hilary, 'Prima Donnas and the Performance of Altruism', in Rachel Cowgill and Hilary Poriss (Eds.), *The Arts of the Prima Donna in the Long Nineteenth Century* (New York: Oxford University Press, 2012), pp. 42–60.

Pugh, Martin, *'We Danced All Night': A Social History of Britain Between the Wars* (London: Vintage, 2009).

Ribeiro, Aileen, *Facing Beauty: Painted Women and Cosmetic Art* (New Haven: Yale University Press, 2011).

Rodmell, Paul, *Opera in the British Isles, 1875–1918* (Farnham and Burlington VT.: Ashgate, 2013).

Rohr, Deborah, *The Careers of British Musicians: 1750–1850* (Cambridge: Cambridge University Press, 2001).

Ronzani, Michela, 'Creating Success and Forming Imaginaries: The Innovative Publicity Campaign for Puccini's *La bohème*', in Christina Bashford and Roberta Montemorra Marvin (Eds.), *The Idea of Art Music in a Commercial World, 1800–1930* (Woodbridge: The Boydell Press, 2016), pp. 39–59.

Rose, Jonathan, *The Intellectual Life of the British Working Classes*, 2nd edn (New Haven: Yale University Press, 2010).

Russell, Dave, *Popular Music in England, 1840–1914: A Social History*, 2nd edn (Manchester and New York: Manchester University Press, 1997).

Rutherford, Susan, *The Prima Donna and Opera, 1815–1930* (Cambridge: Cambridge University Press, 2006).

Salmon, Richard, 'Signs of Intimacy: The Literary Celebrity in the "Age of Interviewing"', *Victorian Literature and Culture*, 25/1 (1997), 159–77.

Sansone, Matteo, 'The "Verismo" of Ruggero Leoncavallo: A Source Study of *Pagliacci*', *Music & Letters*, 70/3 (August 1989), 342–62.

Scaife, Nigel, 'British Music Criticism in a New Era: Studies in Critical Thought, 1894–1945', unpublished DPhil thesis, University of Oxford, 1994.

Scott, Derek, *Sounds of the Metropolis: The 19th-Century Popular Music Revolution in London, New York, Paris and Vienna* (New York: Oxford University Press, 2008).

Scott, Michael, *The Record of Singing*, Vol. 2 1914–1925 (London: Duckworth, 1979).

Seta, Fabrizio Della , 'Some Difficulties in the Historiography of Italian Opera', *Cambridge Opera Journal*, 10/1 (March 1998), 3–13.

Sheppard, Jennifer R., 'Sound of Body: Music, Sports and Health in Victorian Britain', *Journal of the Royal Musical Association*, 140/2 (2015), 343–69.

Shewring, Margaret, 'Reinhardt's *Miracle* at the Olympia: A Record and a Reconstruction', *New Theatre Quarterly*, 3/9 (February 1987), 3–23.

Smart, Mary Ann, 'The Lost Voice of Rosina Stoltz', in Corinne E. Blackmer and Patricia Juliana Smith (Eds.), *En Travesti: Women, Gender Subversion, Opera* (New York: Columbia University Press, 1995), pp. 169–89.

Smith, Barry, *Peter Warlock: The Life of Philip Heseltine* (Oxford and New York: Oxford University Press, 1994).

Snowman, Daniel, *The Gilded Stage: A Social History of Opera* (London: Atlantic Books, 2009).

Søland, Birgitte, Becoming Modern: Young Women and the Reconstruction of Womanhood in the 1920s (Princeton: Princeton University Press, 2000).

Trotter, David, *Literature in the First Media Age: Britain Between the Wars* (Cambridge, MA and London: Harvard University Press, 2013).

Tunbridge, Laura, 'Frieda Hempel and the Historical Imagination', *Journal of the American Musicological Society*, 66/2 (2013), 437–74.

Tunbridge, Laura, 'Singing Translations: The Politics of Listening Between the Wars', *Representations*, 23/1 (summer 2013), 53–86.

Walkowitz, Judith R., *Nights Out: Life in Cosmopolitan London* (New Haven and London: Yale University Press, 2012).

Watt, Paul, 'Critics', in Helen Greenwald (Ed.), *The Oxford Handbook of Opera* (New York: Oxford University Press, 2014), pp. 881–98.

Wearing, J. P., *The London Stage 1920–1929: A Calendar of Productions, Performers, and Personnel*, 2nd edn (Lanham, Boulder, NY, Toronto, Plymouth: Rowman and Littlefield, 2014).

Weber, William, *The Great Transformation of Musical Taste: Concert Programming from Haydn to Brahms* (Cambridge: Cambridge University Press, 2008).

West, Emma, ' "Battle of the Brows": Cultural Stratification in Modern Britain, 1867–1948', unpublished MA dissertation, Cardiff University, 2011.

White, Eric Walter, *The Rise of English Opera* (London: John Lehmann, 1951).

White, Eric Walter, *A Register of First Performances of English Operas and Semi-Operas from the 16th Century to 1980* (London: The Society for Theatre Research, 1983).

Williams, Gordon, *British Theatre in the Great War: A Revaluation* (London and New York: Continuum, 2003).

Williams, Jack, *Cricket and England: A Cultural and Social History of the Inter-war Years* (London and Portland, Oregon: Frank Cass, 1999).

Wilson, Alexandra, 'Modernism and the Machine Woman in Puccini's *Turandot*', *Music & Letters*, 86/3 (2005), 432–51.

Wilson, Alexandra, 'Killing Time: Contemporary Representations of Opera in British Culture', *Cambridge Opera Journal*, 19/3 (2007), 249–70.

Wilson, Alexandra, 'Prima Donnas or Working Girls? Opera Singers as Female Role Models in Britain, 1900–1925', *Women's History Magazine*, 55 (2007), 4–12.

Wilson, Alexandra, *The Puccini Problem: Opera, Nationalism, and Modernity* (Cambridge: Cambridge University Press, 2007).

Wilson, Alexandra, 'Defining Italianness: The Opera that Made Puccini', *The Opera Quarterly*, 24/1–2 (2008), 82–92.

Wilson, Alexandra, 'Music, Letters and National Identity: Reading the 1890s Italian Music Press', *19th-Century Music Review*, 7/2 (2010), 99–116.

Wilson, Alexandra, 'Galli-Curci Comes to Town: The Prima Donna's Presence in the Age of Mechanical Reproduction', in Rachel Cowgill and Hilary Poriss (Eds.), *The Arts of the Prima Donna in the Long Nineteenth Century* (New York: Oxford University Press, 2012), 328–48.

Wilson, Alexandra, 'Gender', in Helen Greenwald (Ed.), *The Oxford Handbook of Opera* (New York: Oxford University Press, 2014), pp. 774–94.

Wyke, Maria, *Projecting the Past: Ancient Rome, Cinema, and History* (New York and London: Routledge, 1997).

Ziolkowski, Theodore, *Classicism of the Twenties: Art, Music, and Literature* (Chicago and London: The University of Chicago Press, 2015).

Websites

Anon., 'Why Are Our Schools Pushing Classical Music to the Margins?', *Gramophone*, 23 August 2016. https://www.gramophone.co.uk/blog/gramophone-guest-blog/why-are-our-schools-pushing-classical-music-to-the-margins?__prclt=bPMFchKQ.

Mitchell, Andrew, 'It's Time to Scotch the Cliché that Opera Tickets are too Expensive': https://www.theguardian.com/music/2015/nov/03/opera-tickets-expensive-cliche-john-humphrys.

Wilson, Alexandra, 'We Need to Move Beyond the Clichés about "Elitist" Opera', *The Guardian* Music Blog, 11 February 2014. https://www.theguardian.com/music/musicblog/2014/feb/11/elitist-opera-cliches-alexandra-wilson.

INDEX